Railways Then and Now

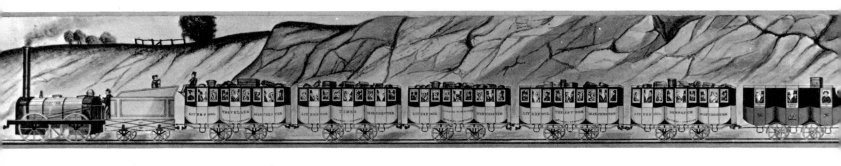

RAILWAYS THEN AND NOW

A World History

O. S. Nock

Crown Publishers, Inc. New York

Half title. Lithographed vignette from the cover of 'The Rail Road. A Comic Song', *c*. 1830. The artist's conception of a train appears to be somewhat confused, for where the locomotive should be he has the type of steam carriage that ran on the roads.

Title page. Trains of first and third class carriages on the Liverpool and Manchester Railway in 1830. The train of first-class carriages is reproduced in colour on pages 26 and 27.

Above. A scene of great animation at King's Cross Station—hard by the offices of Paul Elek Ltd—on the day of a race meeting at York in the 1850s.

Designed by Harold and Adina Bartram and produced by Paul Elek Ltd

© 1975 Paul Elek Ltd

Library of Congress Catalog Card Number: 75-580

ISBN 0 517 520362

Filmset in England by Photocomp Ltd Birmingham

Printed in France by Maison Mame

Contents

The Workings of an Early Steam Locomotive

Coke is put into the firebox through the door at (1) and is
supplied with the air needed to make it burn through the
firebars (2). The boiler contains water up to the level indicated
at (3) which surrounds the firebox in the space between the
inner and outer casings. The heating of the water is further
assisted by the heat of the hot gases from the firebox (4) passing
through the firetubes (5), which are also immersed in the water
of the boiler. Steam collects and builds up pressure in the space
above the water (6) and up under the pressure dome (7), which
houses the safety valve. The regulator handle (8) turns the
regulator (9) to release the steam pressure through the pipe at
(10) into the cylinder (11). The valve gear (not shown) directs
the steam alternately into opposite ends of the cylinder, which is
thus double acting. After the steam has expanded and done its
work in the cylinder, it is exhausted by the returning piston (the
appropriate valve being opened by the valve gear) through the
blast-pipe (12), the narrowed end of which (13) increases the
pressure of the emerging exhaust, and thus its velocity. This
produces a partial vacuum in the smokebox (14) which creates a
draft for the fire through the firetubes, so accelerating
combustion and steam raising.

*Drawing by Clifford Meadway based by kind permission on a
drawing in the possession of Hick Hargreaves & Co. Ltd.*

Preface

The part played by railways in world history over the last one hundred and fifty years cannot be over-emphasised. In the older countries – Great Britain, France, Germany, Austria – the railway became an indispensable tool for industrial development, and for the furtherance of trade. It was a predominant factor in the building of new nations, like the United States of America and Canada, while in Europe it played an invaluable part in coalescing into new nations groups of ancient principalities and kingdoms hitherto independent, as in the case of Italy. Railways began to provide reliable transport where previously there had been the hazards of long, tiresome journeys by road or by coastal shipping; railway engineers found the means of piercing great mountain ranges, crossing great tracts of desert and, in the older countries, immensely speeding up communications between the major centres of population.

Although there were from quite early days some proposals for alternative means of traction, it was above all the development of the steam locomotive that brought to the railroads of the nineteenth century their overwhelming superiority over every other form of transport. They introduced the era of really cheap transport. In Great Britain the basic fare was one penny a mile. One could travel in greater comfort or at higher speeds on payment of higher fares, but from 1844 onwards there was at least one train a day from 'anywhere to anywhere' at the Parliamentary fare. The early locomotives were not very powerful, and the tracks had to be made as level as possible, to avoid steep gradients. This made necessary the construction of some stupendous engineering works, great bridges, deep cuttings, long tunnels, and the architecture was worthy of the pioneer achievements taking place in many lands. Locomotives were designed and ornamented more like *objets d'art* than as pieces of machinery.

As the years of the nineteenth century passed by more and more countries built railways. In India they formed an integral part of the master pattern of British development. In the United States President Lincoln ordered the construction of a transcontinental line to assist in consolidating the Union; in Canada the promise of a transcontinental railway ensured the incorporation of British Columbia within the Confederation of Canada. Railways across Europe were used for conveyance of mails to and from the Far East; and in his colonising work in southern Africa Cecil Rhodes once exclaimed 'The railway is my right hand'.

Railways attained the era of their first pre-eminence in the first decade of the twentieth century, when locomotives had for the first time run at more than 100 miles per hour and journeys could be made between important cities at average speeds of 55 to 60 miles per hour. But with the development of the motor car and the great improvements made to the surface and alignment of main roads railways began to face strong competition that not even the gradual change from steam to diesel or electric traction was able to combat effectively. For a time, particularly after World War II, it seemed as if railway activity was so much on the decline that there was little future for it. But in the 1960s a new era for railways began to dawn, first in the mass haulage of heavy minerals. The continuing demand for coal and iron ore in the highly industrialised countries was exhausting the indigenous supplies and means had to be found for transporting from huge deposits in remote parts of the world; from Labrador, from the Canadian Rockies, from virgin tracts of Queensland and Western Australia. Entirely new railways have been built to form part of a colossal planned output of minerals, and assist in its conveyance over thousands of miles of Arctic wilderness, desert, or primeval forest land.

At the same time, in the crowded lands of Western Europe, the eastern corridor of the U.S.A. and in Japan the potentiality of railways for greatly increased speed began to be developed. Journey times at 90 to 100 miles per hour from one city centre to another were introduced, and are now seen as a solution to road congestion and the uncertainties of air transport that are inevitable in conditions of bad weather. And this is not enough. Still faster rail services are now being planned. The prospects for railway development are now as exciting as in the pioneer days of the 1840s and 1850s, but with the vital difference that there is more than a hundred years of experience to guide the planners of today. When the 150th anniversary of passenger travel by rail is celebrated, in September 1975, the world will indeed be across the threshold of the second era of railway pre-eminence.

Part 1

The Beginnings

One hundred and fifty years ago construction of what became the first public railway in the world was in full swing, between Stockton, Darlington and Bishop Auckland in County Durham, in north-eastern England. The Act of Parliament authorising its construction had received the Royal Assent on 19 April 1821, but the way was then far from clear to go ahead, despite all that had been done earlier in England to develop rail-ways. The Stockton and Darlington was no brainchild of a single man, or group of men; it was the outcome of many years of experimenting, trial and error with all the various components that were to make up the steam railway of the 1830s. The locomotive was of course the most spectacular unit, but that in itself stemmed from the much earlier development of running on rails.

Simple industrial enterprises in many parts of England required the transport of heavy loads from their points of origin to places where established forms of conveyance were available; and at the end of the eighteenth century that meant by water – by river, by canal, or by sea. Horses represented almost the only form of traction on land and, taking their cue from the ancient wagonways, the industrialists of the day laid down primitive forms of rail- or plate-ways, on which it was found that horses could pull much heavier loads than on the rough, deeply rutted roadways of the period. As early as 1733 Ralph Allen, the West Country magnate, constructed a wooden

rail-way to convey stone from his quarries on the heights south of Bath to the River Avon. Iron rails were used at the Coalbrookdale Ironworks, in 1767, and there were other primitive forms of rail-way in the latter part of the eighteenth century.

The purpose of rails was not only to provide smooth and easier running; it was to guide the vehicles, and while some of the early rail- or plate-ways were used with plain wheels, as used on ordinary roadways, others had flanged wheels – admittedly of a rather primitive type. It was in conjunction with vehicles having flanged wheels that William Jessop, in 1789, produced his grand invention of the edge-rail. It was epoch-marking in two respects: first, that it did not rely on continuous support from underneath and, secondly, that it was scientifically designed to provide strength in depth between the points of support, at each end. It was cast, in lengths of about 2 feet 6 inches, and rested at the joints on massive stone blocks, set deep into the ground. With no more than detailed improvements the Jessop rail became the established form of track until steam traction began to take the place of horses.

Astonishing though it may seem the earliest attempts to harness the power of steam in England extend back into the seventeenth century, and in the closing years of the reign of Queen Anne the primitive steam engines of Thomas Newcomen, a native of Dartmouth, were coming into use for pumping water from the Cornish tin mines. Their use extended to France, and at the Science Museum in London there is a model of one that was installed in France at Fresnes, in 1739, which successfully replaced a plant previously worked by twenty men and fifty horses. A model of a Newcomen engine belonged to the Natural Philosophy Class at Glasgow University. This needed repair, and during the session of 1763–4 Professor John Anderson asked his mathematical instrument maker to attend to it. This man was a clever, but frail and retiring, youngster of twenty-seven, James Watt by name, and to repair the Newcomen engine was a job after his own heart. Up to that time he had had little experience of steam; but in his studious way he had read of experiments in France that had to some extent paralleled the Newcomen development, and he immediately began making tests. He found the boiler was large enough only to supply steam for a few strokes and as, for tuition purposes at the University, it was desired to keep the engine running continuously he gave thought to how the consumption of steam could be

Rail-ways before steam: an engraving of 1773 by Will Beilby, of Newcastle, showing a loaded coal wagon descending a gradient by gravity. The horse follows, ready to haul the wagon uphill when required.

lessened, as well as to the provision of a larger boiler. Watt was evidently taking his time over the job for, while the original request was made to him in the session of 1763–4, it was not until a year later that the solution came to him, in May 1765.

Fifty years later, in the evening of his life, he spoke of the occasion to a Glasgow engineer, Robert Hart, who fortunately recorded his words verbatim. This is how Watt himself described one of the great classic moments in British engineering history:

'It was in the Green of Glasgow. I had gone to take a walk on a fine Sabbath afternoon. I had entered the Green by the gate at the foot of Charlotte Street – had passed the old washing house. I was thinking upon the old engine at the time and had gone as far as the Herds house when the idea came into my mind, that as steam was an elastic body it would rush into a vacuum, and if a communication was made between the cylinder and an exhausted vessel, it would rush into it, and might be there condensed without cooling the cylinder. . . . I had not walked further than the Golf house when the whole thing was arranged in my mind.'

So came the separate condenser, and at this one stroke he had secured a possible cut in steam consumption to roughly one-quarter of its previous volume. Watt's famous invention was not applied to the art of traction on railways, but was a vital step in the development for the way in which it led to the introduction of the high-pressure engine, in Cornwall. The Cornish mine-owners' reliance on the partnership of Watt and Matthew Boulton, following the indisputable success of their engine at 'Wheal Busy', a tin mine near Truro, rankled deeply, and in this spirit of independence arose the mighty Richard Trevithick. Not for him the moderate steam pressures of James Watt, and the scientific use of the separate condenser. He raised the pressure to several times atmospheric pressure, and allowed it to escape after each stroke. By working at high pressure Trevithick could obtain as much power as, or more

than, the Watt engines did while using much smaller cylinders and pistons, and Watt's separate condenser and all its appurtenances were rendered unnecessary.

Following his success with the high-pressure engines Trevithick's thoughts soon turned to other means of utilising steam, and to locomotion. Samuel Homfray, owner of the Penydaren Ironworks near Merthyr Tydfil, his partner with a half-share in the patent rights for the high-pressure engine, took a bet that Trevithick's 'puffer' could not haul a load of ten tons of iron over the nine-and-three-quarter miles of the old plate-way from the works to the canal at Abercynon. In response to this bet Trevithick set about building the very first steam locomotive. It was designed on similar lines to the pumping engines, with only one cylinder, and with a crank and connecting rod to produce rotary motion it had a large flywheel to make the motion continuous and avoid stalling on the dead centres. The cylinder was only 8½ inches in diameter, but it had a very long stroke, and extended into the boiler barrel, while the piston rod and the guide for the cross-head projected far out to the rear, reminding one of a trombone at its fullest extent. The locomotive set out on the trial on Tuesday, 21 February 1804, conveying ten tons of iron and five wagons, and with seventy men in addition riding on the wagons. Several times they had to stop to cut down trees – no one had thought to check that there were proper clearances for the locomotive to pass – and elsewhere some large rocks lay on the track; but the run was successfully made in four hours and five minutes and Homfray won the bet. Unfortunately, however, it was not in Trevithick's remarkable nature to persevere steadily on one project. The development of the steam railway locomotive passed into other hands, and for more than ten years its progress was slow, halting and a series of disjointed individual efforts, mostly in the north and north-east of England.

Below left. The original drawing of Trevithick's locomotive of 1804 which won the bet at Penydaren on 21 February 1804.

Richard Trevithick (1771–1833), the great Cornish pioneer, from an oil painting by Linnell.

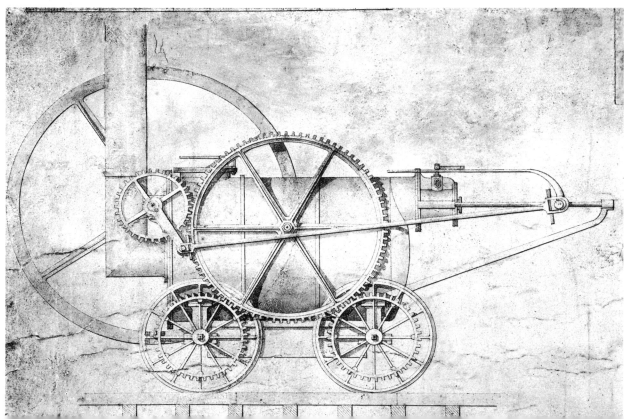

Below. A drawing by Thomas Rowlandson of the test track on a piece of waste ground near the site of the present Euston Station, London, on which Trevithick's locomotive *Catch Me Who Can* was demonstrated in 1808.

Bottom. Hetton Colliery in 1822, showing early Stephenson locomotives at work – a lithograph by J. D. Harding.

Up to this time three men had, directly and indirectly, contributed to the development of the steam locomotive: Newcomen, as the pioneer of steam pumping engines; James Watt, for the way his 'invasion' of Cornwall antagonised the 'locals' and undoubtedly sparked off Trevithick's venture, and, of course, Trevithick himself. Then, in 1811, a north-country enginewright, Blenkinsop by name, made two important steps towards future development. He was the first to attempt any co-ordination between

the design of track and locomotive. Trevithick's locomotive had smashed up the plate-way, and eye-witnesses had also reported that there seemed to be a certain amount of wheel-slip. Blenkinsop thought that the only satisfactory way for a locomotive to pull a heavy load would be to use a geared driving wheel working in a rack fixed on the track. This idea was adopted on a wagonway running from Middleton Colliery to the outskirts of Leeds. His locomotive is reported to have hauled ninety tons on a level stretch of track and taken fifteen tons up a gradient as steep as 1 in 20; but it was a clumsy and expensive arrangement, and involved heavy wear between the gear wheel and the toothed rack.

Blenkinsop's second step forward was to dispense with the gigantic flywheel of the Penydaren engine, by having two cylinders driving alternately through cranks and gears on to the main axle, which carried the toothed driving wheel engaging in the rack on the permanent way.

At about the same time, William Hedley's celebrated locomotive *Puffing Billy* was put to work at Wylam Colliery in Northumberland. Like the Blenkinsop engine at Middleton Colliery it had two cylinders, and an elaborate linkage on top of the boiler transmitted the thrusts downward to an axle midway between the main axles carrying the flanged rail wheels. But whereas Blenkinsop had put the entire driving force on to the one axle carrying the gear wheel Hedley distributed the drive, by a train of gears concealed beneath the massive frame, to both main axles, and dispensed with the toothed drive.

Over this stage in the development of the loco-motive there persists to this day some confusion over priorities of invention, sustained by the various rival claimants to the credit of having *really* invented the steam locomotive. But by the time the Blenkinsop engines were at work at the Kenton, Fawdon and Cox Lodge collieries and *Puffing Billy* was in service at Wylam, the man who was to epitomise and con-solidate the whole development was building his first locomotive at Killingworth; his name was George Stephenson. There was a world of difference between the parentage, education and status of those who had hitherto pioneered the origins of steam traction, and the humble colliery mechanic who now began to come into the picture. For while men such as Trevithick, Blenkinsop and Hedley were none of them engineers in the professional sense, they all had a measure of status in their daily work, and the backing that status provided; but Stephenson at first had none. He had nevertheless something that counted for infinitely more: he had character, a calm resolve and perseverance that brought him to the notice of his superiors, and a great capacity for making and keeping friends. Moreover he had also the priceless attribute of 'vision'. By his steady persistence and attention to detail he achieved some-thing of a reputation as a mechanic and colliery enginewright, and for a man of the humblest birth that might have sufficed for a lifetime's work. But Stephenson saw a future for steam traction far beyond the trundling of picturesque chaldron wagons to and from the banks of the Tyne.

Largely through his own modest but steadfast personality, as well as by the quality of his work, he came to enjoy the patronage of two men who were to set him on the road to fame. There was first of all Lord Ravensworth, owner of the Killingworth colliery, who provided the money for Stephenson's first locomotive; and in this relationship between one of the great founder engineers of the steam age and one of the great north-country landowners, seeking greater efficiency in the coal mines which he had enterprised as a profitable alternative to farming, can be seen, written in microcosm, the story of the industrial revolution which transformed first Great Britain and then the world. Then there was Nicholas Wood, a mining engineer of high professional status, who introduced George Stephenson at the critical moment when the Quaker colliery magnates of Darlington were considering the laying down of a railway. Stephenson's first locomotive, built in 1814 and named *Blucher*, had many points of similarity with Hedley's *Puffing Billy*, in that the drive was through gearing arranged underneath the boiler, and that it ran on a smooth track. The name of the Killingworth locomotive was interesting, because the machine was at work nearly a year before the Prussian general played his part in consummating the great victory of Waterloo. Some months before the battle Stephenson had become dissatisfied with *his Blucher*, chiefly through the noisy and unreliable functioning of the gear drive, and in 1815, in partnership with Ralph Dodds, viewer at the Killingworth colliery, he took out a patent for dispensing with gears. Each cylinder drove on to a separate axle; the cranks were at right angles to each other, and this disposition was maintained by an endless chain passing over a toothed wheel on each axle. This arrangement worked well, and formed a basic feature of what became known as the Killingworth type of locomotive.

In 1820 the manufacture of rails took a major step forward. Not far from Killingworth, at the Bedlington Ironworks, Birkinshaw produced wrought iron rails for the first time by the process of rolling. Stephenson had already been turning his attention to the track and had invented the 'Stephenson and Losh' rail which incorporated a half-lap joint between adjacent rails, thus reducing the wear on the locomotive that butted joints caused. Now the frequency of joints could be greatly reduced for the rolling process produced rails in lengths of 18 to 20 feet – much longer than was possible with the old cast rails.

There could have been rivalry between the products of Wylam and Killingworth collieries had it not been for a personal incident that took place in 1815. At Wylam Timothy Hackworth was enginewright, as devout a Christian as he was a diligent workman. One Sunday he chose to attend a religious service instead of going to the colliery, and was subsequently discharged. He obtained a job as foreman smith at the Walbottle colliery in 1816, and remained there for eight years. Had he remained at Wylam, among

locomotives, there is little doubt that the inventive skill that he afterwards displayed would have been exercised in the development of the Hedley locomotives; as it was, things remained virtually stagnant at Wylam after his departure, and the entire development became centred upon Killingworth, at the hands of George Stephenson with the approbation of Nicholas Wood.

The appointment of George Stephenson as engineer to the Stockton and Darlington Railway Company in 1821 was the outcome of a long controversy going back to 1810, when the project of providing a link between the Bishop Auckland coalfield in County Durham and tidewater at Stockton-on-Tees was first mooted. For many years the advocates of a canal had held the field. As constructed, and opened for traffic on 27 September 1825, the Stockton and Darlington Railway was a curious mixture of modes of traction. The distance from the Old Etherley colliery, just to the north-west of Bishop Auckland, to the quayside at Cottage Row, Stockton, was twenty-five miles, and while the first twenty miles inland was through relatively level country, with no gradient exceeding 1 in 104, two major ridges had to be crossed in the concluding five miles, involving inclines of around 1 in 30 in crossing first the Brusselton, and secondly the Etherley ridges. No locomotives could be expected to haul a load on such slopes, and stationary engine houses were built at the respective summits, from which trains could be hauled up the inclines by rope. Over the rest of the line, while locomotive haulage was envisaged, and provided for in the Act of Parliament authorising the line, the company was at first almost entirely dependent upon horses. Like the private railways further north the Stockton and Darlington was primarily conceived and projected as a coal-carrying railway; although the Act provided for the conveyance of passengers, they were at first quite a minor consideration.

Before referring to the working of the line the actual job of construction needs some particular mention. George Stephenson was 'engineer'. This did not merely involve laying rails and building locomotives. The original survey had been made by a man named Overton, but it was necessary for Stephenson to check the route, and then to carry out all the constructional work – building embankments, excavating cuttings, and in several places erecting bridges both under and over the route. In two places there were rivers to be crossed, and here one found the humbly-born enginewright of Killingworth designing structures that would elsewhere have required the skill and experience of professional engineers of high status. Across the little river Gaunless, near St Helens Auckland, Stephenson built the first iron railway bridge in the world. The elegant and advanced design, incorporating four fish-bellied wrought iron girders, suggested a master hand rather than a self-taught mechanic. The bridge over the river Skerne near Darlington was a massive single masonry arch, with beautifully proportioned wing walls.

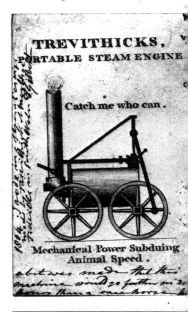

Admission card to Trevithick's railway, 1808, inscribed by Davies Gilbert who, under his original name of Davies Giddy, was an enthusiastic supporter of Trevithick in his earliest Cornish experiments.

George Stephenson (1781–1848), from an oil painting made at the time of the construction of the Liverpool and Manchester Railway.

For the rails, it would no doubt have been very profitable to Stephenson personally to use the 'Stephenson and Losh' patent type throughout; but he specified instead the rolled type from the Bedlington Ironworks, and used the short lengths of his own patent type for making up odd lengths, and at points of crossing. Although he himself had no doubts about the eventual use of locomotives for all traffic, when the line was opened there was only the historic 'No. 1' *Locomotion* available, and this was retained

S. & D.R. N° I. 1825.

Top. A sister engine of the *Locomotion* in the U.S.A.: the *Stourbridge Lion*, built by Foster and Rastrick of Stourbridge, Worcestershire, in 1828.

Above. *Locomotion*, 1825, Stockton and Darlington Railway No. 1. The engine is shown displayed on a pedestal in Bank Top Station, Darlington, Co. Durham.

for coal traffic. It was generally of the Killingworth type, and included a number of detail improvements. When the Act of Parliament authorising construction of the line was passed in 1821 it was to be free to all who chose to put their wagons on it and haul them with their own horses, providing they paid the tolls stipulated by the Act. These charges were originally 4d per ton per mile, for coal intended for land sale, but only ½d per ton per mile for coal intended for shipment at Stockton. The original Act was passed before George Stephenson was appointed engineer and, while he accepted the idea of horse traction

as an expedient until sufficient locomotives were ready, he was constantly emphasising the advantages to be derived from steam traction.

Passenger service on this first public railway was provided entirely by horse-drawn coach. After some early experiments, a number of old stage-coach bodies were bought and mounted on under-frames with flanged wheels. These coaches were hired to various contractors, who horsed and worked them, paying agreed tolls to the railway company for use of the line. For the run of twelve miles from Stockton to Darlington the 'inside' fare, limited to six passengers, was 2s; outside, from fifteen to twenty persons could be accommodated and they were charged 1s each. Before very long traffic on the line increased to such an extent that the company had to take over the entire haulage, and the toll-paying contractors disappeared.

Before even the Stockton and Darlington Railway was opened there were important moves towards the construction of railways in America and on the continent of Europe. Furthermore, the reputation of George Stephenson was increasing to such an extent that he was being consulted on other projects in England. At the beginning of the nineteenth century the greater part of the American population was centred along a relatively narrow strip of territory behind the Atlantic coastline. Behind this was ranged the barrier of the Allegheny Mountains, and beyond that lay a vast region then undeveloped and almost unexplored. It was nevertheless a land that seemed to offer immense possibilities for development. The pioneers who had ventured thus far had found the valleys of the Mississippi, Missouri and Ohio rivers. Communications on these great waterways had largely determined the pattern of industrial development, settled the location of towns, and indicated that trade would inevitably follow the transport facilities naturally offered by these immensely wide rivers. But the general course of the rivers was from north to south, whereas it was urgently necessary to establish communications between these 'new' areas beyond the Alleghenies, and the ports along the Atlantic seaboard. Somehow the mountains had to be crossed, and the thoughts of the pioneers somewhat naturally turned towards canals.

Not of all of them, however. As early as 1812, while the experiments of Blenkinsop and Hedley were still taking place and before Stephenson had built a single locomotive, an American, John Stevens by name, was convinced that the future lay in steam locomotive power, and advocated steam railways in opposition to canals. His efforts were unavailing in the case of the Erie canal linking the Hudson river with Lake Erie, but when a scheme was projected from Philadelphia to Pittsburgh, cutting through the very heart of the Allegheny range, support for Stevens' views led to the formation of the 'Pennsylvania Society for the Promotion of Internal Improvement', which deputed one of its members, William Strickland, to visit England and investigate

Sketch by Dobbin of the ceremonial opening of the Stockton and Darlington Railway, 27 September 1825.

Below. Hedley's *Wylam Dilly*, photographed *c.* 1860 with two of Hedley's sons.

the situation in railway development – particularly as regards steam locomotion. However, Strickland's recommendation, which was duly adopted, gave no place to steam traction but instead involved the use of canals where the country was reasonably level and, over the eleven inclined planes of the mountains between Hollidaysburg and Johnstown, a cable-hauled railway. On this, the 'Portage Railroad', the canal boats were lifted bodily out of the water onto the railway wagons. The entire journey of about four hundred miles took anything between five days and a week.

In the meantime other American interests had been looking at British steam locomotives. The Delaware and Hudson Canal Company and the newly-formed Baltimore and Ohio Railroad both sent representatives to England, but towards the end of the 1820s British locomotive practice was in its infancy. The American visitors, however, saw enough of railway development to draw certain conclusions that were to prove the guiding points of American policy for many years to come. They saw the Liverpool and Manchester Railway under construction. Now the circumstances surrounding the promotion and building of this line were very different from those of the colliery railways in the north-eastern counties, and equally from those of the Stockton and Darlington. A major point with the Liverpool and Manchester was the conveyance of passengers and mails. Professional engineers of the highest status – notably

John Rennie – strove hard to secure the post of 'engineer'; but after lengthy struggles, and parliamentary enquiry, George Stephenson was preferred. When Horatio Allen, from the Delaware and Hudson Canal, and the three-man deputation from the Baltimore and Ohio saw the works in progress Stephenson, with his son Robert, and his pupils John Dixon and Joseph Locke, were at something of a critical stage.

13

The Americans saw that the British were doing something that was not then practicable in the U.S.A. The carefully graded road-bed, substantial track, large viaducts and deep cuttings just could not be afforded. In England, and particularly in the busy industrial region of South Lancashire, capital was plentiful, distances short, and potential traffic density high. In America it was then just the reverse. Although the country was rich in unexploited natural wealth there was little ready cash. Nevertheless, to get things started the Delaware and Hudson Canal Company imported four steam locomotives of what could be termed the British 'colliery' type, a direct derivative from the primitive efforts of Hedley and George Stephenson.

In their appreciation of these pioneer machines the Americans also include the name of Timothy Hackworth, who was last mentioned in transferring his services to Walbottle Colliery, Northumberland. Hackworth and Stephenson became close friends, and in 1824, while construction of the Stockton and Darlington Railway was in full swing, Stephenson was called into consultation over the proposed Liverpool and Manchester Railway, and was away from County Durham for long periods. While the civil engineering side of the work was progressing well Stephenson was worried about locomotives and the machinery of the stationary engine houses, and in May 1825 Hackworth was appointed locomotive superintendent, a post that included the stationary engines as well.

motives gave a lot of trouble, and the Stockton and Darlington Railway was fortunate in having so painstaking and devoted a mechanic as Timothy Hackworth to carry out the numerous day-to-day adjustments and repairs that were necessary to keep them going. In so doing he began to develop ideas of his own in locomotive design and construction. A very important suggestion of his was incorporated in the *Locomotion* and the three others that followed it. In referring to the locomotives built by Stephenson at Killingworth the use of a chain and sprocket wheel to keep the two driving axles in correct relationship was mentioned. Hackworth suggested instead a simple coupling rod between cranks on the axles, and this device, first used on the *Locomotion*, became standard throughout the world.

But Hackworth's main concern was with the steaming. The boilers would not stand up to continuous running, and trains had to stop frequently while steam pressure in the boiler was restored. At one time things got so bad that the company was seriously thinking of abandoning the use of locomotives altogether and working the traffic entirely by horses, and it was at that stage that Hackworth asked permission to build a new engine 'in his own way', rather than continue 'tinkering' with the Killingworth type. If that permission were granted, Hackworth told the board, 'I will engage that it shall answer your purpose'. The result was a very large new locomotive, running on six wheels instead of four, and having all six coupled together. Apart from

On the Baltimore and Ohio Railroad in 1829: an artist's impression of one of the early trains at Mount Clare Station, Baltimore.

At the time of his appointment there was not a single locomotive on the line, and the historic No. 1, *Locomotion*, had arrived from Newcastle only a few days before the ceremonial opening of the railway on 27 September 1825. There were three more locomotives of generally the same design. The first of these, *Hope*, arrived in November, and the next, the *Black Diamond*, was delivered in April 1826, followed by the *Diligence* in May. These early loco-

size however, Hackworth incorporated a major development in the boiler. The previous engines, like those of Hedley and the early Stephenson products at Killingworth, had a single flue; but Hackworth in his new engine had a U-shaped flue. The firebox was at the front end, and the flue ran the length of the boiler, did a U-turn, and then came back to terminate in a direct connection to the chimney. The heating surface was thus doubled, as compared with that of a Killingworth engine; but a peculiarity was that the fireman had to be accommodated on a tender propelled in front of the engine, while the driver was at the rear end on another tender carrying the water supply. Such was the *Royal George* locomotive, put into service in November 1827. Quite apart from the two-tender peculiarity it was a great success and certainly saved the day for the steam locomotive on the Stockton and Darlington Railway.

In 1818 a French Government surveyor of mines, M. de Gallois, visited the wagonways at Wylam and Middleton collieries and saw the locomotives of Hedley and Blenkinsop at work, and returned to France to present a paper to the *Académie des Sciences* entitled 'Notice sur les Chemins de fer Anglais'. His advocacy of railways led to the construction of the first railway in France. Like the pioneer railways in north-eastern England it was built for the conveyance of coal, from the mining districts around Saint-Etienne, about thirty miles to the south-west of Lyons. The Saint-Etienne and Andrezieux Railway was projected in 1821. The application to build was not granted until February 1823, and then by King Louis XVIII personally. The line was only twelve miles long, but it took a terribly long time to build, and coal traffic, all drawn by horses, began in May 1827. It was not until five years later that the company began to convey passengers, still with horse traction; in fact locomotives were not used on this line until 1844. In the meantime another group

of industrialists in the Saint-Etienne district was enterprising a railway north-eastwards to Lyons. This line was opened for traffic in 1830. There was much apathy and opposition to travel by railway in the district—and this, it must be recalled, was some little time before there was any thought of using locomotives in France. Some people in the Saint-Etienne district declared that they preferred to travel by canal because they could fish in it as they went

along! In 1833 an eminent Frenchman declared that railways would never be of any practical use; their construction was more a matter of scientific amusement than of any general usefulness. This however was not the view of the mine-owners of Saint-Etienne, and in 1828 there was authorised a lengthy extension of the Andrezieux line down the valley of the Loire for over fifty miles, to Roanne. It is very interesting to see the striking parallel to British pioneer work, in that the railways of France originated in small, private industrial ventures, and that it was some years before any railway was constructed in or near the capital city of Paris.

By the end of the 1820s the 'world' railway situation was that the railroad section of the Delaware and Hudson Canal, the Baltimore and Ohio, and parts of the 400-mile Philadelphia and Pittsburg scheme were operating in the U.S.A.; there were the French horse-powered lines radiating from Saint-Etienne; and in England the Stockton and Darlington was struggling through to a modicum of success with steam traction, while the much more ambitious Liverpool and Manchester Railway was approaching the time of its official opening. The Liverpool and Manchester Railway included, both in its construction and its equipment, so much that was fundamental in the future development of railways that it demands the most careful study. George Stephenson was the engineer, and he had as assistants in the construction of various sections of the line William Allcard, John Dixon, and Joseph Locke—all three men who were to achieve great distinction in subsequent railway building. Stephenson had a vision of railway development far beyond the small local projects that had so far been undertaken in England. He foresaw the creation of a network of direct trunk railways that would connect up all the major centres of industry and population; and while he did not try to simplify things to the point of extravagant absurdity by settling his routes by drawing a straight line on the map between the two towns he had to connect, he planned the Liverpool and Manchester with easy gradients and a minimum of curvature. It was a line intended for fast running.

Not far from the Liverpool terminus there was a tremendous cutting at Olive Mount, where the rock was so sound that Stephenson made the sides literally vertical; there was a beautiful viaduct of eight arches over the Sankey Canal, and all the smaller bridges both under and over the line were massively and elegantly constructed in stone; and the wayside stations were little architectural masterpieces in themselves. Surpassing all, however, were the adornments at the first Liverpool passenger station. There the tracks were spanned by the huge Moorish Arch that lent an air of almost oriental grandeur to the cutting that it spanned. The way Stephenson, the humbly born enginewright of Killingworth, came to include such refinements in the lineside works of the Liverpool and Manchester Railway might seem quite inexplicable were it not for the fact that by the time he was appointed engineer a number of very influential and affluent men were backing him, and that it was felt essential to set the seal upon this great pioneer railway with appropriate ornamentation. It was all carried out in superb taste and was recorded by some of the leading artists of the day.

Stephenson nevertheless paid the price of having a direct route in the exceptional and unprecedented difficulties he encountered near Manchester, where the line had to cross Chat Moss, an immense peat bog some twelve miles square. Stephenson had to carry through the construction of the line across this vast agglomeration of spongy, vegetable pulp, of unknown depth, in the face of intense and powerful opposition right up to its final completion. Where the rail level was only just above the level of the moss, the expedient of laying the line on a floating mattress of brushwood and heather worked well. But near the Manchester end, where a shallow embankment had to be formed, the mattress sank under the weight of earth. Week after week of tipping seemed to produce

no result, and a board meeting was held on the site to consider abandoning the attempt and building a long deviation to avoid the Moss altogether. But Stephenson urged 'press on', until after many more weeks of tipping the embankment began to rise, firm and solid above the level of the bog.

Then there was the question of locomotives. While Stephenson had been so involved in all the preliminaries and with the construction of the line Hackworth had gradually improved the locomotive stud of the Stockton and Darlington to a state of reliability; but it was the reliability of a mainly mineral line, on which no great speeds were called for, and large six-coupled locomotives like the *Royal George* with a tender at each end were not ideally suited to the kind of running that was anticipated on the Liverpool and Manchester Railway with the passenger and mail trains. The troubles experienced with the original locomotives of the Stockton and Darlington Railway were common knowledge in Liverpool, and the people who were constantly working to discredit Stephenson urged that locomotives should not be used. They argued that horse or cable traction would be more reliable. Again, however, those who had faith in Stephenson won the day; and while it was agreed that cable traction would be necessary on the steep, though short, inclines from the passenger station at the Moorish Arch, down through the tunnels to the docksides, steam locomotives would be employed for all traffic over the rest of the line. It was the first railway in the world of any kind, mineral or passenger, that was to have steam exclusively from the very outset. The problem was to decide the most suitable type and the directors decided to offer a prize of £500 for the best steam locomotive to fulfil certain running conditions.

Perhaps the most momentous development so far in the entire history of the steam locomotive took place in 1827, not through any of the engineers who had been hitherto pioneering railways, but at the suggestion of a non-technical man, Henry Booth, secretary to the Liverpool and Manchester Railway.

Booth, then styled 'treasurer', reported to a board meeting of the company that he had discovered 'a method of producing Steam without Smoke.' George Stephenson was in attendance and said that if successful the idea could be highly beneficial to the company. He was instructed to make experiments necessary to test the idea. The main feature was to have more than one flue, each fed from a separate 'fireplace', thus increasing the heating surface without resorting to the clumsy 'return flue' arrangement introduced by Hackworth. This worked well on a new engine put into service in 1828, called the *Lancashire Witch*, but it was no more than the first step towards the multi-tubular boiler used on the 'competition model' for the Liverpool and Manchester prize money, entered by the infant firm of Robert Stephenson & Co., a partnership between George Stephenson, his only son Robert, Edward Pease, the Darlington coal owner who had provided wealthy backing for the Stockton and Darlington Railway, and Michael Longridge, the proprietor of the Bedlington Ironworks. In the competition engine the tubes were quite small; there were twenty-five of them, and they all carried the gases of combustion from a single fire. Another feature of the *Lancashire Witch* was incorporated in the 'competition' engine, namely having the cylinders inclined, instead of vertical, and thus presenting a much neater arrangement. There was one very important change from previous practice in the layout of the machinery of the *Rocket*: only a single pair of wheels was used for the drive. The rear pair of wheels, under the firebox, were of smaller diameter, and were not in any way coupled to the leaders. The *Rocket* was designed for fast running, and the absence of connecting rods between a multiplicity of driving wheels, as in the *Royal George*, made for a free-running machine; and in England for much of the nineteenth century the 'single-driver' locomotive was highly favoured for express passenger work. In this respect, as in so many others, the *Rocket* was a pioneer. The remaining feature of prime importance was the blast-pipe, a narrowing cone leading to a small orifice through which the exhaust steam was passed, and which, by imparting great speed to the exhaust, acted as a draught on the fire. There was at one time great controversy, and indeed acrimony, over who invented the blast-pipe – whether it was George Stephenson in the Killingworth days, or Hackworth, or even if Hedley had a hand in it. But the basic principle could be traced back to Trevithick's Penydaren engine of 1804. Apart from this however, the *Rocket* was the first embodiment of *all* that was considered basically essential in a steam railway locomotive.

Its only serious competitor in the trials of 1829, held on the main line of the Liverpool and Manchester Railway, at Rainhill, Lancashire, was Hackworth's own engine, the *Sanspareil*, which was a four-coupled machine designed to his established principles, with the return-bend type of flue, vertical cylinders, and the tender with the fireman travelling on it propelled in front. It had his own rather fierce version

The 'Grand Competition' of locomotives for the Liverpool and Manchester Railway at Rainhill, Lancashire, 1829. The three competitors, *Rocket*, *Novelty* and *Sanspareil*.

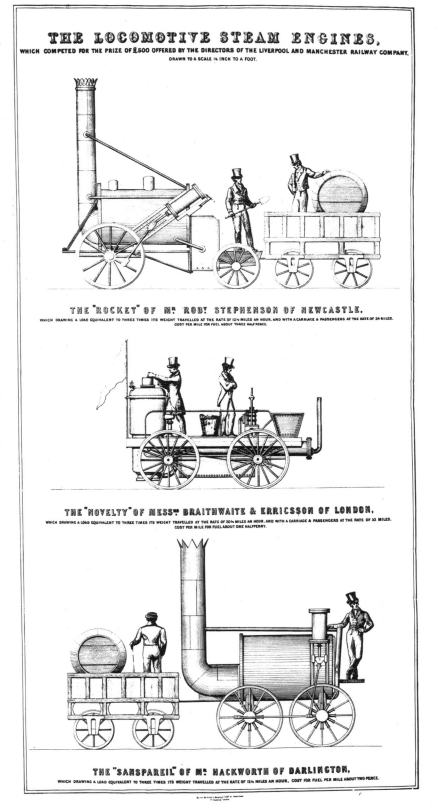

THE LOCOMOTIVE STEAM ENGINES,

WHICH COMPETED FOR THE PRIZE OF £500 OFFERED BY THE DIRECTORS OF THE LIVERPOOL AND MANCHESTER RAILWAY COMPANY.

DRAWN TO A SCALE ¼ INCH TO A FOOT.

THE "ROCKET" OF M.ʳ ROB.ᵗ STEPHENSON OF NEWCASTLE,

WHICH DRAWING A LOAD EQUIVALENT TO THREE TIMES ITS WEIGHT TRAVELLED AT THE RATE OF 12½ MILES AN HOUR, AND WITH A CARRIAGE & PASSENGERS AT THE RATE OF 24 MILES. COST PER MILE FOR FUEL ABOUT THREE HALFPENCE.

THE "NOVELTY" OF MESS.ʳˢ BRAITHWAITE & ERRICSSON OF LONDON,

WHICH DRAWING A LOAD EQUIVALENT TO THREE TIMES ITS WEIGHT TRAVELLED AT THE RATE OF 20¾ MILES AN HOUR, AND WITH A CARRIAGE & PASSENGERS AT THE RATE OF 32 MILES. COST PER MILE FOR FUEL ABOUT ONE HALFPENNY.

THE "SANSPAREIL" OF M.ʳ HACKWORTH OF DARLINGTON,

WHICH DRAWING A LOAD EQUIVALENT TO THREE TIMES ITS WEIGHT TRAVELLED AT THE RATE OF 12½ MILES AN HOUR. COST FOR FUEL PER MILE ABOUT TWO PENCE.

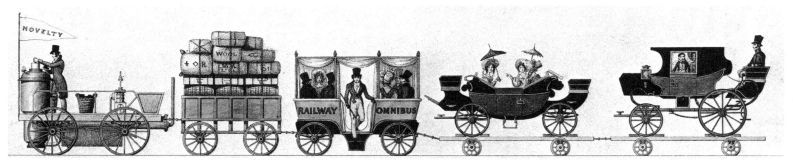

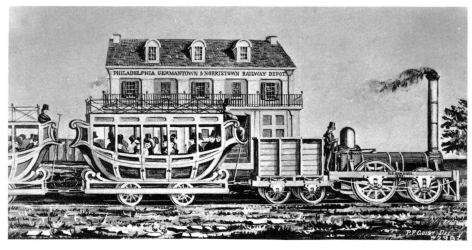

Top. Wishful thinking by
Charles Vignoles, a strong
supporter of the *Novelty*.
Vignoles made this delightful
drawing of how the locomotive
might have been used on the
Liverpool and Manchester
Railway. But it broke down
in the Rainhill trials, and
never worked on the line.

Above. The locomotive *Old
Ironsides*, which could be
described as of the
Stephenson *Planet* type, was
the first built by the great
Matthias W. Baldwin, founder
of the Baldwin Locomotive
Company, in 1832, for the
Philadelphia, Germantown and
Morristown Railroad. It was
the first railway to operate in
Pennsylvania, and this
reproduction of a painting by
P. F. Goist shows a train
leaving the old depot at
Ninth and Green Streets,
Philadelphia, in a service that
was inaugurated on
26 November 1832.

Above right. The *Rocket*,
winner of the Grand
Competition at Rainhill, 1829,
was modified in regular service
on the Liverpool and
Manchester Railway by
having the cylinders moved
down to a near-horizontal
position, so as to improve the
riding. This photograph shows
the locomotive as received at
the Patent Office Museum for
preservation in 1862.

of the blast-pipe, which sometimes resulted in live
coals being thrown from the chimney. It did reasonably well until the pump feeding water into the boiler
failed, and put an end to its running. After fulfilling
all the conditions laid down for the trials – the only
competitor to do so – the *Rocket*, driven by Robert
Stephenson, made an exhibition run with one carriage
and some passengers, and attained the speed of
24 miles per hour. Locomotives of the *Rocket* type
became the first passenger engines of the Liverpool
and Manchester Railway, while four-coupled engines
were developed for goods trains which did not
demand such fast running. A handsome tribute has
recently been paid to this early development in a
highly authoritative work by John H. White, Jnr.,
*American Locomotives: an engineering history 1830–
1880*, in which he writes:

'It was the British who perfected the basic design of the
locomotive and introduced the separate firebox, multi-tubular
boiler, direct connection to the wheels, blast-pipe and other
fundamental features that remained with the steam locomotive
to the end of its production. American improvements – mainly
in running gears – were hardly as fundamental or as far-
reaching as the work of the British designers who had
perfected their basic design by 1830.'

Lest we should place too shining a halo on the
locomotives of the Liverpool and Manchester Railway we should mention that the 'basic design' was
quickly found to be in trouble, not only in those
exported to the U.S.A. but on the comparatively
perfect track at home. It was a matter of riding,
rather than of fundamentals. Stephenson's built a
four-coupled engine for the Mohawk and Hudson
Railroad in 1831. The short wheelbase and lack of

any leading wheels caused it to rock and derail
easily on rough track, while the limited size of the
boiler made it incapable of hauling a heavy load on
steep gradients. On the Liverpool and Manchester
Railway, the high, inclined position of the cylinders
on the *Rocket* type of locomotive caused an uncomfortable shouldering action when a good speed was
being worked up, and an attempt to remedy this
was made by moving the cylinders to an almost
horizontal position. But Robert Stephenson introduced an entirely different conception of engine layout
in 1830, by virtually turning the machinery back to
front, and putting the cylinders between instead of
outside the frames, and beneath the smokebox.
This new locomotive was named *Planet*, and it formed
the starting point for a long succession of British
designs with inside cylinders. But although a few
locomotives of the *Planet* type were exported to the
U.S.A. it made no headway, because of the nature of
American tracks.

With the opening of the Liverpool and Manchester
Railway the conveyance of passengers in steam-
hauled trains became a major consideration. Hitherto,
on the early railways in England, France and America
freight and minerals had been the prime traffic and no
particular attention had been given to facilities for
the reception of intending passengers, or to the
vehicles in which they were conveyed. But by the
year 1830 the vision of railways as the pre-eminent
means of transport of the future was beginning to
open up – certainly in England and America, though
not yet in France. Proper provision was necessary
for passengers and so the railway station was born.
There was no functional pattern; every problem
had to be solved in its own terms. The station was

essentially a part of the new system just as much as the track and the locomotives. Inevitably it made an impact (the first impact!) on the prospective traveller, and to the average passenger the way he and his family, his goods and luggage were received probably made a greater impression than the subsequent 'wonder' of being conveyed along the line at 30 miles per hour.

Liverpool Crown Street was in many ways the father of all railway stations. It was simple and functional; the era of magnificent ornamentation was still some years ahead. There was a good, solid building which contained the various offices, booking hall, waiting rooms and so on. There was only one platform, but two additional running lines, and these three tracks were spanned by an all-over roof, which on the farther side rested on a plain masonry wall. The roof was entirely of timber. Passengers entrained in comfort, completely protected from the weather. It was far otherwise when the journey itself started.

On the Stockton and Darlington Railway the original passenger service was provided by single carriages which resembled stage coaches, in which the more affluent patrons travelled inside and the rest outside. No one questioned the distinction. People travelled the length and breadth of England 'outside' on stage coaches. The only difference on steam railways was that one could get smothered in smoke and cinders. On the Liverpool and Manchester Railway provision was made for three classes of passengers. Going 'first class' one had a vehicle like a stage coach, enclosed and comfortably appointed; the 'seconds' had a canopy overhead, though the sides, above the waistline, were open, while the

'thirds' were little more than open trucks with wooden benches to sit on. These early English carriages were compact little things, and the long chimneys of the locomotives towered above them – not that the chimneys were excessively tall in themselves. George Stephenson and his colleagues were indeed establishing the physical parameters within which the British railway system was to be constructed, in height, width, and the rail-gauge of the rolling stock. Furthermore, the early line-side structures were so massively constructed as to deter anyone from altering them when, in later years, the physical restrictions of the Stephenson railways were realised and greater elbow room, both upward and outwards, would have been an advantage.

The Americans started from the beginning in more spacious ways. On their early railways there was practically nothing in the way of over-line crossings. Locomotives and carriages built in the U.S.A. were much taller. On the Mohawk and Hudson Railroad, and on the Baltimore and Ohio, double-deck carriages were built in the early 1830s. The Imlay design on the latter line even went to the extent of providing a canopy for the passengers seated on the roof.

The French railways in the Saint-Etienne district are believed to have applied the 'gravity' principle of working even to passenger trains, an extension of the technique used on the Stockton and Darlington Railway. On the main line of that railway the coal trains were equipped with what was called a 'dandy cart'. When the train reached a descending gradient the horse was unhitched and led back to ride in the 'dandy', and the train ran by gravity. Judging from some old prints in French railway archives, passenger trains on the Saint-Etienne and Andrezieux line,

A primitive steel-engraving showing the early Paris–Versailles line, from a popular broadsheet of the time.

consisting of two or more 'double-decker' coaches, were run by gravity on the descending gradients, with the driver sitting on the leading coach. Like the British and the earliest Americans, these French coaches were four-wheelers; but in the U.S.A. the rough tracks that made British-built locomotives so unsuitable were equally bad for light four-wheeled carriages. From the early 1830s the pioneer American railroads began to develop the long carriage, borne on two four-wheeled bogies, or 'trucks' as they are known in America. This design provided a degree of flexibility on sharp curves, but also adapted itself easily to inequalities or irregularities in the track. Very soon it became the standard design for both passenger and freight vehicles.

Another very important distinction between British and American railways became apparent early on. Reference has already been made to the relatively straight and level tracks engineered in Great Britain, and to the massive excavations, embankments, and viaducts needed to provide such roads. While the Americans had necessarily to build their early railroads on a minimum of capital, and consequently were forced to use heavy gradients and sharp curvature to reduce the costs of construction in hilly country, there were locations where bridges could not be avoided, and some of these were very large. For such instances where the cost of brick or masonry structures in the British style would have been prohibitive, the material most readily to hand was used, with great ingenuity of design and skill in construction –

Stephenson was engaged on improvements to the very simple four-wheeled engines working the traffic on the Liverpool and Manchester Railway, as a manufacturer he was aware of the widely differing conditions abroad that offered scope for export business; and when the deputation of engineers from the Baltimore and Ohio Railroad visited Newcastle in 1828, and told him of the intention to include curves of a 400-foot radius on the main line, he put forward for their consideration a type of locomotive very different in its wheel arrangement from anything then running in England. He suggested a locomotive with a single pair of driving wheels at the rear end, and the front to be carried on a swivelling truck, or bogie, that would readily adapt itself to the sharp curves. An engine called the *Brother Jonathan*, the first ever to be built new in the U.S.A., was constructed on this principle in 1832, and certain locomotives of the traditional Stephenson type were rebuilt on similar lines. They had excellent tracking qualities, and as vehicles were ideal for the characteristically rough American railroads. Robert Stephenson & Co. did not export a *new* engine of this design until 1833, when they received an order for one for the Saratoga and Schenectady Railroad. It was the first 'bogie' engine ever built by Stephenson's.

The problem of hauling loads up steep gradients was one that the earliest British locomotive engineers had quite openly evaded. Cable haulage had been used on the steep inclines of the colliery lines in north-east England, and at the western end of the

The locomotive *Atlantic* was built for the Baltimore and Ohio Railroad in 1832. It was subsequently preserved, and it operated under its own power at the railroad's centenary celebrations in 1927. The coaches shown in the picture are exact replicas of those used in 1832.

namely timber. The technique of building timber trestle viaducts, some of tremendous height, and some on continuous curves, was developed to an astonishing degree; and although there were occasional accidents, and sometimes damage by fire, these timber viaducts played a vital part in the railway development in the nineteenth century all over the American continent.

Returning now to locomotives, while Robert

Liverpool and Manchester Railway; but in 1836 a small American locomotive, the *George Washington*, built by William Norris for the Philadelphia and Columbia Railroad, achieved something that was quite new in railway traction. Near Philadelphia there was an inclined plane, roughly half a mile long, on which the track rose 196 feet. This was an inclination of 1 in 14, which at that time was considered far too steep for any locomotive to haul a load. But on a certain Sunday in July 1836, the *George Washington*, hauling a load of ten tons, plus twenty-four persons, climbed that steep gradient in a fraction over two minutes, at an average speed of 15 miles per hour. It is true that the little engine was not hauling much more than its own weight but, as a distinguished engineering journalist, Zerah Colburn, said, 'In 1836, such a feat as was achieved by the *George Washington* took the engineering world by storm, and was hardly credited'–despite, one might add, the actual name of the locomotive! Be that as it may, the fame of William Norris spread far and wide, and he exported many locomotives of a similar type to Europe.

In the meantime attention in England had also been centred on the production of locomotives that would be able to run safely at higher speeds. The *Planet* type, although much smoother in its action than the *Rocket*, still showed a tendency to 'yaw' at any speed, and in 1833 Robert Stephenson & Co. developed this type into one of the classics of British locomotive history, by adding a pair of carrying wheels under the firebox, and turning the 2–2–0 of the *Planet* into a 2–2–2. This arrangement was patented, and the design became known as the *Patentee*. The extra pair of carrying wheels worked wonders with the riding, and before the decade was out locomotives of this type were running safely at nearly 60 miles per hour on the sound British tracks. Six-wheeled Stephenson locomotives of this same general type were the first ever to run in Belgium, Germany and Russia. But before discussing these important develop-

ments the story must be told of how railways came to these European countries, recalling that in the critical year of 1832 France, although having a mineral railway in the Saint-Etienne district, had not yet adopted steam traction.

In Belgium the construction of railways was a matter of urgent national policy. The geographical boundaries of the new independent sovereign state that emerged from centuries of foreign domination in the revolution of 1830 left Belgium cut off from the mouth of the river Schelde, and the great port of Antwerp was feared to be in danger of losing its trade. First class communication with the Rhineland seemed a vital necessity. Leopold of Saxe-Coburg, crowned King of the Belgians in July 1831, took a personal hand in pressing for the construction of a comprehensive system of communications 'from the sea coast and the Schelde to the Meuse and the Rhine, answering to the wishes and requirements of the entire country', and on 1 May 1834 there was enacted a measure unique in the history of railways, providing for state ownership of a new national railway system. The main line was to run from Ostend to Liège and the Prussian frontier with a central junction at Malines, about fifteen miles to the north of Brussels. From these, branches were to be constructed, northwards to Antwerp, and southwards to the capital. It was the latter section from Brussels to Malines that was completed first. It was not only the first railway in Belgium, but also the first on the continent of Europe to use steam traction.

The Belgian Government called in George Stephenson as consultant, and the first locomotives were all British. As might be expected the orders were placed with Robert Stephenson & Co., but the firm was very busy at the time, and while building two of the locomotives at Newcastle the order for the third was transferred to the newly-established firm of Tayleur & Co. of Newton-le-Willows in Lancashire. (This

Right. The first excursion trip of the *Best Friend* on 15 January 1831.

Below. Friedrich List, architect of a plan for a complete railway network for the Germanic states.

Opposite top. Scene at the ceremonial opening of the *Ludwigsbahn* on 7 December 1835. The first steam locomotive in Germany, *Der Adler*, built by Stephenson. The driver is an Englishman named Wilson.

Opposite bottom. The first locomotive to run in the State of Mississippi, built in England in 1834, and shipped to Natchez, Mississippi, in 1837. Later it carried soldiers, cannon and supplies during the Union Army's siege of Vicksburg.

firm later became the world-famous Vulcan Foundry.) The two locomotives built at Newcastle were of the *Patentee* 2–2–2 type and were named *La Flèche* and *Stephenson*. The Tayleur engine was four-coupled, with a pair of leading wheels under the front end; it was named *L'Eléphant*. All three locomotives were in steam when the royal opening of the line took place on 5 May 1835. It was considered appropriate that the first train should have an English driver, and during the ceremonies both George and Robert Stephenson were decorated by King Leopold. The steam railway certainly had an auspicious send-off in Belgium, but the Brussels and Malines line was not really prepared for the popularity that descended upon it. There was only a limited number of carriages, and so many people wanted to make the journey, just for the ride, that speculators bought up blocks of tickets and sold them at black-market prices! The carriages themselves were very crude, being even more open than the 'thirds' on the Liverpool and Manchester Railway, and one had to climb into them by loose ladders. Nevertheless, railways were now launched on a national scale in Belgium, and a year later the line was completed to Antwerp.

It may come as something of a surprise to learn that the earliest ideas of a steam railway system for the Germanic states, as they then were, were conceived in America, by a Württemberg man named Friedrich List, exiled in Reading, Pennsylvania. He was a man of outstanding intellect and administrative ability, but his liberal views had made his native country too hot for him, and in the U.S.A. he quickly established himself as a coal-mining proprietor. In 1831 he built a non-steam railway from Tamaqua, Pennsylvania, to Port Clinton on the Schuylkill Canal—a distance of twenty-one miles—and seeing the rapid growth of these settlements into towns of considerable size and prosperity List had the idea of building railways in his own homeland. Even so, he had attained a position of eminence in the U.S.A. and might in other circumstances have been reluctant to leave; but in 1832, when he was 43 years of age, the President of the U.S.A., then Andrew Jackson, invited him to become American Consul in Leipzig, and so he returned to Germany and soon after published a plan for a complete railway network for the Germanic states.

At first the atmosphere did not seem propitious. List's plan was greeted by an outpouring of pamphlets

from learned circles (some of which were bought up and burnt by the early railway promoters). Among the more absurd utterances they contained was the following, emanating from the Bavarian College of Physicians:

'The rapid movement must inevitably generate in the travellers a brain disease, a special variety of the *Delirium furiosum*. If travellers are nevertheless determined to brave this fearful danger, the State must at least protect the onlookers, for otherwise these will be affected with the same brain disease at the sight of the rapidly running steam wagon. It is therefore necessary to enclose the railway on both sides with a high, tight board fence.'

Train spotters please note!

Then at the University of Erlangen in Bavaria, a certain Professor Kips issued a pamphlet in which he attacked the proposed railways not from any human considerations, but for their likely effect on horse-breeding. From the military point of view, he argued, it would make cavalry and artillery impossible. 'In case of war, enemy cavalry could swarm into Bavaria without the state army being able to put up any resistance unless cavalry horses could be brought from *abroad* at high prices.' He then went on to dilate on the dangers should lightning strike the rails, which he said would interrupt communications for weeks and months. His final shot was 'Though everything delude and deceive, the post office and the licensed coachman will put an end to the thing.'

In February 1834, however, Ludwig I, King of Bavaria, gave the Royal Assent to the construction of a railway four miles long from Nuremberg to Fürth, known as the *Ludwigsbahn*. Stephenson's won the order for the first locomotive after a German firm found it could not meet the delivery date. The locomotive they supplied, the first ever to run in Germany, was *Der Adler*, a very small edition of the *Patentee* type already in use on the Liverpool and Manchester Railway. The *Patentee* weighed 11·45 tons, and *Der Adler* no more than 6·6 tons. The line was opened, with much pomp and circumstance, on 7 December 1835. Stephenson's supplied the driver as well as the locomotive and this Englishman, named Wilson, was considered so important that his pay was nearly double that of the manager of the railway. It is interesting to note that so far as traction was concerned, arrangements were exactly the reverse of those on the Stockton and Darlington, in that the

Above. Ludwig I, King of Bavaria, who in 1834 gave assent to the construction of the first railway in Germany, the *Ludwigsbahn*, from Nuremberg to Fürth.

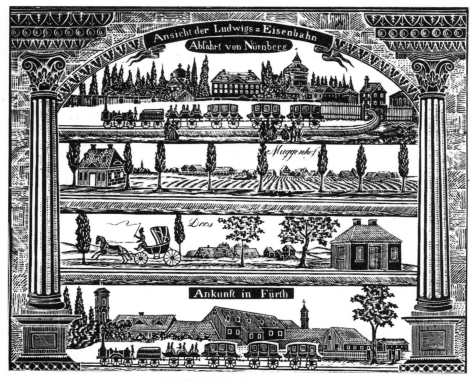

Above. A curious print showing the route of the *Ludwigsbahn*, starting from Nuremberg, passing through the intermediate stations of Muggenhof and Doos, and ending at Fürth.

Right. Canada: the pioneer Champlain and St Lawrence Railroad, opened in 1836, issued notes with values in English, French, American and Spanish currency.

Opposite top. Hand-coloured engraving showing the scene at the opening of the Liverpool and Manchester Railway, 15 September 1830. The Moorish Arch is in the background.

Opposite bottom. The London and Greenwich Railway, London's first. It ran entirely on a brick viaduct.

Overleaf top. A train of first class carriages on the Liverpool and Manchester Railway, and the mail coach, 1830. There are striking parallels with the stagecoach, down to the 'coachman' seated atop the front and rear carriages, and the luggage stowed on the roofs.

Overleaf centre. A coal train on France's first railway, the Lyons and Saint-Etienne, opened in 1829.

Overleaf bottom. Brunel's South Devon Atmospheric Railway: the view at Exeter Station from a series of contemporary watercolours of scenery along the line.

from Leipzig to Dresden, seventy-one-and-three-quarter miles, which was opened in April 1839, and which included the first railway in Germany, near Oberau. Six months earlier the development of railways had received a tremendous fillip, which swept away all the gloomy prognostications of timid and pessimistic hearts. At the end of October 1838, a railway sixteen-and-a-half miles long had been opened between Berlin and Potsdam. The ceremony was performed by the Crown Prince of Prussia, Friedrich Wilhelm, who later married Victoria, Princess Royal of the United Kingdom, and became still later the first Emperor of the united Germany. At the opening of the Berlin–Potsdam Railway he declared: 'No human arm will ever stop the progress of this car, which will roll through the world.' Alas for Friedrich List the approbation of the Crown Prince of Prussia was not enough to offset the ridicule, ingratitude, and ostracism he received from most of his contemporaries; saddened and impoverished he took his own life at Kufstein in 1846, at the age of 57.

In the 1830s the colony of Canada consisted of little more than the settlements along the St Lawrence river; Nova Scotia and New Brunswick and Prince Edward Island were quite separate colonies. One of the great problems of Canadian commerce had always been the freezing of the St Lawrence river for many months during the winter and the need was felt for some efficient means of transport between Quebec and the ports on the Atlantic seaboard in the British colonies. As early as 1832 there had been proposals for a railway from Quebec to St Andrews, a port on the Bay of Fundy. In January 1836 interested parties, encouraged by the support of the Lieutenant Governor of the Colony of New Brunswick, sent a deputation to England to present a petition to King William IV, and enter into negotiations with the imperial government. This was no local project, but a trunk line some five hundred miles long – by far the most extensive and ambitious railway proposal yet launched anywhere in the world. No colonial interests could possibly furnish the necessary finance.

The result was that the British Government made a gift of £10,000 to pay for the cost of a survey. But the route that was proposed – an almost straight line from Quebec to Halifax, Nova Scotia – came up against the question of the unresolved frontier between Canada and the U.S.A., and a strong protest came from the United States government. The Americans looked on the proposed railway as a strategic threat – an interesting foreshadowing of the immense strategic importance that railways were later to acquire. In the event of trouble, troops could be landed at Halifax and rushed quickly to Quebec, or Montreal, whatever the state of the St Lawrence estuary; and until the boundary question was settled the route of such a railway could well have passed through American territory. The imperial government in London, anxious to avoid an open dispute, ordered a halt to the work and the project for the 'Intercolonial Railway' hung fire for the next twenty years.

one steam locomotive was used for hauling passenger trains, while the goods trains were drawn by horses. Unlike the pioneer railways in England and the U.S.A. the first steam railway in Germany was never part of the national network subsequently built up.

Despite the dire prophecies of physicians and other 'wise men', the *Ludwigsbahn*, like its counterparts in England, set the ball rolling in Germany. In April 1837 a short line five-and-three-quarter miles long, and pioneered by Friedrich List, was opened between Leipzig and Alten, and this proved to be only the first stage of the first main line in Germany. This was

Liverpool to London, by the Grand Junction & Birmingham Railway _____ 210 __ 10

London to Dover, over the London and Greenwich Viaduct or Railway
the Plan for its continuation to Dover being now in the House of Commons } 72 __ 4

Dover to Calais, by Steam Vessels _____ 21 __ 2

Calais to Paris, by Railway (commenced by the French Government) _____ 180 __ 8

Total   M. 483   H. 24

The Steam Vessels, after the Railway is completed, will, it is contemplated, be restricted from navigating the Thames above Deptford, by which numerous accidents on the River will be prevented.

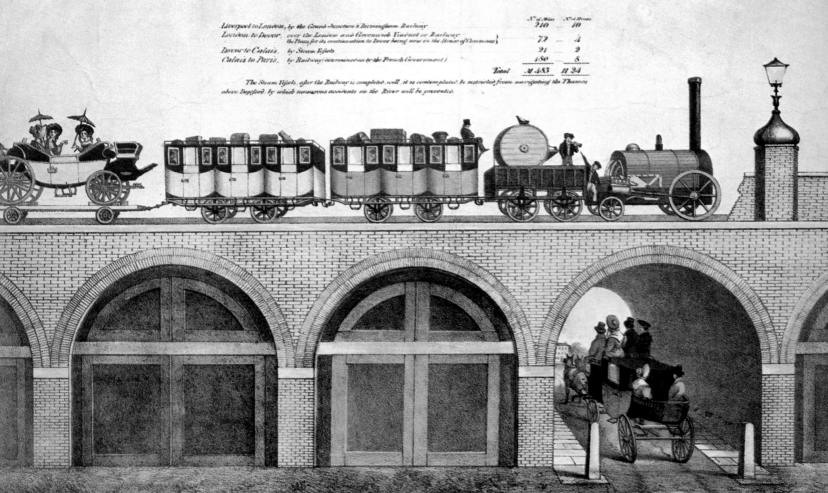

In the meantime, however, a railway in the conventional style of the early pioneers had been approaching completion. This was the Champlain and St Lawrence Railroad, a line fourteen miles long extending from Laprairie, on the right bank of the St Lawrence opposite to Montreal, to St Johns on the Richelieu River. A specially-built steamer, named *Princess Victoria* after the heir to the British throne, provided a connection with Montreal and the locomotive which took part in the grand opening on 21 July 1836 was a 0–4–0 built by Stephenson's, called the *Dorchester*.

The years 1835–40 were of immense importance in the development of railways everywhere. While railways on the continent of Europe were just beginning, with Austria, France and Russia opening their first steam lines in 1837 to add to those of Belgium and Germany, Italy and the Netherlands followed suit in 1839. Great Britain was fully launched on the construction of a national network – not, I hasten to add, through any central co-ordinated planning, but by a series of individual, quite unconnected private enterprises, which in their aggregate effect were soon to produce the same result. While many of these projects had their origins in provincial cities, the overall effect was to make London the focal point of the developing network, with lines building up, or proposed, to Dover, Brighton, Southampton, Bristol, Birmingham and East Anglia, with northward continuation to Liverpool and Manchester, to Leeds, York and Newcastle, and with eventual penetrations into Scotland. There were cross-country lines between Newcastle and Carlisle, and between Edinburgh and Glasgow, and much consideration was being given to the route for conveying the Irish Mail between London and Dublin. By the year 1840 the railway map of the world would indeed have looked a little odd, with a close concentration of activity in one small island, and no more than a few small enterprises elsewhere – except of course in the U.S.A. where a number of lines were under construction along the Atlantic seaboard.

The British philosophy of railway building, which had been highlighted in the contrast between the layout of the Liverpool and Manchester line and some of the earliest railroads in the U.S.A., continued in full measure on trunk routes under construction in the late 1830s and for a few years thereafter. Perhaps its clearest expression was in the attitude to gradients. George Stephenson considered that the maximum inclination for any steam-worked railway was 1 in 330 if the locomotive was to maintain a reasonable speed when running uphill. The London and Birmingham, on which his son was engineer, was built to this specification; and although it ran through country that could be considered flat compared to that traversed by some of the pioneer American railroads, it involved some tremendous engineering works: long tunnels north of Watford and under the Kilsby ridge, near Rugby, and enormous excavations in the Tring and Blisworth cuttings. It is certain that if the railway had been built no

more than fifteen years later it would have been taken up hill and down dale on much steeper gradients and the cost of construction would have been a mere fraction of that actually involved. Certainly, the superb line that eventuated from Stephenson's work was of lasting benefit to many succeeding generations of railway managers and engineers, but it was obtained at a heavy price, not only in money, but also in human endurance – physical and mental alike.

In building the original main line of the Great

Western from London to Bristol, the great Isambard Kingdom Brunel carried the philosophy of easy gradients almost to the point of a fetish, yet with two very curious contradictions. From Reading, thirty-six miles to the west of London, instead of following the natural route of old, through established centres of population like Newbury, Hungerford and Devizes, he chose to make a wide sweep to the north to obtain an almost gradeless alignment through the Vale of the White Horse, by-passing even the smaller towns that lay to right and left and securing a gradient no steeper at any point than 1 in 660, until reaching the watershed between the catchment areas of the Thames and the western Avon. Then he suddenly dropped down a slight escarpment on a slope of 1 in 100 for a mile and a half. This, however, is a minor point compared to his unusual solution of the physical problem which confronted him at a point some ninety-six miles west of London, where today the train enters the Box Tunnel – at one and the same time a phenomenon, a legend, and a monumental work of civil engineering.

At that point the railway was crossing the southern flanks of the extensive limestone plateau of the Cotswold Hills, characteristically high and level in the interior, and dipping to the river valleys in precipitous escarpments. One such valley lay immediately beyond the high ridge known generally as Box Hill, and the railway had to reach river level in that valley to proceed westwards to Bath and its

of 1 in 100, almost entirely in tunnel. It was considered a most daring, foolhardy piece of work at the time, and in view of the simpler and less costly alternative available one can indeed question why Brunel chose the tunnel and that steep gradient, when he had taken such care to avoid such features on the major part of the line. Herein, however, lies the legend: every year, on Brunel's birthday, the rising sun shines through the tunnel from end to end! It is more than a legend, it is a fact. Brunel was nothing if not a showman, and one draws the inescapable conclusion that it was a piece of consummate personal planning. Unless he had had the slope at 1 in 100 the sun's rays could not have penetrated; the tunnel had to be straight from end to end, and sited at precisely the right angle. The tunnel itself is a superb piece of engineering, with a stupendous classical entrance at the west end in full view of the Bath road, where it crosses the railway.

Questions of personal vanity apart, however, the men who were building the English railways in the late 1830s were deeply conscious of the new era they were inaugurating. Some years later an eminent newspaper said: 'Railway termini and hotels are to the nineteenth century what monasteries and cathedrals were to the thirteenth century. They are truly the only real representative building we possess . . . Our metropolitan termini have been leaders of the art of our time.' It could indeed be said that the grandeur of early railway architecture in England

terminus in Bristol. To an engineer intent on securing the easiest of gradients the logical course would seem to have been to top the ridge, possibly in a deep cutting, and then to contour gradually down the escarpment, losing height over a distance of seven or eight miles. Instead, however, Brunel took a wide sweep to the south and tunnelled deep under Box Hill to reach the floor level of the valley in no more than two miles, once again resorting to the steep gradient reflected the grand, expansionist outlook of the age, which was followed as railways developed overseas on an even more elaborate and spectacular scale on the continent of Europe, in the U.S.A. and still later in the Empire of India. At the start of what could be called the 'main line era', as distinct from the early industrial activity in the north, some of the builders were inclined to overreach themselves, as in the colossal ornamentation that marked the approach to Euston station, the terminus of the London and Birmingham Railway. As early as 1838, H. N. Humphreys, writing in the *Architectural Magazine*, compared the whole line to the aqueducts of Rome, and considered that it far eclipsed the latter, while having the additional merit of not having been built with slave labour. He was clearly overawed by the architectural work at Euston, but thought that on the grounds of fitness to its purpose Stephenson's engineering along the line was superior to Philip Hardwick's architecture; but another commentator referring particularly to the Doric Arch felt that the national character had been involved in the execution of the project. So much so indeed that when Euston was first built it was regarded not as a railway station but as a spectacle. Visitors used to flock to it in omnibuses, and examine it with all the careful scrutiny of architectural sightseers.

Of course there were some who considered it, and certain other ornamental works on the early railways, a shocking waste of money. In 1843 A. W. N. Pugin, writing *An Apology for the Revival of Christian*

Architecture in England, said of Euston:

'The Architects have evidently considered it an opportunity for *showing off what they could do* instead of *carrying out what was required*. Hence the colossal Grecian portico or gateway, 100 feet high, for the cabs to drive through and set down a few feet further, at the 14-inch brick wall, and sash-window booking office. This piece of Brobdingnagian absurdity must have cost the company a sum which would have built a first-rate station, replete with convenience, and which would have been really grand from its simplicity.'

Certainly the very pinnacle of ostentation and grandeur in early railway station architecture was touched in the Doric Arch at Euston, and in the years immediately following there was work at Derby, Bristol, Newcastle and Brighton. Later magnificent stations were built in the U.S.A., Europe, India, Australia and South Africa, but in the early days the evolution of stations took place almost entirely in Great Britain.

The constructional characteristics of the early British main line railways had a profound effect on locomotive development, which extended to much of Europe, but not to North America. In England the tracks were not only made relatively straight and level, with the under-line structures massively built in brick or stone, but on plain, open line every attempt was made to keep the road-bed firm, rigid and well drained. The aim was to secure smooth running and, by minimising the interaction between track, locomotives and rolling stock, to cause the least disturb-

Above. Isambard Kingdom Brunel, first chief engineer of the Great Western Railway, and staunch upholder of the broad gauge of 7 feet.

Below left. The *Pioneer*, first locomotive of what became the Chicago North Western. It was built in 1836 and after serving two other railroads was bought by the Galena and Chicago Union, and so in 1848 became the very first locomotive to operate in Chicago.

Opposite top. The London and Birmingham Railway: building the cutting and retaining wall at Camden Town, in the lithograph by J. C. Bourne. The line was opened throughout in 1838.

Opposite bottom. A cartoon of early days in England: a narrow escape of the Queen's Staghounds on the Great Western Railway. There was more earnestness than jest about the regard of the G.W.R. for hounds, and until the 1950s – the *nineteen* fifties – the following notice appeared in the working timetables: 'Every care should be taken to avoid running over PACKS OF HOUNDS, which, during the Hunting Season, may cross the Line.'

Below. Early example of
one of the famous 'One-arm
Billies', built by William Norris
of Philadelphia in 1837. It was
the first locomotive of the
Baltimore and Ohio to have a
horizontal boiler.

Opposite. A Norris engine
exported to England, working
on the notorious Lickey
Incline, near Bromsgrove,
Worcestershire, where the
gradient is 1 in 37 for two
miles. This is part of the
Birmingham and Gloucester
Railway, constructed to the
British standard gauge of
4 feet 8½ inches, which made
an end-on confrontation with
Brunel's 7 foot gauge of the
Great Western at
Gloucester.

ance to the machinery. Few of the early methods of
track laying came anywhere near to this ideal when
speeds began to rise from the 40 miles per hour to
the 50 miles per hour range. The Stephenson technique of laying on stone blocks had the disadvantage
that the individual blocks 'settled' unevenly into the
ground and required constant fettling to keep the
track true to level. In one place where a cutting had
been blasted from the solid rock the rails were spiked
directly, and some people thought they would last
forever. On the Great Western Brunel used what was
termed a 'bridge' rail, supported from end to end on
continuous baulks of timber, and resting on piles
driven deep into the ground to provide additional
support and rigidity. And in keeping with this constant quest for rigidity locomotives were designed
with compact short wheelbases, with all wheels
carried in a single frame, and having only the springing
of each pair of wheels available to take up any
irregularities in the track.

No description of the actual works would be
complete without paying a tribute to the men who
built them. I am not referring here to the engineers,
or even to the contractors, but to those cornerstones
of the early railways, the down-to-earth navvies.
In England and Scotland the contractors were
fortunate in having a certain quantity of first class
labour ready to hand. Many men had been employed
in the making of embankments and cuttings for canals.
This is how they got their name, for 'navvy' was a
colloquialism for 'navigator'. Men of this type

formed the backbone of the contractors' forces.
The work they did each day was prodigious. Thousands of them would be working as teams on a single
cutting or embankment, and the contractors saw to it
that they were highly paid. There were few labour
troubles, and when their bosses secured overseas
contracts the men were glad enough to go with them,
to form the spearhead of the workforce.

In America the developing situation was exactly

the opposite. The pioneer railroads just could not
afford the fine grading and alignments of the English
tracks – still less to provide massive road-beds once
the 'right of way' had been established; for American
conditions the British type of locomotive was useless.
Something quite different from the short-wheelbase,
rigid-framed six-wheeler was needed to travel safely
on the light, cheaply-laid American track, to mount
steep gradients and negotiate sharp curves. At first
speed was a purely minor consideration. The evolution

of the 'American' type of locomotive to meet these
conditions is one of the great stories of railway
mechanical engineering. While the British were
developing the *Rocket* and *Planet* types into the 2–2–2
which lasted so long in Great Britain itself, and was
exported to many European countries, the Americans,
faced with very different track conditions, worked on
the simple basic principle of three-point suspension.
(A three-legged stool is stable no matter how uneven

the ground, while four or more legs will wobble unless the ground is level.) The first American locomotives built on this principle were of the 4–2–0 type, with a single pair of driving wheels at the extreme rear end, axleboxes mounted on the main frames, and a bogie or truck swivelling on a single pivot point at the front end. The most successful engines of this design were those built by William Norris, builder of the *George Washington* locomotive and manager of the American Steam Carriage

and most surprisingly for the Birmingham and Gloucester Railway in England, for use on the Lickey Incline, of all places. This was a precipitous descent of two miles, at 1 in 37, at Bromsgrove in Worcestershire, which it was thought quite impossible to operate with ordinary locomotives. But although the wheel arrangement on the Norris 4–2–0s gave good tracking, the single pair of driving wheels and the limited adhesion weight that could be placed upon them restricted the tractive power. Just as

Company of Philadelphia. His standard pattern had outside cylinders and a 'hay stack' type of firebox, popular on some early British designs. Norris was so confident of his design, and so eager to promote an export trade in locomotives, that in March 1838 he issued a nineteen-page prospectus in English, French and German.

Locomotives of his standard 4–2–0 design were built for the Berlin–Potsdam Railway, for Austria,

Stephenson, Hackworth and other British pioneers secured increased tractive power by coupling the axles, so the Americans developed the 4–2–0 into a 4–4–0, by having four coupled wheels at the rear end. The principle of the three-point suspension was retained because the suspension of the coupled driving axles was connected through an equalising level to a single point on each side of the main frames. This type was the most popular wheel arrangement in nineteenth-century America. It was well suited to all kinds of service, passenger, goods or shunting, and it became in fact the national engine known universally – outside Europe! – as the 'American' type. Nothing like it was seen in Great Britain for very many years and its distinction was further accentuated from very early days by the mounting of large cabs for the enginemen, at a time when most European locomotives had no cabs at all. A further point of difference was the use on many American locomotives of

W^{M.} MASON & Co BUILDERS TAUNTON MASS.

huge 'balloon' chimney stacks, including spark-arresting apparatus where wood was the standard fuel.

In the early days of railways in many parts of the world far-sighted engineers felt that the rail gauge of the first British railways was likely to have a constraining influence on the design of locomotives and the accommodation that could be provided in the carriages. George Stephenson had built his earliest locomotives to the gauge of the old wagonways in the collieries of north-eastern England. The Liverpool and Manchester Railway had been the same. Stephenson had no doubt that all these British railways would be connected up one day, and he had no hesitation in recommending the same gauge for them all – the rather odd 4 feet 8½ inches. On the continent of Europe, largely through the early British influence, the majority of the railways were built to the same gauge; but at first there was considerable diversity in North America. Some roads were built to 4 feet 8½ inches, others to 5 feet 6 inches, and some to 6 feet. How far this diversity might have continued it is difficult to imagine had not things been brought to a crisis point in Great Britain itself, as a result of the adoption by the Great Western Railway of a gauge of no less than 7 feet, on the recommendation of their dashing and unorthodox chief engineer, Brunel. It might have seemed that such a decision was flying in the face of established convention and all the canons of practical politics; but Brunel was unshakable in his arguments and the board of the Great Western decided to adopt the broad gauge

in October 1835. At the time there was probably not much more than one hundred miles of the 'standard' gauge in operation, but the situation was to change dramatically in the ensuing ten years, and the seeds were sown for the serious confrontation that led to the setting up of a Royal Commission on Railway Gauges.

Before this, however, there had been important developments elsewhere. The year 1837 saw the beginnings of railways in two more European countries. Some time previously the Czar of Russia, when in England, had visited the Middleton Colliery railway, seen several of Blenkinsop's primitive locomotives at work, and been duly impressed. Then in 1834 an Austrian engineer, Franz von Gerstner, went to Russia to inspect some mines. Strangely enough though the first proposal he made for a Russian railway was not connected with any industrial enterprise but was purely for pleasure. A new entertainment centre had just been established at Tsarskoe Selo, about fifteen miles from St Petersburg, and Gerstner sought a concession to build a railway connecting the two. The Czar gave it readily, and in March 1836 the Petersburg and Pavlovsk Railway Company was formed. The Austrian engineer recommended a gauge of 6 feet, but all the earliest equipment was obtained from England. There were three locomotives, one each from Robert Stephenson, Timothy Hackworth, and Tayleur & Co. The rivalry between Hackworth and the Stephensons stemming from the Rainhill trials of 1829 was still manifest in contemp-

adventures young John Hackworth had in getting the locomotive to St Petersburg in the depths of winter. All normal routes were frozen over, and they had to land their cargo at the nearest port on the Baltic that was open and make the rest of the journey by sleigh, across the snow. At one stage they had to run the gauntlet of a pack of wolves. The engine itself was a large and handsome 2–2–2, and it was duly steamed in November 1836, at Tsarskoe Selo, in the presence of the Czar himself. Young Hackworth was introduced to the Emperor who expressed himself delighted and amazed at the development of the locomotive. He recalled that the only previous occasion he had seen one was twenty years earlier at Middleton Colliery.

Before being put into public service a year later the engine had to be put through a baptismal ceremony, according to the rites of the Greek Orthodox Church. This was done in the presence of an assembly of the public. Water was obtained from a nearby marsh in a golden censer, sanctified by the immersion of a golden cross amid the singing of a choir and the intonations of priests, while a hundred lighted tapers were held round it. This was followed by the invocation of special blessings upon the Czar and the imperial family, and fervent supplications that on all occasions of travel by the new mode they might be swiftly and safely conveyed. Then came the due Administration of the Ordinance by a priest bearing the holy censer. Meanwhile a second priest, carrying a huge brush, and dipping it in the holy water, dashed

orary accounts of the locomotives exported to Russia in 1836.

The Stephenson engine was a conventional 2–2–2 of the *Patentee* type, and on trial it was claimed to have run at 65½ miles per hour–in 1836! Hackworth went one better, and announced that 'This engine is constructed on an improved principle, and finished in the best manner. She has been tried on the premises, and propelled at the rate of 72 miles per hour . . .' This was really stretching things, because 'on the premises' presumably meant in Hackworth's factory. Where there would have been space, and suitable track, to run a locomotive up to 72 miles per hour, is indeed a mystery. Hackworth's learned biographer, Robert Young, makes no mention of this extraordinary speed claim; but he does record some of the

each wheel of the locomotive with the sign of the Cross, ending with showers of water all over the engine and the men on the footplate! When the public trial of both the Stephenson and Hackworth engines was made in October 1837, several thousand people gathered to watch, and many spectators crossed themselves at the sight of the two locomotives as if they had been demons. As in every other country where these pioneer railways were installed, not everyone was enthusiastic. The St Petersburg–Pavlovsk Railway was regarded by some cynics as a toy of the Czar, and one man contrasted it unfavourably with other countries where railways had been built for industrial use. The Russian enterprise, he commented, ran merely from the capital city to a tavern! The 6 foot gauge was not perpetuated: for

Left. Prussia: the opening of the Berlin and Potsdam Railway by the Crown Prince, later the first Kaiser of the united Germany, 1838.

Opposite top. An early and very typical example of the 'American' type of locomotive, designed to ride easily and safely on the pioneer tracks of the U.S.A.

Opposite bottom. 'Lost at Gloucester' was the universal explanation for anything that got mislaid on the railways of Great Britain at the time of the gauge controversy. Everything had to be trans-shipped from broad to standard gauge, or vice versa, at Gloucester.

the trunk line from St Petersburg to Moscow a gauge of 5 feet was preferred and this became the Russian standard.

The beginning of railways in the old Austro-Hungarian Empire also took place under imperial patronage, but in a rather different way from that in Russia. By the year 1835 two powerful financial groups, led by Solomon Rothschild and Baron Sina, were both seeking concessions to build railways. Rothschild got in first, with authority to build a line

Two historic Austrian locomotives now in the railway museum at Vienna: the *Ajax (left)*, built in England in 1841 by Jones, Turner and Evans for the Kaiser Ferdinand's Northern Railway, and the *Steinbrück*, built in 1848 by Haswell.

Opposite top. 'The great international railway suspension bridge over the Niagara River connecting the United States and Canada, the New York Central and Great Western railways, 1859.'

Opposite bottom. Fire following a derailment near Versailles in 1842. The death toll in this great French disaster was greatly increased by the fact that the passengers were at that time locked in the carriages.

from Vienna northward across the Danube to Florids-dorf and Wagram. The Emperor Ferdinand granted this concession only six months after he had succeeded to the throne, and the line was at first known as the Vienna–Bochnia Railway; but in 1836, by an astute move, Rothschild changed the name to 'the Kaiser Ferdinand's *Nordbahn*', and by this evidence of imperial identification, hoped to block the aspirations of Baron Sina's rival financial group. The first section of the *Nordbahn* was opened in November 1837; in the following January regular steam-hauled train working began and by July 1839 it had been extended as far as Brno, a distance of eighty-one miles. As in the case of so many early railways the first locomotives were all British-built. The engine working the inaugural train was a *Planet* type 2–2–0 by Robert Stephenson & Co., and a total of sixteen were supplied, some by Stephensons, and some by Tayleur, over the next three years. But Austria was early in the field of locomotive building, and several firms that were to achieve great fame were being established in the 1840s.

The year 1837 was also notable for the opening of the first railway in France to be a 'common carrier', as distinct from the private and mainly industrial lines in the neighbourhood of Saint-Etienne. The new French railway ran from Paris to Saint-Germain, a distance of thirteen miles, and was originally planned for steam operation throughout but had, for a period of twelve years, a diversity of traction methods.

Like the first railway in Russia it was favoured with a royal opening, by Queen Marie-Amélie, in the absence of King Louis-Philippe. One feels, however, that royal attendances at railway opening ceremonies – so frequent in early days in Europe – were evidence more of fashionable interest in the latest mechanical wonders of the age than of any appreciation of the transforming social, political and economic consequences that the growth of railways was to have. Perhaps if they had been able to foresee these consequences – the political and social ones at any rate, if not the industrial ones – they might have taken steps to ostracise, rather than patronise, the railways – as indeed the Duke of Wellington tried to do in England. At a time of great social unrest he feared that railways would assist in the moving of radical agitators from one part of the country to another.

Naturally the opening of the Paris–Saint-Germain railway attracted a good deal of attention, and admiration for the courage of the Queen, then fifty-five years old, for venturing to embark on this novel form of transport. As in Russia, there were many who were not enthusiastic. One leading statesman described the railway as a plaything, good for nothing but to take students and their *grisettes* out to the Forest of Saint-Germain. But like early railways elsewhere it survived the critics. A contemporary account describes how a certain ceremony attended the departure of the trains. A bell was tolled, upon which a gate was opened through which the first class passengers passed to their seats in the train, watched by the second class passengers from behind a barrier. Not until all the first class travellers were comfortably settled were the second class allowed to entrain, being given entrance through a separate gate on to the platform. While great care was thus taken to segregate passengers of the different classes their welfare was looked after in other ways. Men were stationed at intervals along the line, not only to invigilate on the condition of the permanent way but 'to retrieve and restore to the management such objects as travellers in their excitement or jubilation might let fall from the train'!

Originally the line terminated at Le Pecq, on the opposite side of the river to Saint-Germain. Apart from the question of crossing the river there was a very steep slope on the Saint-Germain side which it was considered would be impassable for steam locomotives. An omnibus was run to connect with the trains, but passengers regarded the extra charge of 25 centimes for the bus ride as something of an imposition, because the second class railway fare from Paris was only 1 franc for the thirteen-mile journey. Nevertheless, this arrangement lasted for ten years, after which a novel and costly alternative was brought into use. This was an application of the 'Atmospheric' system of traction, invented by Samuel Clegg and the brothers Samuda in 1839. Even at that early stage in railway history the many objections to the steam locomotive, with its puffing noise, dirt, and supposed danger, had encouraged inventors to put forward methods of doing without it, and the

Above. One of the earliest locomotives of the Paris–Orléans Railway. Note the curious near-horizontal guide wheels.

Left. A very early 2–2–2 express locomotive of the Northern Railway of France, *La Scarpe*, built in 1842, pictured here at Lille.

Opposite top. Dashing complacency on the part of the railway travellers contrasts with the consternation of the horses and their passengers in this watercolour of a train on the Southern Railway of Austria in 1847.

Opposite bottom. London's first underground railway, the Metropolitan: the Bellmouth Junction, Praed Street, showing one of Gooch's broad-gauge 2–4–0 tank engines.

Atmospheric was one. A cast iron tube was laid between the rails, and by means of stationary pumping engines the air was exhausted from the tube. The motor carriage of a train had descending from it a piston which fitted closely into the tube. Along the top of the tube was a slit about $2\frac{1}{2}$ inches wide, which was closed by a flap of leather, secured to the tube along one side of the slit, and forming a continuous hinge. The air was exhausted from the tube in front of the train, and the suction created on the piston

Top. The Kraanbrug bridge across the Delfshavensche Schie near Rotterdam.

Above. A contemporary watercolour of Shakespeare Cliff, Dover, showing the viaduct and a train of the South Eastern Railway, *c.* 1850.

drew the train along. The bar carrying the piston pushed the leather flap aside, and it resealed immediately afterwards.

While Clegg and Samuda were experimenting to translate their ingenious principle into a practical working proposition, two other European countries had opened their first railways. One of these was Holland, where a company had been formed in 1837 to build a railway from Amsterdam to Rotterdam;

but the first engineer had experienced such difficulties with landlords, involving countless law-suits, that by the opening of the year 1839 little had been done, and he had to resign. Then the Government appointed the distinguished engineer F. W. Conrad 'engineer director', and he was able to get the first division of the line – that between Amsterdam and Haarlem – open in September 1839. It was a stretch of only ten-and-a-half miles, but it was a beginning. Quite apart from the trouble experienced in obtaining the necessary land the constructional difficulties were of a special and unusual kind. It was Chat Moss over again. The spongy soil made it necessary to build the railway on faggots – not just over one or two short sections, as Stephenson had to do, but over practically its entire length. There were places where conditions were even worse where the route crossed pools of water. There layers of faggots alternated with beds of rubble, often to the number of seven layers of each. The layers were held together by stakes and wattles, and then the earth was laid on the top – the 'earth' being composed chiefly of sand from the sea beach, covered with turf.

There was another engineering problem which in its extent was peculiar to Holland. With no hills and dales to negotiate, the railway was carried at a level very little above the surface of the ground; yet there were innumerable navigable waterways to cross, used by sailing ships large and small. To have crossed these with bridges of conventional type would have involved the making of large inclined ramps to give the necessary clearance for the masts of ships, or even of smaller sailing craft. The spongy nature of the ground precluded any such approaches, quite apart from the undesirability of the steep gradients involved; and so Conrad designed bridges in which a portion could be swung completely clear to give uninterrupted passage for waterborne traffic. Each particular location had to be treated on its merits; there could be no standard design. The route involved crossing the Leyden canal, many smaller canals, and the river Rhine. In the first three divisions, from Amsterdam to Haarlem, Haarlem to Leyden, and thence to The Hague, there were no fewer than fifty-eight bridges, and in tendering for the work the competing contractors were required to furnish exact scale models of the structures they proposed, and in the case of the successful tenderer the models became the property of the railway company. It is fortunate beyond measure that many of these models, of exquisite craftsmanship, have been preserved, and are on display in the Netherlands Railway Museum at Utrecht.

Conrad devised his own type of permanent way, with particular regard to the land the line had to traverse. He was a member of the Institution of Civil Engineers in London, and studied English practice closely. The result was something very similar to Brunel's track on the broad-gauge Great Western Railway. He used a 'bridge' section of rail, very like Brunel's, carried on continuous longitudinal timbers of Riga red deal, with cross-sleepers of the same timber halved into them. Regardless of what was being done in Belgium where the English 4 foot 8½ inch gauge had been adopted, Conrad chose a gauge of his own, nominally 2 metres, but this appears to have been from centre-line to centre-line, and the actual gauge of the rails was about 6 foot 4½ inches. The ballasting was composed of sea shells. The first locomotives were British built, by Longridge & Co. at Bedlington, Northumberland. A replica of *De Arend* ('the Eagle') is on display in the Railway Museum at Utrecht. They were of the 2–2–2 type, generally similar to the classic Stephenson *Patentee* type, with outside frames throughout. It was interesting to find Conrad saying in his paper, 'After the opening of the second division, several of Stephenson's new patent locomotive engines were added to the stock of the Company, and after ample trial of their qualities, they were considered to be the best engines in the service.'

In travelling to the south of Europe to note the beginning of railways in what is now Italy, it has to be remembered that the entity as we know it today did not exist until 1861. A large part of the northern territory, in Lombardy, formed part of the Austrian Empire; Sardinia was an independent and powerful force, with much more than a foothold on the mainland, while in the south there were the Papal States and the dual Kingdom of the Two Sicilies. It was in the south, with the eventual idea of building a line along the Bay of Naples, that the first 'Italian' railway was projected. The first section, just five miles long, was opened between Naples and Portici in October 1839. It was extended to Caserta by 1843, and to Capua by 1844. In the meantime there had been some activity in the north. As early as 1837, the year of Austria's own first railway, a line had been projected from Milan to Venice, known as the Lombard–Venetian Railway. But this northern part of 'Italy' was very unsettled at this time, both politically and strategically, and progress was slow. The first section of the line authorised was opened between Padua and Fort Malghera in 1842, and the line across the lagoon into Venice itself completed in 1846. But development was hindered by the constant suppression of Lombard and Venetian enterprise by Austrian strategic needs, and the railway network of Italy progressed very slowly. Although our information is rather vague it seems certain that the first steam locomotive to run in 'Italy', on the Naples–Portici line, was a Stephenson 2–2–2 of the *Patentee* type; and Stephenson's records show that the firm had a similar locomotive working between Milan and Como shortly afterwards.

Before passing on to the critical and dramatic period of the railway mania and the gauge war in Great Britain, reference must be made to the rapidly developing situation in the United States. On the continent of Europe, although six countries had steam railways in operation by the year 1840, their extent was very limited. It was the same in Canada. Only in the U.S.A. was the network spreading to anything like the extent of that in England, and then

almost entirely along the eastern seaboard, with penetrations into the hill ranges that separated the east coast from the country bordering on the Great Lakes. The vast areas lying to the west were completely devoid of railways until the strategic weakness of the west coast was realised at the time of the American Civil War, and in 1862 under a decree signed by President Lincoln himself construction of the Union Pacific Railroad was authorised, and the work pushed forward at break-neck speed. This,

The dawn of railways in Italy: an iron bridge at Civitavecchia.

however, is to anticipate the story, and in the early 1840s in addition to the Mohawk and Hudson and the Baltimore and Ohio, mentioned earlier, the principal American railways of the period were the Louisa, progenitor of the Chesapeake and Ohio; the Erie; the beginnings of the Norfolk and Western; and the Philadelphia and Reading.

Of these the Erie was by far the most extensive, and it is of particular note that this was built on the 6 foot gauge, the widest ever adopted on the North American continent. Its original name was the 'New York and Erie', and although the company was formed in 1833 the first section was not opened until 1841. This was from Pierpont, New York, to Goshen; but despite many difficulties, necessitating financial reconstructions, the line reached Dunkirk on Lake Erie in May 1851. It was then the longest stretch of line under one management, not only in the U.S.A. but in the whole world – 450 miles. In later years the Erie became of interest in another respect, in that by extensions it reached Chicago by what could be called a 'middle' route, traversing territory between the rugged mountain terrain of the Pennsylvania through Philadelphia, Harrisburg and Pittsburgh, and the 'water-level' route of the New York Central, via Albany, Syracuse, Buffalo and Cleveland. Yet the Erie, in its later years, was never a powerful competitor for the through passenger business between New York and Chicago. Nevertheless, the very fast running that was to characterise the rival New York

41

Central and Pennsylvania routes was very much a thing of the future. Despite rumours of very high speeds achieved by the British-built locomotives on the St Petersburg and Pavlovsk Railway, of which there was never any confirmation, speed as such was a purely minor consideration on all railways outside Great Britain in the period from 1835 to 1845; but in England particularly events combined to force the pace.

There was first of all the orgy of railway promoting

the grand scale, with the inevitable results!

While financiers grappled with the 'mania' and strove to keep the established companies clear of the maelstrom of wild speculation, engineers and operating men were approaching the 'battle of the gauges'. The 'big four' of the Great Western – Charles Russell, the chairman, Charles Saunders, the secretary, Brunel, and his locomotive superintendent, Daniel Gooch – were extending the broad gauge far beyond the original main line from London to Bristol; but the

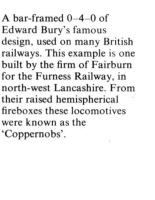

A bar-framed 0–4–0 of Edward Bury's famous design, used on many British railways. This example is one built by the firm of Fairburn for the Furness Railway, in north-west Lancashire. From their raised hemispherical fireboxes these locomotives were known as the 'Coppernobs'.

that followed the spectacular financial success of the early well-planned and sagely-backed railways. Less scrupulous promoters saw the chance of quick profits in the railway game. Men who began on solid ground lost their heads through early success, and turned to the wildest speculation. Railways were proposed in the most unlikely localities; simple people were induced to invest, having little knowledge of what was sound or otherwise, and they lost all they possessed. A remarkable number of entirely spurious schemes were put forward, mostly without the slightest intention of proceeding one step beyond the collection of subscriptions from gullible investors. With the splendid results from the first railways widely publicised there was a general rush to 'get rich quick', with little regard for the enormous gulf that lay between the working of companies like the Liverpool and Manchester, the Newcastle and Carlisle, and the London and Birmingham, and the ephemeral outfits that were being proposed on all sides. The greatest and most spectacular crash of the 'railway mania' was that of George Hudson, a linen draper of York, who from some skilful and fortunate investing in the early days of railways in his vicinity rose to control a positive railway empire, an association of companies that between them built an admirable network north and eastwards from Leeds. Unfortunately his integrity was not beyond question, and when success was followed by difficulties in certain of his companies he resorted to 'fiddling' on

standard-gauge network was growing much faster. Points of contact were growing; interchange of traffic meant shifting goods and luggage from one train to another, and at major junctions the complexities grew. The storm centre of this gauge confrontation was at Gloucester, in the west Midlands, and it became the standard excuse for any delays, damages or other frustrations. Any freight that failed to arrive was always 'lost at Gloucester', no matter how far away the route of the particular consignment may have been! It was not purely a railway matter. The times were uneasy. Europe was torn with wars and threats of revolution, and no one could be sure how long it would be before Great Britain was involved. There was a constant fear of invasion, and the military authorities were already looking to railways as an aid to rapid movement of troops. The inconvenience of a break of gauge disturbed the War Office. So, from a variety of uneasy thoughts a Royal Commission on Railway Gauges was set up. While the Commissioners accepted the technical superiority of equipment already in use on the Great Western Railway, it could not in their view outweigh the far greater mileage of railways built to the standard gauge. Recommendations were made for eliminating the broad gauge; but first the Board of Trade, and then Parliament, so watered down the report, that not only was the existing extent of the broad gauge left unaltered, but subsequent extensions to it were made, down to the year 1877.

It was not finally eliminated until 1892.

Having secured reprieve from summary execution, in the 'live and let live' situation sanctioned by the British Parliament, the Great Western proceeded to cast the decision of the Gauge Commissioners back into their teeth, in the development of some remarkably fast train services, crowned by two phenomenally fast individual runs. By the year 1848 the morning mail train from London was booked to run the 53 miles to Didcot in 56 minutes, start to stop, on the first stage of its run to the west, and this high speed, which no section of standard gauge railway could approach at the time, earned for the train its nickname of *The Flying Dutchman*, after the celebrated winner of both the Derby and the St Leger in 1849. The name was adopted officially by the G.W.R., though never to the extent of being printed in public timetables. Among railwaymen it survived for more than a hundred years, being applied in the 1950s to the 8.30 a.m. express from Plymouth to London. The running of the *Dutchman* in the late 1840s was an everyday task for Daniel Gooch's broad-gauge engines. What they could do when *really* opened out was shown when the *Great Britain*, a development of the basic 2–2–2 type, ran from London to Didcot in 47½ minutes, making an average speed of 67 miles per hour from start to finish. This involved running at about 70 miles per hour for 40 minutes on end – a world record that was not surpassed for very many years.

Leaving out of consideration for the moment the advances in design and constructional techniques that had made such speeds possible, less than twenty years after the Rainhill trials and the triumph of the *Rocket*, Brunel was not averse to trying alternative methods of traction, despite the brilliant successes achieved by his locomotive superintendent, Daniel Gooch. This brings me back to the Atmospheric system, referred to in connection with the Paris and Saint-Germain Railway. There it was a question of the steep gradient. Brunel also had the problem of steep gradients when he surveyed the South Devon Railway, from Exeter to Plymouth, and was faced with the succession of steep hills and deep valleys lying between the heights of Dartmoor and the sea. The Atmospheric appealed to him, because the tractive power applied to a train could be increased almost at will, by installation of additional stationary engine houses on the difficult sections. So, the man who had gone to enormous expense to secure easy gradients between London and Bristol went ahead regardless of hill and dale in South Devon, and built a railway that was more like a giant switchback than anything else.

At first the Atmospheric worked well on the level twenty-mile stretch round the South Devon coast beneath the red sandstone cliffs of Dawlish and Teignmouth. Then problems began to occur with the leather strap that sealed the tube. Rats found the leather a delicacy, the sea air assisted in its deteriora-

The epitome of broad gauge elegance and power on the Great Western in England: one of Daniel Gooch's 4–2–2 express locomotives with 8-foot driving wheels, a design of 1847.

tion, and the result was catastrophic. With numerous points of leakage the pumping engines could no longer create vacuum in the tube in advance of the trains. They were frequently stranded in open country, and with no ordinary form of motive power available the delays were crippling. Fortunately the Atmospheric was confined to the relatively accessible section between Exeter and Newton Abbot. Installation had not been completed farther west, and with

roads fairly near at hand, stranded passengers could be rescued. It would have been far otherwise in the hilly country of the southern slopes of Dartmoor, where the track was often many miles from a road, or indeed from any habitation. So the costly experiment with the Atmospheric on the South Devon line ended in September 1848, after little more than twelve months' operation. The short section of the Paris and Saint-Germain, up the steep final incline

A view of Potsdam station showing one of the English-type 2–2–2 locomotives on the turntable.

meal extension of the railway network, through individual and unconnected private enterprise, as was currently taking place in Britain. But in 1842, possibly with strategic considerations in mind, France as a nation adopted a policy of railway building designed to evolve a scientifically-planned and non-competitive system. One might see in this a reflection of the differing political traditions in the two countries, represented on the one hand by the rigorously centralised administrative and legal system left by Napoleon I and, on the other, the evolution of Parliament and parliamentary liberties in Great Britain. Immediate state operation was not envisaged, but the land and the road-bed on which the permanent way rested were provided at the expense of the State, and 99-year concessions were granted to the operating companies that equipped the various lines. Paris was to be the hub of the entire national system, and the country was parcelled out into a series of sectors to give each group a monopoly in its own area. Although a number of smaller individual companies constructed lines under the Government concessions, by the year 1857 most of these had been incorporated into one or another of six large systems, as follows:

Railway company	Date of incorporation
Northern (Nord)	1845
Eastern (Est)	1845
Paris–Orléans (P.O.)	1838
Western (Ouest)	1855
Paris, Lyons and Mediterranean (P.L.M.)	1857
Southern (Midi)	1852

from Le Pecq, seems to have been more fortunate, for there the Atmospheric is reported to have survived for twelve years.

Apart from activities on the Saint-Germain line the 1840s witnessed a very important development in France. The initial stages, with the introduction of the mineral railways at Saint-Etienne, and the inauguration of regular passenger working between Paris and Le Pecq, seemed to foreshadow a piece-

The grouping of railways, which caused an upheaval in Great Britain in 1923, was completed in France by 1857. The Midi was the only one of the original six that did not enter Paris. It operated south of a line on the map running roughly from Bordeaux, through Toulouse to Narbonne, and made connections to the north via both the Orléans and the P.L.M. The name of the Paris–Orléans, although apt enough when the line was first projected in 1838, became something of a misnomer since from the bifurcation at Orléans its two main lines ran to Bordeaux on the one hand and Toulouse on the other. However, these routes, and the final extent of the French railway system,

were very much things of the future in the 1840s. In this period, nevertheless, the foundations were well and truly laid, not least in the guaranteeing by the state of very substantial dividends to the large companies. It was originally intended that no competition for internal traffic should exist, though in actual fact it did not work out that way.

The first French railway of any main line importance to be completed was that between Paris and Rouen. It was sponsored by an English banker, Sir Edward Blount, and one can guess that this line did not at first form part of the French master plan. Blount was also one of the moving spirits in the London and Brighton Railway, and the two enterprises formed part of a scheme to set up communications between London and Paris. In any case the Rouen line was well on the way to completion before the French national plan was drawn up. It was very much an English affair, with Joseph Locke as engineer and Thomas Brassey as the contractor, and the spearhead of the labour force were English navvies of Brassey's own selection. It was when he was engaged on this line, and the going was particularly tough, that an onlooker exclaimed, 'Mon Dieu! Les Anglais, comme ils travaillent!' – and work they did, compared with the French and Italian labourers who made up the gangs.

Part 2

The Years of Expansion

By the year 1850 railways had arrived. There was no longer any doubt about the advantages and potentialities of the new method of transport, whether it was for trade and industry, pleasure, or strategy. In England it was the evidence of the Quartermaster General of the Army that had carried immense weight during the sitting of the Royal Commission on Railway Gauges, and had influenced the commissioners to no small degree in reaching their decision. By 1850, in the countries that already had some railways, plans were being made for considerable extensions; those that had no railways as yet were seeking means, and finance, to introduce them. Despite the early use of horses and cable traction, and such excursions into the unorthodox as the Atmospheric, the steam locomotive – of which all the basic features were embodied in the *Rocket* – was the foundation of all railway workings; and it remained so, with scarcely a serious challenger for main line work, for a further seventy years. In the

other problems that were to assume critical proportions in the next quarter-century.

In Great Britain the 2–2–2 type was becoming established as the standard for passenger working from the later 1830s. Improvements in design were centred upon the chassis, to obtain better riding as a vehicle, on the valve gear, for better distribution of steam and economy in fuel, and upon experiments to make possible the use of raw coal as a fuel instead of going to the expense of coke. But two passing phases of considerable importance must be noted. In 1841 Robert Stephenson had patented his celebrated 'long-boiler' type of locomotive. The idea was to obtain more perfect combustion and more economical use of the fuel. At the same time early station and yard layouts, and the size of turntables, were already making it undesirable to increase the wheel spacing of locomotives, and so Stephenson placed all the wheels of his 'long-boilered' locomotives ahead of the firebox, giving a somewhat

eyes of the public, as well as for railway management, it was the cornerstone of the whole edifice of railway development; and upon it were lavished ornament and artistic style, as well as engineering skill and the craftmanship of the new race of mechanics. At this stage in the story it is therefore appropriate that special attention should be given to the development of locomotive design, for it was not only to set the pace for many years, but its very success brought

ungainly appearance, and in certain cases a dangerous 'yawing' action that led to derailments. Nevertheless, the long-boilered type was extensively adopted in Great Britain and exported to the continent of Europe. As a freight engine engaged on intermittent duty it was economical and successful, but for fast express work it was not satisfactory.

The second passing phase was the patent rear-driver locomotive of T. R. Crampton. This was in

Skill and artistry in English timber bridging: one of Brunel's trestles carrying the Cornwall Railway across a tidal creek of the Lynher River, a few miles west of Plymouth, Devon.

Top. A striking French example of a Crampton locomotive, on the Northern Railway, built in 1858.

Above. One of the French 'Crewe'-type engines built at W.B. Buddicom's factory, shown in a contemporary caricature.

some ways an English version of the Norris type, with a single pair of driving wheels at the rear end. Crampton did not use the three-point suspension principle which was coming into general application in America, but adopted the rear-driver arrangement to place the large wheels clear of the boiler. Then, he postulated, the boiler need not be pitched high, to clear the driving axle; it could be enlarged as required, and a much steadier riding locomotive should result from the low centre of gravity. Experience with locomotives of the Crampton type in Great Britain was not happy. They rode 'hard', and caused damage and excessive wear on the track. But they became very popular in France and were in fact the standard type of express locomotive on several systems for many years, and were synonymous with railway travelling. The phrase *prendre le Crampton* was a French colloquialism for going by train. A magnificent specimen of one of these engines, from the Eastern Railway, has been preserved, and is at the French railway museum at Mulhouse, in Alsace.

Of the conventional 2–2–2 type with inside cylinders there were three principal variations in the classic design. The Stephenson *Patentee* of 1833 had outside frames throughout, of what were known as the 'sandwich' type. The origin of this design could be traced back to the earliest colliery locomotives, in which the machinery, wheels and boiler were carried on two massive baulks of timber. The sandwich frames were also mainly of timber, which formed the

'meat' of the sandwich, with the 'slices of bread' consisting of wrought iron plates on each side. Gooch used sandwich frames in his high-speed broad-gauge engines, but the weight at the front end was too great to be carried on a single axle, and his famous engines had two pairs of carrying wheels ahead of the 8 foot diameter driving wheels. In contrast to the American 4–4–0 locomotives, in which extreme flexibility was demanded, the Gooch 4–2–2s on the Great Western had all four axles carried on a single sandwich frame. There was no leading bogie, or truck. Another successful form of frame design was that known as the 'Jenny Lind', from the name of a celebrated 2–2–2 built for the Brighton Railway by E. B. Wilson & Co. of Leeds. The 'Jennies' had outside bearings for the leading and trailing wheels, and inside bearings for the drivers. The designer of the original *Jenny Lind* was David Joy, one of the most colourful and delightful characters in the British locomotive world of the nineteenth century.

Finally, there were the 'Bloomers' of J. E. McConnell, locomotive superintendent of the Southern Division of the London and North Western, one of the very few British railwaymen of that era who was prepared to play Brunel and Gooch at their own game of speeding. In his new inside-frame 2–2–2 express engine which appeared in 1851 he 'cleared away the decent skirting of an outside frame, and exhibited the whole of his wheels to the gaze of the traveller', thus evoking the contemporary fashion from which the design got its nickname. 'Bloomers' eventually came in three sizes – 'large', 'small' and 'extra-large'.

Nicknames apart, the 'Bloomers' of all sizes were extremely successful, and they settled the argument, for all time, as to what made a smooth and easy-riding locomotive. While the Stephenson long-boilered type yawed their way along and at times came off the road, and the Cramptons smashed up the track with their low centre of gravity, the 'Bloomers' rode like a swing, easily and comfortably, and their drivers took full advantage of this to make them 'fly'. They had large boilers, and the wheels were well spaced out on a lengthy rigid wheelbase. It must not be forgotten, however, that the 'Bloomers' ran on one of the straightest and best-maintained tracks in the world. One can quite imagine that they would not have taken kindly to the tracks that were customary in the U.S.A.

The Southern Division of the London and North Western was the historic London and Birmingham. Crewe, Cheshire, was the home of the locomotive works of the Grand Junction which had been amalgamated with the London and Birmingham to form the London and North Western in 1846. There the mainspring of Northern Division locomotive activity was the 'foreman of locomotives', Alexander Allan, who built a range of reliable, if small, engines of the 2–2–2 and 2–4–0 types. Large numbers of the Allan 'Crewe' type of engine were built for use on several of the French railways by a former Grand Junction locomotive superintendent, W. B. Buddicom, who went to France and set up a locomotive manufactory near Paris. Crewe was entirely a railway town. Before the advent of the railway and the decision of the Grand Junction to site its works there, it had been nothing but a village. An entire town was built by the railway, and for many years Crewe was governed from the railway's headquarters at Euston. For a time church services were held in the works on Sundays by clergymen whose stipend was paid entirely by railway directors.

The Pennsylvania Railroad, the premier line of the U.S.A., was one of the very few American railways

tinted. A builder armed with a portfolio of such prints could then go to a prospective buyer and say in as many words, 'How would you like one like this?'

The centres of the locomotive building industry in the U.S.A. became concentrated in Philadelphia and Paterson, New Jersey. In a census taken in 1860 it was estimated that three-quarters of the entire locomotive production of the United States was in those two cities. The industry naturally had its good and bad times but, in contrast to the situation in Great Britain, it never had to face strong competition from railway-owned workshops. In 1855 Rogers was the firm with the largest production, with

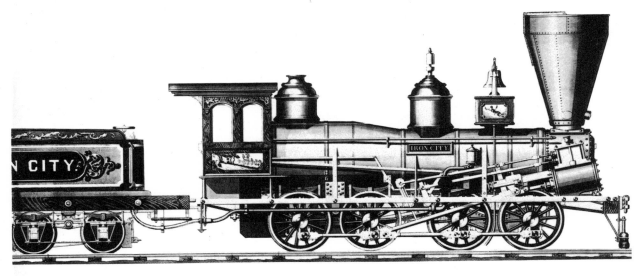

An American giant of 1857: a Baldwin 0–8–0 of the flexible-beam-truck type, the *Iron City*, in a beautiful example of an early lithograph, by Rosenthal of Philadelphia.

that manufactured its own locomotives to any appreciable extent. This activity did not begin until the year 1866. Before then the establishment of a strong independent locomotive building industry early in American railway history had had a direct influence on the design and appearance of the motive power used. The commercial firms controlled design far more tightly than the early British locomotive builders were ever able to do, and this influence continued in the U.S.A. for many decades. It is true that Robert Stephenson had one foot planted firmly in each camp. He was engineer and consultant to many railways, and at the same time a locomotive manufacturer; but in less than fifteen years after Rainhill there were railway engineers like Gooch, McConnell and Alexander Allan coming into prominence and telling contractors what they wanted, when they were not actively preparing to make locomotives themselves. In the U.S.A. it was business houses like Baldwin, Rogers and Norris who were setting the standard. The industry developed at great speed, when many of the railways with names that later became household words were little more than schemes on paper. The railway projectors knew little of engineering, and the builders soon realised that to sell their products it was no use talking technicalities or even displaying working drawings. As a result there grew up the practice of producing beautifully executed pictorial lithographs—exquisite examples of mechanical draughtsmanship, artistically

eighty-two locomotives in a year. It is interesting to compare the respective outputs of the three biggest firms in the U.S.A. up to the year 1860, thus:

Numbers of locomotives produced

	Baldwin	Norris	Rogers
1840	9	15	7
1855	47	75	82
1860	83	40	88
Total to 1860	988	1000	979

While the 'American' type, the 4–4–0 with outside cylinders, remained the most popular for both passenger and goods services, the increase in freight traffic, even as early as 1840, brought demands for a more powerful type. Conventional six- and eight-coupled engines were capable of moving heavy loads, but were frequently in trouble on sharp curves. On poorly-built tracks they 'burst the road'–that is, they turned the rails over, tearing up their fixtures from the sleepers.

M. W. Baldwin's invention of the 'flexible-beam-truck' locomotive in 1842 has been glamourised and dramatised into one of the great legends of American railway history. The story goes that the idea came to him during a sleepless night when his many creditors were going to foreclose the next day. It is however generally known that he had been working on ideas to increase the tractive effort of locomotives for

Below. St Louis' Great Levee
along the Mississippi
thronged with paddle steamers
and crowded with warehouses,
at the time of the 'Great
Railroad Celebration'.

Bottom. The old Union Depot
of the Milwaukee Railroad in
Chicago, which was located at
the foot of Reed Street: note
the horse-drawn street cars and
the long line of waiting cabs.

some time; but the flexible-beam-truck idea put the
two front driving axles of an eight-coupled engine
on a truck in which the axles could slide laterally
when on a curve, but would remain parallel to the
rigid, conventionally-mounted rear driving axles on
the main frame. Like all Baldwin's ideas, the details
were carefully worked out and the engines so equipped
were enthusiastically received. This type of locomotive
was in production for fifteen years, during which time
about 300 were built.

In the meantime the American passenger station
was developing, generally in a style quite different
from its European counterparts. A popular type
was that sometimes referred to as the train barn.
There was a distinction in terms: the 'station'
referred to the offices, waiting rooms, concourse and
so on, while the part containing the tracks and the
platforms was the 'train shed'. In the 'train barn'
type the train shed and station were combined in one
compact block, and the trains went through large

50

doorways at each end. The locomotives were housed inside the station at night, and the doors were closed (in case the engines got loose and broke away!). In many towns in the U.S.A. tracks ran down the main street, and the stations were built over the tracks in the middle of the town, forming an obstruction to such road traffic as there was. Where larger stations were built on special sites, very elaborate and highly ornamented edifices were provided for the 'station' portion, but the train sheds – often at a

could pale into insignificance. The book also contains an entertainingly detailed picture of the celebration itself.

Though the author could in his mind's eye see the future westward progress of the railroads, he had no hesitation in declaring that:

'In distance, in geographical position and the advantage of climate, the Ohio and Mississippi Railroad must forever stand without a rival.'

lower level – were indescribably dark and airless, filled with all the odours fascinating to devotees of the steam locomotive but repugnant to the great majority of travellers. There was no encouragement, either then or now, for that British pastime once described as 'station sauntering' – just the pleasure of watching the coming and going of trains.

In the gradual growth of the great American railway network, the projection of the massive transcontinental routes and the emergence of the great railway empires were still, in the 1850s, things of the future. The principal development of the period before the Civil War was the establishment and improvement of direct routes between the eastern seaboard and the growing cities of the Middle West, Chicago and St Louis. A classic book describes the 'Great Railroad Celebration' that took place in 1857 on the opening of the Ohio and Mississippi Railroad, which completed the route of the Baltimore and Ohio from New York to St Louis. The overwhelming sense of the accomplishment of reaching the Mississippi which it reflects is an interesting reminder to us of the great scale and pace of development in the U.S.A. in the second half of the nineteenth century, when in a few decades this mighty achievement

Accordingly,

'No railroad celebration has ever been projected in the history of the country on a scale so magnificent and costly as this. The preparations were commensurate with the grandeur of the Great National Highway which it opens up.'

Four days before the festivities in St Louis were to take place special excursion trains departed from all over the east bringing senators, mayors, senior officials from other railways and other distinguished guests – some two-and-a-half thousand in total. The bulk of the guests set out from Cincinnati on the last leg of their excursion journey on 4 June, in two trains. They reached Illinoistown, opposite St Louis on the east bank of the Mississippi, at midnight, but 'hundreds of pine torches which had been planted in the ground on each side of the track, for several hundred yards, brilliantly illuminated the scene. Our arrival was instantly announced to the citizens across the stream by the firing of cannon from the bluffs. Four large and elegant Mississippi River steamers . . . had been moored to the levee on the Illinois side of the river . . . These, brilliantly illuminated, presented a very pretty spectacle in the darkness of the evening.'

Left. An English station scene of the 1860s, London and North Western Railway. The locomotive, No. 1080, is one of John Ramsbottom's 'DX' class of mixed traffic 0–6–0s – one of the first examples anywhere in the world of engineering mass-production. First introduced in 1858, no fewer than 943 examples were built, all at Crewe Works.

Above. Advertisement for the steamer route from San Francisco to New York, via Panama, in the days before the building of the transcontinental routes.

The guests were immediately escorted aboard these, where they were fed and put up for the night. Those who felt inclined could watch 'plentiful displays of fireworks . . . the great city across the river, lighted up by its thousands of gas burners, and its long levee brilliant with the glare of torches, Roman candles, Grecian fires, or other pyrotechnic devices.'

The next day, following a river excursion during the morning, there was a procession several miles long past scenes of exuberant popular festivity to

the city's fairground. 'Amid this exciting pageant, the ladies of the "Mount City" shone with resplendent lustre as they waved their handkerchiefs, and smiled a pleasant welcome to the guests.' On arrival at the fairground the guests found three 300-foot tables laden with sixteen different kinds of cold meat, strawberries, ice-cream, Charlotte Russe and a variety of drinks – towards which 'many a longing eye and watering mouth' were turned in the course of the two-hour opening speech. Following the meal, speeches continued until nightfall. A further reception took place the next evening in the city's theatre, and the following month guests from all over the west attended return celebrations in Baltimore, Washington and other east coast cities.

In 1860 the U.S.A. was plunged into the excitement, uncertainty and disruption of civil war. Particularly in the south the new railways played a considerable part. Trains were used to hurry up supplies and reinforcements; tracks were torn up, locomotives sabotaged, and in one well-remembered incident a locomotive was stolen and driven away, only to be recovered when it stopped, completely denuded of fuel. The war caused a galloping inflation in the prices of locomotives, so desperately were they needed. A standard American 4–4–0 cost about £2,000 (at prevailing exchange rates) at the beginning of the war, whereas nearly three times that price had to be paid in 1864. Apart from all the drama, the raiding and counter-raiding (and the profiteering) the war

Top. Elegant French station architecture: the façade of the Gare du Nord, Paris.

Above. Railwaymen: a pointsman on the Western Railway of France.

had demonstrated the immense value of railways in opening rapid lines of communication, and transporting men and materials in large quantities. Although many railroads in the war areas were badly damaged in the course of the fighting, it was also shown how quickly resolute and fearless men could carry out sufficient repairs to run the trains through, albeit at much reduced speeds.

Among the railways at the centre of Civil War events was the Louisville and Nashville. This line ran almost due north and south, through country in which some of the most sustained and bitter fighting of the war took place. It was a vital supply line to both sides. Its tracks were torn up, its bridges destroyed, its trains wrecked. But then in 1862 the city of Nashville was captured by the Federal army, and made the headquarters of the United States Military Railways. It was on these railways that General Sherman based the strategy for his tremendous sweep into Georgia. Over more than 400 miles of single line an army of 100,000 men was kept supplied. The Confederates, defeated and driven out of Atlanta, retreated, wrecking the railway as they went. Track was torn up, bonfires were made of the sleepers, and when the rails became hot enough in the fires they were twisted round trees. Locomotives were isolated, without any tracks to run on, and there was one instance where a whole shedful of 'strandees' were captured, and carted over forty miles of open country, devoid of rails, to where they could be used again.

When the war was over a disadvantage greater even than the actual lack of communication was the variation in rail gauges that existed. Despite the uproar that had occurred in Great Britain in the 1840s, in the 'battle of the gauges', the earlier American railways had been built with little thought for future transportation needs. At the time of the Civil War there were substantial mileages of 4 foot 8½ inches; 5 foot; 5 foot 6 inches and 6 foot gauge, but the war had underlined the urgent necessity for having a uniform gauge throughout the country, and by 1865 a process of standardisation, to 4 feet 8½ inches, was already under way. Some railways were however very heavily committed, none perhaps more so than the much-battered Louisville and Nashville, with main lines of 1,500 miles laid to the 5 foot gauge.

In Great Britain one of the most spectacular events of the nineteenth century was the conversion of the remaining sections of the broad-gauge Great Western, from Brunel's 7 foot gauge to the accepted standard, in a single weekend in May 1892. The route mileage involved was 171. But this notable achievement had been anticipated in a far more spectacular way six years earlier on the Louisville and Nashville, when the entire 1,500 miles was converted from 5 feet to 4 feet 8½ inches *in a single day*. Of course the actual mechanics of the operation were much simpler than on the Great Western: with flat-bottomed rail nothing more was needed than to withdraw the dog spikes from one rail on each sleeper and move the rail across 3½ inches, whereas the Great Western men had to cut the cross-ties and slew the longitudinal transoms across more than 2 feet. But on the Louisville and Nashville the organisation must have been superb. It is interesting to recall that the man responsible, Reuben Wells, was the master mechanic of the railway, a locomotive man rather than a civil engineer. Shortly afterwards he left railway service and joined the Rogers Locomotive and Machine Works, as plant superintendent. He remained in this office until 1907.

The war had effects on railway working and development far beyond the borders of the United States. In the early days of the war British sentiments, both at home and in the colonies, were on the side of the Confederate states of the south. This did nothing to reduce the thinly veiled tension that prevailed along the boundary between the Union territories and the British colonies in the north. The entry of America into the Napoleonic War on the *French* side in 1812 had not been forgotten, and in the

Above. Sandford Fleming, engineer-in-chief of the Intercolonial Railway, Quebec to Nova Scotia, completed in 1876; first engineer-in-chief of the Canadian Pacific, retired in 1880 before major construction started.

Left. Railwaymen: a head guard on the South Eastern Railway, England. The locomotive is one of a type nicknamed 'the gunboats', because of the plain stove-pipe chimney, reminiscent of a cannon.

Left below. Platform porters on the South Eastern Railway, showing very typical English passenger coaches of the 1870 period.

emergency of 1861 it was felt essential in Canada to make one more attempt to get the project of the Intercolonial Railway off the ground, and ensure rapid communication between Quebec and the ports in the maritime colonies at all times of the year. In the autumn of 1861 a deputation from Canada, New Brunswick and Nova Scotia sailed for England to try and secure financial help from the imperial government. An incident occurring at this time, in which a Union warship fired on a British ship, the *Trent*, and seized two Confederate leaders journeying to Europe in search of diplomatic support, immensely strengthened the hand of the deputation from the British North American colonies who were in London at that very time. Not only did they secure a loan of £3,000,000 towards the building of the Intercolonial Railway, but this was followed by the appointment of the very distinguished Sandford Fleming as engineer, acting on behalf of the imperial government and of the British American provinces. This was a great step forward, so far as Canada was concerned, and the other outcome of the *Trent* incident was equally felicitous for railways. Lord Palmerston had sent a strongly-worded ultimatum to Washington and the reply was awaited with the utmost excitement in the United Kingdom. The L.N.W.R. had promised to convey the Queen's Messenger and the vital despatch to London within five hours of its arrival at Holyhead. The speed at which the special was run from Holyhead was extremely important for the future development of railways. One of the very picturesque outside-cylindered 2–2–2s of the 'Lady of the Lake' class was waiting, and with the special train of three light coaches she set out to make a non-stop run to Stafford, then the divisional point between the Northern and Southern Divisions of the L.N.W.R. John Ramsbottom, the outstanding chief mechanical engineer, had recently laid down the first water troughs in the world at Aber, on the North Wales coast, by which locomotives could pick up water without stopping, and the engine allocated to the *Trent* special, named *Watt*, was able to run the 130½ miles to the Trent Valley Junction, just south of Stafford station, in 144 minutes, at an average speed of 54·3 miles per hour. Then the train was handed over to the Southern Division, where one of McConnell's extra-large 'Bloomers' was waiting. So far as speed was concerned this engine had an even harder task, for after engines had been changed in no more than 1½ minutes and the special was under way once more, only 141½ minutes remained for the 133 miles to Euston if the five-hour promise was to be kept. But although there were as yet no water troughs on this stretch of line the McConnell engine was a much larger and more powerful engine than *Watt*, and despite a loss of ten minutes because of fog those 133 miles were covered in 139½ minutes, an average of 57 miles per hour. It was the fastest long-distance run that had yet been made in Great Britain – and that meant anywhere in the world, at that time. Before the special had stopped the Queen's Messenger, carrying the precious despatch box, had jumped from the saloon, raced across to a waiting carriage and pair, and was driving through the station gates on his way to Downing Street before the train came finally to rest! The reply was conciliatory, and the crisis was at an end. In the general rejoicing over the peaceful end of the *Trent* affair the dramatic conveyance of the despatch received much commendation, particularly the part played by the water troughs.

Another momentous railway outcome of the Civil War was in the U.S.A. itself. In 1862 when the result of the war was still very uncertain President Lincoln became anxious about the isolated and almost undefended situation of the Pacific coast. The Confederate States had many friends in Europe, and he feared a hostile attack in their support, launched from the west coast. In July 1862 Congress therefore passed an Act creating the Union Pacific Railroad Company and authorising construction of a line extending, as first projected, across the State of Nebraska, beginning from the western bank of the Missouri river, which formed the boundary between Iowa and Nebraska. The Act provided for land grants and bond issues to aid in financing the construction, but despite the generous terms capital was not attracted to this proposal. Congress became so alarmed that this urgent and strategic railway had not even been started that in 1864 they doubled the land grants, and liberalised other features of its financing. And so a start was made, and the first rail was laid in the Missouri Valley in July 1865. The Union Pacific must be one of the very few privately-owned railways to have been inaugurated by direct Government instigation. Its development was dramatic. Once started, the construction was pushed ahead in a shipwreck hurry and the westward progress of the line soon extended far beyond the original concession made by Congress in 1862.

There was good reason for this haste, even if it came somewhat belatedly. Out in California railway construction had started in a limited way in 1855, with the laying of the first rail of the Sacramento Valley Railroad, in August of that year. Then in 1861 the Central Pacific Railroad of California was incorporated, with the intention of building eastwards across the State of Nevada and ultimately forming a link with the east. In the unsettled conditions of the Civil War no work was actually done for two years. But the initiative of Congress in 1862 in launching the Union Pacific project no doubt spurred the western company into action, and the Central Pacific made the first move towards the construction of the very first transcontinental railway across the U.S.A., at Sacramento in 1863. When two years later the Union Pacific really got going it became a race between the two companies as to which could construct the greater mileage. Clearly, the greater the mileage the larger the revenue one or other of the companies would derive from the transcontinental traffic. Apart from all the natural hazards, such as the wild undeveloped country, and constant attacks from Indians, the Central Pacific was enormously

54

TWENTYFIVE TON PASSENGER ENGINE.
LAWRENCE MACHINE SHOP
LAWRENCE MASS.

Gordon McKay, Agent   John C. Hoadley, Supt.

handicapped by the fact that all materials and rolling stock had to be transported by sea. The Panama Canal was not then dreamed of, and so everything had to go round the very tip of *South* America, round Cape Horn – a voyage of some 15,000 miles.

Once started, the Union Pacific went ahead at great speed and laid roughly 1,000 miles of track in three years. The Central Pacific had much the harder task from the constructional point of view, in cutting through mountainous country in Nevada. The Central Pacific, despite its somewhat misleading name, was the western section of the great transcontinental railway authorised by President Lincoln in 1862, to open up the west of the country; but this in fact merely gave national impetus to a project that had been initiated in the previous year by four merchants in Sacramento, California. These four had had no previous experience of railways, but were anxious to have a line eastward over the Sierra Nevada range to further trade. Collis P. Huntingdon and Mark Hopkins were hardware merchants, Charles Crocker was in the dry goods business, and Leland P. Stanford was a grocer. Although dynamic energy, tenacity of purpose and a zest for sheer hard work possessed them all, yet their audacity was quite beyond belief. By June 1864 the rails had reached no further east than Newcastle, thirty-one miles from Sacramento; and then work ground to a halt for lack of labour. It was then that Crocker took personal command of the whole job. When his Irish navvies went on strike for higher wages, he promptly replaced them with Chinese.

As on the Canadian Pacific in later years the Chinamen flocked into Sacramento for the work. In their coolie hats, blue denim blouses and flapping trousers they looked a strange sight on a railway construction contract; but they did their work well, and when Crocker was criticised for putting them on masonry work he replied, 'Why not? Didn't they build the Chinese Wall, the biggest piece of masonry in the world?' All went well until the coming of winter, and then in the High Sierras storm succeeded storm until snow lay 20 feet deep on the level, and 60 feet in the drifts. Half the men were kept busy shovelling to keep the completed part of the line clear. Men, materials and even locomotives were hauled on sledges over the snow. At the summit of the range a tunnel 1,650 feet long had to be driven. It took a year to complete, not for want of effort, but for scarcity of gunpowder. The Civil War had absorbed practically all supplies, and the price of what remained was sky-high. Before the work started $2.50 for a keg of gunpowder was normal; before the tunnel and its approach cuttings were finished Crocker was having to pay $15 a keg.

Then came the race to join up with the Union Pacific, whose construction gangs were forging west across the Laramie plains. Crocker organised the Central Pacific gangs to the last detail. Sleepers were laid ahead on the carefully levelled road-bed; a train of sixteen cars loaded with rails and enough material for two miles of line was pushed up to the 'end of steel', men climbed up and threw off all the fittings, while others rolled off the rails. As soon as the materials train had been unloaded and was pulled back, light hand cars were placed on the track and loaded with the specific quantities of rails and fittings to make up eight complete lengths. Two horses with riders were attached, a crew of Chinamen jumped on the car and off they went at a tearing gallop to the appointed place. With this magnificent organisation, track was laid at the rate of nearly one mile per hour. In twelve hours, from dawn till dusk, more than ten miles were laid; and just to prove it was well and truly done, at the close of the day a locomotive was driven at 40 miles per hour over the entire new section. So the Chinese – 'Crocker's pets', as they were called – raced eastwards to meet the rival gangs of the Union Pacific.

Of course, life at the front, as it were, was but one aspect of the advance. Nor far behind followed a much larger community bringing up supplies and generally providing a base of operations, which attracted also the motley collection of freebooters and opportunists, hangers-on and droppers-out, that one would expect to find in such places. A contemporary witness describes one of the short-lived townships that sprang up to serve this community all along the line of the Union Pacific's progress. This was Benton in 1868.

In the middle of the desert 'as if by the touch of Aladdin's lamp' a city of twelve thousand people sprang up in two weeks. 'The streets were thronged with motley crowds of railroad men, Mexicans and

Opposite top. 'Seats for five persons.' Persons of many shapes and sizes crowd a British third class carriage in an entertaining oil painting *c*. 1860.

Opposite bottom. 'Five minutes for refreshment'. A chaotic scene at an American railway station in the days before the dining car.

Below. Track laying on the Union Pacific.

Indians, gamblers, "cappers" and saloon-keepers, merchants, miners and mule-whackers.' Among the places that employed some of them and entertained most of them were twenty-three saloons and five dance halls. The biggest of the dance halls was the 'Big Tent', measuring 100 feet by 40, which was dismantled and erected in each new town – like most of the buildings: houses presenting impressive facades of red brick, brownstone or stucco were actually

Left. Laramie, Union Pacific Railroad: a photograph taken in 1868 shortly after the building of the railway. Although little more than open land at the time, Laramie already had a windmill, water tank, twenty-stall round house and machine shop, the foundations of what was to become a major railway centre.

Below. A striking example of North American trestle viaduct construction—Dale Creek on the Union Pacific. It was built with pre-cut Michigan timber, 700 feet long and 126 feet high where it crossed the stream, and had to be guyed with ropes and wires against Wyoming winds and the shock from trains passing across it.

Opposite top. Building the Union Pacific: temporary and permanent bridges at Green River. In the background is the spectacular Citadel Rock.

Opposite bottom. An early excursion party at the Devil's Gate Bridge, on the Union Pacific. The timbers used in the first temporary bridge are prominent on the river bank.

built of pine in sections beneath these outer skins. The Big Tent had 'a splendid bar supplied with every variety of liquors and cigars with cut-glass goblets, ice-pitchers, splendid mirrors . . .' Part of the space was devoted to dancing, with 'a full band . . . in attendance day and night,' while 'all the rest of the room is filled with tables devoted to monte, faro, rondo coolo, fortune wheels, and every other species of gambling known.' When the writer visited the same place a short time afterwards 'there was not a house or tent to be seen; a few rock piles and half-destroyed chimneys barely sufficed to mark the ruins; the white dust had covered everything else, and desolation reigned supreme.'

Mention was made earlier of the danger from Indians. It was on the Union Pacific that the danger of attack was a real problem. At an early stage the Central Pacific made an arrangement with the tribes of the areas through which it was to pass. The Union Pacific, cutting straight across the buffalo trails that meant all to the Sioux and the Cheyennes, could not hope for any such accommodation. Many commented on the military character of the enterprise. Construction workers were as ready to wield a gun as to use a pick-axe, and in fact large numbers of them had served in the Union army. The construction trains were well stocked with arms and ammunition, and box-cars and cabooses had double walls filled up with sand between them. At times up to half the work-force was needed to keep watch against Indian attack, and hundreds of lives were lost. Perhaps among the

most gruesome of many terrible tales that are told is the story of the Plum Creek Massacre of 1867. The man to whom we owe our knowledge of the story was himself scalped during the 'massacre' and his scalp, which he managed to retreive in the course of his escape from his Indian pursuers, ended up in Omaha Public Library Museum, a lasting memorial to the events he described. William Thompson was sent out from the little station of Plum Creek, Nebraska, at 9.00 in the evening on the day in question, to investigate the cause of a break in the telegraph lines. The explanation came home to him and his two companions in no uncertain terms when they arrived on the scene; some of Chief Turkey Leg's Cheyennes had used lengths of telegraph wire to tie a large piece of timber to the track. Leaping with his fellows from their vehicle just before it collided with the obstacle, Thompson was shot through the arm and failed to escape the pursuing Indians. It was at this stage that he lost, then recovered, his scalp. His attacker rode off, leaving Thompson for dead. Thompson then watched the rest of the night's events.

The Indians were prising up the ends of a pair of rails, piling sleepers beneath them. A westbound freight train struck the obstacle at 25 miles per hour and plunged from the track, catching fire. The driver and fireman were killed, but four of the crew, aided by the darkness, managed to escape and run back along the track to attract the attention of the driver of a following freight train. They jumped aboard as the train rapidly reversed to safety, evacuating Plum

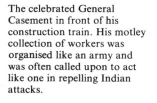

The celebrated General Casement in front of his construction train. His motley collection of workers was organised like an army and was often called upon to act like one in repelling Indian attacks.

Creek on the way. Lineman Thompson watched as the Indians cavorted about with increasing frenzy around the now burning train under the influence of a case of whisky they had broken open, dressing themselves up in an extraordinary assortment of hats and other finery which had been part of the train's cargo, and using whole rolls of cloth as streamers to unroll behind their galloping horses. Eventually he was able to drag himself to a settlement fourteen miles away in the opposite direction from Plum Creek. But when the timid inhabitants of the settlement returned the next morning and surveyed the scene through binoculars, the Indians were still there, milling around the smoking remains of the train.

By the end of 1868 it was generally accepted that the meeting point between the two railroads would be in Utah somewhere in the neighbourhood of the Great Salt Lake, and the rival construction gangs raced to meet each other round the northern shores of the lake. The 'meet' eventually took place on 10 May 1869, at Promontory, Utah, and on that day a golden spike was driven to mark the completion of the first transcontinental railway.

Now had arrived the great moment in American history which would weld together east and west and make America the thoroughfare of the world; when, as the chronicler of the Baltimore and Ohio celebrations in 1857 foresaw:

'The steam-whistle which greets the early morn upon the shores of the Atlantic, will roll on in one continuous strain through mountains and across rivers and prairies, until its voice is lost in the roar of the Pacific; beginning with the rising of the sun, and following his pathway across the vast expanse of a hemisphere until he disappears through the golden gates of California.'

Elaborate preparations were made for communicating the news of this historic event simultaneously to all the great cities of the Union by telegraph. The telegraph station at Omaha, the centre of communications, sent out a sequence of messages as follows. Eager enquirers were first told: 'To everybody. Keep quiet. When the last spike is driven at Promontory Point, we will say "Done".' Then came 'Almost ready. Hats off, prayer is being offered,' and a few minutes later 'All ready now. The spike will soon be driven. The signal will be three dots for the commencement of the blows.' Finally three dots and the word 'Done' hummed along the wires to the multitudes waiting to hear them, like modern Americans waiting for a space launch. In San Francisco the blows of the hammer at Promontory were echoed on the bell of the City Hall; in Omaha and New York 100-gun salutes were fired; San Francisco and Chicago had the longest processions in their history; and everywhere there were great public celebrations and rejoicing.

As well as arousing government interest in the

The last spike: the historic link-up at Promontory, Utah, on 10 May 1869, between the Central Pacific (locomotive on left) and the Union Pacific.

61

Country station scene on the Union Pacific Railroad in early days. The locomotive is the *McQueen*, a typical 'American' type built by Schenectady: note the highly burnished brasswork and the antlers on the headlamp.

Opposite top. Washington, D.C., in 1863, during the Civil War, with many wood-burning locomotives stored for safety, to prevent their falling into Confederate hands in the event of a raid on Alexandria, Virginia. The Capitol can be seen in the distance.

promotion of railways, the Civil War gave them a new economic impetus by disrupting traffic on the Mississippi and depriving it of its position as the main artery of commerce for the cities of the Middle West. Its aftermath threw up the first of the great railway barons, Cornelius Vanderbilt.

Vanderbilt, a typical rags-to-riches exemplar of the American Dream, had already built up a great steamboat empire when, in 1865, he saw that the future lay with railways. He sold up his entire shipping interests to invest in railways and in a few years welded together the great New York Central by buying up component lines in stock market operations that gave contemporaries the impression of one who 'created values, earned dividends and invented wealth as if by magic.' His son who succeeded to the empire created a profound sense of shock when he revealed that its total value was then 100 million dollars. Private fortunes on this scale had never been seen before.

For the rest of the nineteenth century much of American railway history appears as a battle of financial giants. Huge fortunes were made out of government funds and land grants, spectacular stock market manipulations and, more rarely, the sound operation of giant railway undertakings. The Erie Railroad, known at one time as 'the scarlet woman of Wall Street', was perhaps more subject than any other to the activities of speculators. One of the most famous episodes in its financial history

concerned the notorious Daniel Drew. In 1866 the company was short of funds, as it often had been before, and Drew, though employed by the company as Treasurer, made it a loan on his own account of 3 million dollars, taking convertible bonds as security. He then sold massive amounts of Erie stock in forward contracts, despite the fact that the market was rising. Onlookers watched tensely as the day of reckoning approached: where would Drew obtain the shares he had contracted to hand over, at prices well below their current value? Surely he would be ruined. But at the eleventh hour Drew converted his bonds and flooded the market with the shares thus created, bringing the price down from 90 to 50, and emerging with several millions in profit. A year later Drew and Vanderbilt battled for control of the Erie in a fantastic duel involving astonishing manipulations of the stock market, injunctions and counter-injunctions in the courts, flights across state lines, and brazen attempts at corruption in the legislature. From the battle an equally notorious third party, the financier Jay Gould, emerged in control.

Many of the great companies succumbed to bank-ruptcy in the 1870s and emerged under soberer and more astute control such as that exercised by the railway baron whose name is best known to posterity, J. Pierpont Morgan. Another later baron, James J. Hill, associated with Morgan in many enterprises, from being a small-time agent for a semi-moribund paddle steamer company, built up his mighty Great

Northern company on a foundation of hard-headed business and railroading acumen. For a time Hill was also associated with the Canadian Pacific and, as we shall see, it was he who brought in one of the greatest railroad giants of all time, William Cornelius Van Horne. But at times the American railroad business continued to look like a game of monopoly capitalist roulette, until there came the days of tighter regulation, and then of crippling competition, beyond the turn of the century.

Canada's first great transcontinental railway was inspired by political considerations, like the U.S.A.'s. John A. Macdonald, first premier of the Dominion of Canada, was very anxious for the two colonies of British Columbia and Vancouver Island to join the Confederation of the eastern provinces that had been formed under the British North America Act of 1867, and on 7 July 1870 an agreement was signed in Ottawa, in which the very first clause read:

'The Government of the Dominion undertakes to secure the commencement simultaneously, within two years from the date of the union, of the construction of a railway, from the Pacific toward the Rocky Mountains, and from such point as may be selected east of the Rocky Mountains towards the Pacific, to connect the seaboard of British Columbia with the railway system of Canada, and further, to secure the completion of such railway within ten years from the date of such union.'

In this manner was born one of the most famous railways of the whole world, the Canadian Pacific.

Much was to happen, however, before the last spike of this great high road of the British Commonwealth was driven in 1885, and I must return to the mid-1850s to show how British commitments elsewhere in the world led to the creation of another great railway system.

Among all Britain's increasingly diverse overseas interests at that time India was pre-eminently first. It was at one and the same time a source of great potential wealth, explosive in its domestic affairs, and gravely susceptible to outside influences, if not direct aggression. In the early 1850s Imperial Russia was seen as the greatest danger, and Britain fought the Crimean War of 1854–5 as much to block the way to India as to stop immediate aggression upon Turkey. The city of Constantinople was seen as one of the outer bastions of defence of Britain's increasing commitments in Asia. In India, the railway network was planned very much on a strategic basis, and although the establishment of three different rail gauges might have seemed to be in direct contradiction to what the military authorities had argued during the 'battle of the gauges', in Great Britain itself the Indian network was conceived as a system of broad-gauge (5 feet 6 inches) lines, covering the main arteries of traffic, with metre-gauge lines acting as feeders from the secondary areas, where considerations of cost did not warrant the construction of broad-gauge lines, and a series of quite subsidiary lines on the 2 foot gauge serving hill stations and remoter districts. The three gauges were planned as a single entity with appropriate facilities for interchange as necessary.

The principal Indian network built up rapidly. Strategic considerations dictated emphasis on lines that led towards the North-West Frontier, for supplying armies that might be involved in a campaign in Afghanistan. But conveyance of the mails to and from London was a major consideration and in 1848 two large railways were authorised, one originating at Calcutta and one at Bombay, with a view to connecting up the two cities by rail. Both railways, the East Indian and the Great Indian Peninsula, retained their original names for nearly one hundred years. So rapidly was construction of the East Indian Railway pushed ahead that in 1868 its total mileage was greater than that of the London and North Western – 1,354 against 1,328. The travel habit grew at great speed among the native population in India, so much so that facilities were virtually overwhelmed, and overcrowding in the third class accommodation became a serious embarrassment, and an issue for political agitators.

The Great Indian Peninsula – the 'G.I.P.' as it was always known among those of us concerned with Indian railways – provided an astonishing example of the changed attitude towards steep gradients. Less than twenty years after Robert Stephenson had committed the London and Birmingham Railway to colossal engineering works to ensure easy gradients in the south of England, James J. Berkley was surveying the formidable mountain barrier of the Western Ghats, which ran parallel to the coast about fifty miles inland from Bombay. It was enough to intimidate the boldest of railway engineers, including as it did bold mountain scarp, towering peaks of bare black rock, deep canyons, valleys clothed with dense virgin forest, broken only by an occasional torrent. Whereas Stephenson had kept the gradient of the London and Birmingham down to 1 in 330, except in the first mile out of Euston, where cable haulage was used on the 1 in 70 gradient up to Camden Town, Berkley laid in lengthy gradients of 1 in 37, to be worked by steam locomotives. It is an eloquent testimony to the development that had taken place in locomotive design in the intervening years that this could be done. On each of the Ghat inclines a reversing station, or zigzag, was included. The line climbs steeply, roughly parallel to the line of the escarpment, and comes to a terminal siding. Then the direction of running is reversed, and the ascent continues in the opposite direction to that in which the train was previously travelling. In the face of immense difficulties, in addition to those associated with the nature of the terrain – including the absence of a trained labour force, and alternate drought and monsoon flooding – through communication to Calcutta, via the Thul Ghat route, was eventually established, on 8 March 1870.

Berkley's surveys, which set out the astonishing inclines over the Ghats, were made at a time when locomotive engineers in several parts of the world

Dr Karl Ritter von Ghega (1801–60), engineer of the Semmering line, leading south from Vienna through the easternmost ranges of the Alps into Styria.

Right. Ascending the Ghats: a reversing station at Poona Ghat on the Bhor Ghat, on the main line of the Great Indian Peninsula Railway, eastbound from Bombay.

were taking up the challenge of very severe gradients. Three very interesting cases may be considered alongside each other. In Europe, the Giovi Incline, between Genoa and Turin, had been constructed, while in Austria the need to provide railway communication between Vienna and Trieste (the latter then within the Austrian Empire) involved crossing some of the easternmost ranges of the Alps. It was a strategic as well as a commercial need, as part of the policy of maintaining communication between

while Ghega had seen plenty of examples of the rough and ready type of construction that was all that could be afforded in the pioneer days of American railroading, no such expedients were applied on the Semmering. It was built to standards equal to the finest in England at that time. It is sad to recall, however, that while the engineering planning was extremely thorough the same foresight had not been shown for the welfare of the huge labour force that came to be involved. This was mostly composed of

The Kalte Rinne Viaduct–most spectacular structure on the Semmering line, Austria, completed in 1853.

the Baltic and the Adriatic. The great project of crossing the Semmering range began as early as 1837 when the Archduke Johann, General Engineer Director of the Army, instructed four officers to make some preliminary surveys, and also to study what had already been achieved in England. But the comparatively level country, south of the Humber and the Mersey at any rate, was no guide as to what might be done in such a confused and unexplored mountain mass as the Semmering, while political troubles in Austria itself put the project into abeyance. In 1842, however, Dr Karl Ritter von Ghega, a man already well experienced in the construction of Alpine highways, was appointed to make a study of railways in the U.S.A. Ghega came back convinced that the crossing of the Semmering range presented difficulties no greater than some he had seen conquered by the Americans in the Alleghenies and elsewhere. However, it was only after much indecision and delay that construction of the Semmering line was finally authorised in 1848, on the route recommended by Karl Ghega.

It was a tremendous task. The track lay through dense forests on precipitous mountain sides; much reverse curvature had been laid in to keep the gradients down to a maximum of 1 in 40, but the line nevertheless includes in the thirty-six miles from Gloggnitz to Murzzuschlag fifteen tunnels, sixteen viaducts, a hundred small culverts and many substantial lengths of stone retaining wall. Moreover,

Germans, Czechs and Italians, and while they entered upon the task with great enthusiasm, they did so with little regard to their own safety and welfare. The death toll from accident and disease was terrible, and in the six years the line was under construction no fewer than 700 men died. Today the railway is electrified, and I know of no more fascinating ride on a railway than in the front cab of one of the powerful electric locomotives sweeping round the endless succession of curves, through the many tunnels, looking out over a wild mountainous country that even today presents a confused, jumbled mass of rocky eminences, forests and deep ravines which effectively conceal the way in which the railway claws its way up the mountain sides. Most spectacular of the constructional works is the Kalte Rinne Viaduct, with its line of graceful arches superimposed upon a lower line. The line over the Semmering range was completed in 1853 and through railway communication between Vienna and Trieste established in 1857. A modern Austrian writer, Dr Karl Fuler, has epitomised the Semmering railway in the following words:

'Through the immortal renown of Ghega, the problem of the Alpine railway and future similar constructional works was solved; the high mountains were opened up at one stroke, after a quarter of a century, to Stephenson's steam railway, and the realisation of later Alpine railways was no longer a technical but an economic question.'

Top. Late-nineteenth-century period piece in England: a local train London-bound on the Great Northern Railway, drawn by one of Patrick Stirling's 'straightback' 0-4-2 locomotives, near Barnet, Hertfordshire.

Above. The Mont Cenis Tunnel: the special machine devised for the excavation.

Before construction of the Semmering railway had begun the first moves towards the inception of another great railway system, that of Australia, had taken place in the infant British colony of New South Wales, and in 1853 the first locomotives were ordered from England for the pioneer Sydney and Parramatta Railway. An early objective of railway development in New South Wales was, however, the improvement of communications between Sydney and the great plains of the west, between which lay the tremendous barrier of the Blue Mountains. At a distance of about twenty-five miles from the coast appears this almost solid wall of mountains, extending in endless array to left and right and rising to nearly 4,000 feet. The escarpment is tremendous, and to climb Lapstone Hill gradients of 1 in 20 and 1 in 30 were at first proposed. No Australian contractor at that time was prepared to tender for a tunnel nearly two miles long through solid rock, and even if the bore had been driven no one could suggest, in the then primitive state of the colony, how the ten million bricks necessary to line the tunnel could have been transported to the site. So John Whitton, the engineer, used the zigzag technique adopted by Berkley for ascending the Ghats, in India. On the eastern escarpment of the Blue Mountains the zigzag did not extend far, as an easier alternative direct route was found; but on the western side of the range the great Lithgow Zigzag was constructed, and brought into service in 1869. The alignment is still very much in existence today, crossing the lofty viaducts, over which one can drive quite comfortably in a car, while looking down to the present alignment of the railway. Today the mountain slopes are densely wooded, and even from vantage points on the viaducts it is not easy to pick out the original alignment. But when the line was first constructed, the hillsides were quite bare and the full extent of the *double* zigzag and its viaducts presented a magnificent spectacle.

While locomotives had been developed in power to climb such severe gradients they were also becoming much more speedy. But the quality of the track had not advanced commensurately, neither had the means of traffic regulation. In England particularly those responsible for running the trains, and those who provided the tools, did not always see eye to eye, and this disagreement was nowhere more manifest than in the vital matter of controlling the flow of traffic along the lines. A distinguished disciple of the Stephenson school of engineers, Edwin Clark, devised what was known as the 'Two-Mile Telegraph' and it was installed on the London and North Western Railway. Telegraph huts were erected at two-mile intervals along the line, each equipped with a primitive form of semaphore signal, and Clark wanted to make the traffic regulation 'absolute'–that is, a second train was not allowed to enter the 'two-mile' section to the next hut until the man in advance had telegraphed to advise that the preceding train was clear. But the traffic department overruled him, saying they could not work the line unless the system were made 'permissive'. For this the semaphores were constructed with three positions: horizontal for 'stop'; inclined downwards for 'caution'; and hanging vertically down for 'clear'. It was left to the judgement of the man at the telegraph hut whether he stopped a train or gave it a 'caution', according to how long previously the last train had passed. If the train was telegraphed 'clear' from the far end the next train was given the 'all clear'. But as might be imagined, there were many misunderstandings. Not all drivers interpreted the 'caution' in the same way, and there were cases of trains catching up the previous one in a section. Even where 'absolute' working was normally in force there were grievous mistakes, and none more disastrous than that in Clayton Tunnel on the Brighton Line on a Sunday morning in 1861. The details of this sad affair are worth recalling as an example of faulty working in the early days of railways.

The signalling arrangements at Clayton Tunnel were primitive in the extreme. There was a small cabin at each end, each equipped with a single needle telegraph instrument for each line. On the approach sides of the tunnel there were warning signals situated about 350 yards before the portal, worked by hand wheel in the respective cabins. The idea was that a train could be warned of the state of the line through the tunnel; but if the previous train had not cleared, the only means of telling the driver to stop was by the signalman displaying a red flag from his cabin, or a red lamp after dark.

The three trains concerned were an excursion from Portsmouth to London, an excursion from Brighton, and the regular 8.30 a.m. express, and on this particular morning all three were running late. The signalman at the south end of Clayton Tunnel, who had been working greatly excessive hours, became confused by the rapid approach of the second of the three trains and gave the 'red' warning signal indicating that the first train had not cleared the tunnel, too

late to stop the train. As he entered the tunnel the driver thought he saw a flash of red and decided to stop and back his train to the entrance to speak to the signalman; but in the meantime the weary man at the south end received a message 'tunnel clear' from the north end and thought it meant that both the first and second trains were safely through. So he gave the third train the 'all clear' and it entered the tunnel under full steam, to collide inside with the second train which was backing towards the entrance. In the

frightful collision that followed in the darkness of the tunnel twenty-one passengers were killed and 176 seriously injured.

At the time of this terrible accident the Board of Trade inspectorate was constantly urging upon the railway companies the need to abandon the time-interval system of working, and to use space-interval block. The majority of the railway managements then argued that space-interval working was impracticable and would slow up the traffic to such an extent as to cause extreme congestion on the lines. Others argued that the installation of more signals would tend to induce slackness among drivers and lessen the degree of alertness that was needed in running fast trains. Clayton Tunnel was seized upon as a double argument against the principles of the Board of Trade, because in the first place the signal that was provided did not work, and in the second the space-interval block through the tunnel failed to protect the second train. Much, unfortunately, was yet to happen before the inherent soundness of the space-interval block was generally acknowledged.

Linked up closely with the question of regulation along the lines was the matter of brake power. Locomotive engineers were at one time strangely reluctant to put any form of brake on to the engine as such. It was argued that to use anything like a brake-shoe on the running face of the tyre would be injurious to the machinery. There may have been grounds for apprehension in the early days, and a

Eastern Railway of France: the magnificent viaduct at Chaumont, Haute Marne, on the main line from Paris to Belfort and Switzerland.

good deal of trouble had been experienced with broken axles. In consequence, the only brakes on many locomotives running in the sixties and seventies of the last century were on the tender – massive wooden blocks applied by hand by the fireman. The engines had no brakes at all. The trains themselves had 'brake vans' at front and rear, in which the brakes were applied by hand by the guards, and there was a whistle code by which the driver signified to the guards that he wanted the brakes applied. But the great majority of the coaches in a train would be without any kind of brake. This primitive state of affairs persisted on the continent of Europe as much as in Great Britain, and on the early railways in Canada, the U.S.A. and India.

The first major development came in the U.S.A. In October 1846, when in England the 'railway mania' was subsiding, leaving many luckless investors penniless, an eighth child was born in the village of Central Bridge, New York, to George Westinghouse and his wife Emaline, grandson of a German from Westphalia who had emigrated to the U.S.A. in 1755. (The family name was originally Wistinghausen, but by the third generation they had become thoroughgoing Americans.) The newborn baby of 1846 was also named George, and after an exciting early life, and service in the Union Army during the Civil War, he began to show a remarkable talent for mechanical invention. In 1866 he saw a catastrophic head-on collision on the railway between Schenectady and Troy which might have been avoided had means for the prompt

A terrible disaster on the Great Northern Railway of Ireland near Armagh, 12 June 1889: an artist's impression of the scene just after the runaway train, sweeping down the steep incline, had crashed into the train that was following.

and powerful application of the brakes been available, and his fertile brain became concentrated for the time on ideas for better railway brakes. He contemplated a scheme using a continuous chain, and applied by the use of steam; but what really set the remarkable chain of development in motion was an account in an illustrated magazine of the construction of the Mont Cenis Tunnel, connecting France and Italy beneath the Alps. In this the young George Westinghouse read of the use of compressed air to drive rock drills more than 1,000 yards into the solid mountain.

Up to then he had been thinking about ways of applying the brakes on *every vehicle* in a train, not only on the locomotive tender and two brake vans; and the idea of using compressed air was the first step towards the construction of a *continuous* brake. In 1868 a train belonging to the one-time Panhandle Railroad was completely fitted up with the first form of continuous air brake, designed by Westinghouse and built partly with his own hands. It was a typical American 'accommodation' of the day, in other words a train that stopped at all stations, and intermediately too, if anyone flagged it down. But every vehicle in the train had its brake, and there was no need for anyone to be alerted when the brakes were needed. Everything was under the control of the driver. Fortune deservedly favoured Westinghouse on that memorable day. The train started out from the Union Station in Pittsburgh and entered a lengthy tunnel. They gathered speed, and were emerging from the far end at a smart pace when a cart drawn by two horses drew onto a level crossing immediately ahead. The engine whistled; the horses and their driver panicked, and nothing it seemed could prevent their being run down. But the driver of the train made a full application of Westinghouse's air brake, and the train was stopped in an incredibly short distance, clear of the terrified animals. The incident became front page news throughout the length and breadth of the U.S.A., and some of the largest and most influential railways were soon anxious to try the brake. Large orders followed from the Pennsylvania, the Chicago and North Western, and the Union Pacific Railroad.

This however was merely the beginning, and as it happened also, a false start. In July 1871, the young engineer was in Europe seeking support for his invention when he met one of the associate editors of the British journal *Engineering*, Dredge by name, who was preparing a campaign for better brakes on British railways, and he discussed with Westinghouse the draft of a leading article he was intending to publish, setting out the requirements for an improved brake. It went considerably further than Westinghouse had progressed so far, and specified an important feature, which was that if one part of a train became detached from the part coupled to the locomotive *both* parts would automatically be brought to rest. With Westinghouse's original air brake the part detached from the engine would be bereft of all brake power. Westinghouse at once saw the cogency of Dredge's specification, and although it cut across all he had done so far he returned to America and immediately set out to design apparatus that would do what Dredge had suggested. Commercially it was a very courageous thing to do. The American railways were quite satisfied with the original brake and installing it in large quantities, and Westinghouse had now to tell them it had inherent defects and he was now replacing it by a better arrangement.

So was born the 'automatic' air brake, patented in 1873. The air brake came to be generally adopted on the continent of Europe, but in Great Britain a variety of types prevailed for some time. There was general agreement that a brake acting on all vehicles in a train was desirable, but the inclusion of the word 'Automatic' in the title of the improved Westinghouse apparatus was a point on which much opposition became centred. One English railway manager exclaimed: 'No man in his senses would entrust his train to an automatic brake.'

The unsatisfactory state of affairs in the United Kingdom regarding both the use of the automatic brake and the operation of the space-interval system was brought sharply to an end by a great disaster on the Great Northern Railway of Ireland on 12 June 1889, near Armagh. The rear portion of a heavily-loaded excursion train with 800 children aboard broke loose when the driver divided the train in an attempt to handle the situation that arose when his undersized locomotive stalled on an incline. It rapidly gathered speed down the 1 in 75 gradient, to crash into the engine of a regular train following 20 minutes behind by the time-interval system. The trains on the line were not equipped with automatic brakes. Seventy-eight passengers were killed and 250 injured. Public opinion was so shocked that legislation was rushed through Parliament in Westminster, making compulsory on all passenger lines the use of continuous automatic brakes and the space-interval system of block working. Any form of 'permissive' working with passenger trains was henceforth forbidden.

When railways were first projected in the Australian colonies the 'battle of the gauges' in Great Britain was still fresh in everyone's mind, and the pioneers referred their proposals to London. But London persistently urged uniformity throughout Australia, without specifying preference for any particular gauge. At first there was general agreement on the British standard of 4 feet 8½ inches; but then the Sydney and Parramatta line appointed as engineer an Irishman by the name of Shields who promptly sought to revoke the earlier agreement and adopt the Irish standard gauge of 5 feet 3 inches. Shields did not survive long in office, but Victoria and South Australia had committed themselves to the 5 foot 3 inch gauge before his dismissal and replacement by a Scotsman named Wallace, who carried New South Wales back to the British gauge. If the home government in London had taken a tough line it would not have been difficult to alter such con-

The great air brake pioneer, George Westinghouse: an early photograph taken at home, with his wife.

U.S.A.: until rivers could be bridged, the only way to get the construction trains forward in winter was by laying tracks across the ice. This is the first train to cross the Missouri, in March 1879.

struction as had already been done. But Victoria and South Australia dug their toes in and expanded their pioneer lines on the 5 foot 3 inch gauge till that of the former eventually came into confrontation with the tracks of New South Wales across the banks of the Murray River. Even so Australia had not finished with differences in rail gauge when Victoria, South Australia and New South Wales determined to go their several ways. Up in the north-east Queensland was also planning some railways. Cost was a major consideration in this sparsely-populated colony with great distances to be covered, and a survey showed that they could get a considerably greater mileage for their money if they used the 3 foot 6 inch gauge. At that time there was little prospect of any rail link-up with New South Wales, so 3 feet 6 inches it was—and Australia then had three gauges! So it still has today, though much has been done recently to obviate some of the more tiresome break-of-gauge interchange points.

In the then remote colony of New Zealand, the first public railway was projected primarily because of the peculiar geographical situation of the capital city of Christchurch in relation to its port. Lyttleton lies on a splendidly secluded inlet of the sea, at the northern extremity of the Banks Peninsula, and within that harbour there is a cove around which the town was originally built. The disadvantage, so far as communication with the interior was concerned, was that Lyttleton Harbour was ringed on the north side with a chain of hills never much less than 1,600 feet

high, and rising little less than sheer from the sea. No more than a bridle path led over the hills from Lyttleton to Christchurch, and any railway plans for making a connection would involve tunnelling. The provincial commission set up to investigate possibilities sent all the relevant data to a commission in England, which in turn approached Robert Stephenson. The year was 1859, and Stephenson's health was rapidly declining; he passed the matter over to his cousin George Robert, who recommended taking a direct line through the encircling hills, giving a railway little more than six miles long of which, however, nearly one-and-three-quarter miles were in tunnel. The proposals included a branch to Ferrymead, on the estuary of the Avon river. Because of the heavy constructional work involved in the tunnel the section between Christchurch and Ferrymead was completed first, and opened on 1 December 1863. The line through the tunnel was opened four years later.

The first ten locomotives to run on the 5 foot 3 inch gauge lines of the Canterbury Provincial Railways were all built in England, at Bristol. The first three were shipped while the name of the firm was still Slaughter, Gruning & Co. but this was later changed to the Avonside Engine Company. The very first locomotive, with the picturesque 'balloon' smokestack, named *Pilgrim*, was not originally intended for New Zealand at all but was shipped from England in October 1862 for the Melbourne and Essendon Railway Company, in Victoria, which was one of

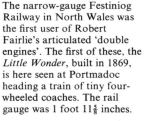

The narrow-gauge Festiniog Railway in North Wales was the first user of Robert Fairlie's articulated 'double engines'. The first of these, the *Little Wonder*, built in 1869, is here seen at Portmadoc heading a train of tiny four-wheeled coaches. The rail gauge was 1 foot 11⅝ inches.

those being built in Australia on the 5 foot 3 inch gauge. But the traffic on this railway was proving much less than anticipated, and when the engine arrived arrangements were made to dispose of it, unused. It thus became engine No. 1 of the Canterbury Provincial Railways.

To visit Ferrymead today is to be very conscious of being on significantly historic railway ground. Passenger trains still run through the tunnel between Christchurch and Lyttleton in connection with the rail ferry service to Wellington; but in early days many settlers first stepped on to New Zealand soil at Lyttleton, and had their first train ride in what was to be their new 'home country' through the tunnel recommended by George Robert Stephenson.

In the seventies of the last century the subject of rail gauges was a thorny one, and on virtually a world-wide scale; so much so that a renowned protagonist of the narrow gauge, Robert F. Fairlie, wrote a book in 1872 entitled *The Battle of the Gauges Renewed*. This time it was not a case of Brunel's 7 foot gauge as against Stephenson's 4 feet 8½ inches, but strong advocacy of much narrower gauges than the British standard – even narrower than that of the 'metre' or 3 foot 6 inch one. It is remarkable to recall that this worldwide movement was sparked off in the first place by the outstanding success of a little slate-carrying railway in the wilds of North Wales. The Festiniog Railway, built to the narrow gauge of 1 foot 11⅝ inches and brought into service in 1836, was not originally designed for steam locomotive traction at all. The slate quarries lay in the hills some thirteen miles from the sea at Portmadoc. There was a difference of 700 feet in altitude between the termini of the line, and it was skilfully laid out to have an average continuous descending gradient of 1 in 92 for a distance of twelve-and-a-quarter miles. As Charles Easton Spooner, its engineer, described it, 'The exertive power is one way only – from Portmadoc (the great slate depot for shipment) to the upper terminus. The down traffic is entirely by gravity.'

As on the Stockton and Darlington and other earlier railways, horses were used to haul the empty wagons up the gradient, and the animals rode back on the loaded trains in a dandy cart. On the Festiniog Railway this method of working might have continued indefinitely had not the traffic on the line increased to an embarrassing extent. Now steam locomotives were required so that much heavier loads could be conveyed in one train. But then there was the problem of the ultra-narrow gauge, and the restricted height and width available. The established leaders of the railway engineering profession such as Robert Stephenson, Brunel and John Ramsbottom all declared that it was impossible to build a locomotive of such small size. But C. E. Spooner found a willing contractor in George England of the Hatcham Ironworks, near London, and four little engines were delivered and put into service in 1863. They were an immediate success, but not powerful enough to provide a long-term answer to the ever-increasing traffic; and it was then that Robert F. Fairlie entered

the scene, with his celebrated 'double engine'. This was virtually two engines in one, with boilers and fireboxes arranged back to back, but with the two fireboxes in one wrapper. Each boiler supplied steam to a separate engine unit, and the composite locomotive had the dual advantage not only of possessing at least double the power of an ordinary locomotive, but also of having a flexible wheelbase which enabled it to traverse sharp curves, and to be controlled by a single engine crew.

Fairlie was not a modest man. He broadcast the merits of his double engine widely, and Spooner was suitably impressed. In 1869 George England built the first 'double engine' for the Festiniog Railway, appropriately named the *Little Wonder*, and it had a positively sensational success. Test runs were made in the presence of a distinguished company of engineers and technical journalists, some of whom were so carried away by Fairlie's oratory as to make the wildest statements in favour of very narrow gauge railways in general, and the 'double engine' in particular. There was talk of converting existing railways built on the 4 foot 8½ inch gauge to the very narrow, and one observer declared that with engines of the *Little Wonder* type he could handle the entire traffic of the London and North Western Railway – then the busiest line in the whole world. This, of course, was an outrageous exaggeration. Certainly the *Little Wonder* did very well, and was ideal for the operating conditions on the Festiniog Railway; and it was the first practical step in a development

of locomotives of the articulated type that were to blast their way over difficult terrain, in developing countries all over the world. Fairlie's slogan became, 'Railways or no railways: narrow gauge, economy with efficiency, *versus* broad gauge, costliness with extravagance.' The question of speed did not enter into his philosophy; it was literally a question of 'railways or no railways'.

There is no doubt that the success of the Fairlie

Railway beginnings in New Zealand: Port Chalmers in sailing ship days, showing the port's first railway station at the shore end of the wharf, about 1875.

'double engine' on the Festiniog Railway started a positive mania for new narrow-gauge railways all over the world. Not all the lines subsequently constructed, particularly those in the Rocky Mountains region of the U.S.A., had so narrow a gauge as the Festiniog. The metre and the 3 foot gauge became common. The 3 foot gauge was also widely adopted in Ireland at a later date, for many picturesque lines built under the provisions of the United Kingdom Light Railway Acts, of 1883, 1889 and 1896. Meanwhile the Festiniog Railway continued to flourish. Additional 'double engines' of an improved design were added to the stock, and in addition to the enormous slate traffic the company started running passenger trains and fostering something of a tourist traffic to view the beautiful country between Portmadoc and the slate quarry desolation of Blaenau Festiniog. One of the 'double engines', much rebuilt, but looking externally very like the original, is still in service on the line today.

The year 1872 saw the birth of what is now one of the most remarkable railway systems in the world, that of Japan. It followed soon after the birth of the Japanese nation as we know it today. For centuries the virtual rulers of the country had been the great feudal lords, autonomous and often at war with one another. But in March 1869, in a deed that stands out as one of the most dramatic in history, the four greatest among the clans – those of Hizen, Chosin, Satsuma and Tosa – gave up all their possessions in an Act that restored the ancient status of the Emperor, and it was the new government of the Emperor that lost no time in making plans for a railway to connect the ancient capital city of Kyoto with Tokyo. Japanese finance was not forthcoming, however, and the state treasury could not afford the outlay required. Instead a proposal was accepted from an Englishman, H. N. Lay, and in 1870 a loan of £1 million was floated on the English market. British engineers were appointed, and in due course work

began on a section of eighteen miles between the port of Yokohama and Tokyo, the first step in a project that eventually became known as the Tokaido Line, after the ancient Tokaido highway that skirted the Pacific Ocean for more than 300 miles.

When the time came for the opening it was much more than a mere railway occasion; it was a symbol of the new national sentiment of Japan. For the first time ever the Emperor Meiji appeared in state robes before the eyes of a public that included foreigners. He rode on the first train from the Shinagawa station, Tokyo, to Yokohama and there he mounted a raised dais to receive congratulatory addresses from a foreign committee, headed by the British Minister. A huge crowd in holiday attire milled round the Little Yokohama station, and once the ceremony was over eye-witnesses have told how the chair in which the Mikado had sat was 'mobbed, kissed and torn in fragments'! The inaugural train was drawn by a little 2–4–0 tank engine built in 1871 by the Vulcan Foundry Ltd, at Newton-le-Willows in Lancashire, and it has been immortalised in a series of quaintly-drawn and beautifully-coloured contemporary pictures, in which the artist was obviously much more at home in portraying the human form and animals than with mechanical items or the ships clustered in Yokohama Bay which form the background to one of the pictures. Later some smart little outside-cylindered 4–4–0s were supplied by Dübs & Co. of Glasgow. On the recommendation of the English engineer who laid out the first line the gauge was set at 3 feet 6 inches. Two years later a line was opened between the ports of Kobe and Osaka – some 300 miles to the south-west of the pioneer line.

The first lines were laid with only a single track, but at a very early stage discussions were held with a view to doubling them, and also to converting the lines already built to the 4 foot 8½ inch gauge. In other respects, however, these first Japanese railways had been laid out in the English style, with substantial,

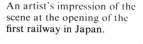
An artist's impression of the scene at the opening of the first railway in Japan.

well-built stations, high platforms and British-built rolling stock. British influence was also embedded in the mechanical engineering practice of the Japanese system thanks to the early work of William Mackersie Smith, famous in railway history for his later career in the British North Eastern Railway. The rebellion of the great Satsuma clan and other political disturbances between 1876 and 1882 delayed the progress of the line, but by 1889 the original Tokaido Line was completed, providing a continuous line of 3 foot 6 inch gauge railway from Kobe, through Osaka, Kyoto and Nagoya to Yokohama and Tokyo.

Although the very first locomotive to run in Japan came from the Vulcan Foundry, most of the rolling stock and the majority of the earliest locomotives were built by Sharp, Stewart & Co. in Manchester. At first there were three classes of carriage, as in Great Britain, and while the 'thirds' and the 'seconds' merely provided different levels of primitiveness some of the 'firsts' were unusual. The interior consisted of one long saloon extending for the entire length of the vehicle, the centre of which was taken up with a table, on which was placed a tea service with all the necessary equipment for brewing a cup of green tea. The carriages had the distinctive double roofs, as used in Australia, as a form of insulation against extremes of climate. Speeds were at first incredibly slow, even after the completion of the line between Kobe and Tokyo; the fastest train took nineteen-and-a-half hours to cover the distance of 440 miles – an average of 22 miles per hour. As a contemporary *littérateur* remarked of the Japanese railway system in general, '. . . it offers a new and surprising sensation to the jaded globe-trotter – that of being absolutely unable to hurry!'

In mentioning earlier the little Dübs 4–4–0s in Japan I was anticipating a most important development in British locomotive practice, and the completion of one of the most colourful and distinctive of the old railways of Britain. I must therefore briefly take the story back about twenty years. The Highland Railway, which originated in 1855 with a short line between Inverness and Nairn, was unique. This claim was not so much in respect of its physical characteristics, though it certainly reached the highest altitude of any British railway at its summit in the Druimuachdar Pass, at the Perth–Inverness county march (1,484 feet). Its distinction lay more particularly in the men who were among the principal sponsors in its promotion. In the early years of the nineteenth century the Highlands of Scotland were in a critically depressed and impoverished state. The aftermath of the two Jacobite rebellions, and still worse of the notorious highland clearances, had certainly broken for ever the old clan system, but not the spirit in which the clan chieftains had regarded their dependants; and in the nineteenth century public-spirited men saw in railways a means of opening up the country, of bringing industry and a revival of agriculture and fisheries to a vast depopulated region. While railways in other parts of Great Britain were promoted by financiers and industrialists,

prominent among the pioneers in the Highlands of Scotland were the Earl of Seafield, Cluny Macpherson, the Earl of Caithness and other important men who in earlier days would have been feudal lords in the clan system.

The Highland was a splendidly-built railway thanks to the meticulous attention given to its construction through the mountain fastnesses by Joseph Mitchell, himself a citizen of Inverness. As a mountain railway it does not, of course, compare in the least with

such tremendous works as the Ghats, on the Great Indian Peninsula, with the Semmering, or with the great Zigzag in the Blue Mountains of New South Wales. But the Highland was not only a symbol of altruistic railway enterprise. Its severe gradients, and the need to maintain reasonably fast services, made it a natural breeding ground for powerful locomotives, and at much the same time as the first railways were being built in Japan the Highland locomotive engineer, the great Welshman David Jones, was introducing some of the most powerful passenger engines yet seen in Great Britain. In 1874 the first of the celebrated 'Duke' class was put into service. It was a 4–4–0 development of Alexander Allan's 'Crewe' type, massively constructed and elegant in appearance. The first locomotives of this type were built by Dübs & Co., and they were clearly the inspiration for other products of that firm, including some of the early 4–4–0s built for Japan. While the 'Duke' class engines were the largest and heaviest passenger engines that had been seen in Great Britain up to 1874, and were probably in advance of any contemporary designs on the continent of Europe, in size and power they were equalled if not surpassed by many 4–4–0s of the 'American' type then running in the U.S.A.

The original network of the Highland Railway was completed in 1870, by the opening of the highly scenic 'Dingwall and Skye' line to the steamer pier of Strome Ferry, on Loch Carron in Western Ross.

British-built tank engine in Japan: one of the popular Class '1800', built by Kitsons of Leeds and first introduced in 1881.

Below. Joseph Mitchell, the great civil engineer of Inverness, who built the Highland Railway through the Grampian Mountains from Perth to Forres, completed in 1865.

But main line railway construction in Great Britain had by no means ceased at that time. Rivalry on the competing routes for the Anglo-Scottish traffic led to the building of one of the most spectacular fast express lines in England through the mountain ranges of the Pennines. The Midland Railway was determined to claim a share of the Anglo-Scottish business and, after an unsatisfactory period of working over L.N.W.R. lines, it decided it must have its own line to Carlisle. But this was easier said than

speed of at least 50 miles per hour from end to end of the new line. There was no way of avoiding heavy gradients in climbing to that high watershed, more than 1,100 feet above sea level, so to maintain the overall average there must be no restriction to high speed downhill. The great general manager of the Midland Railway, Sir James Allport, went with his chief engineer to see the territory that was involved. It was enough to daunt the spirits of the most stout-hearted of men; but Allport was one of those

managerial genii who with unerring judgement can pick the right man for the job. He selected for the survey a young engineer named Sharland, a Tasmanian by birth, to carry through the task of planning the world-famous Settle and Carlisle railway. There were immense obstructions in the way of a straight line route. But for Sharland and the tremendous work force that followed him there could be no compromise; if there was anything in the way they had to span it with a viaduct, tunnel beneath it, or blast clean through. The result was some of the most spectacular civil engineering ever seen on the railways of Britain – or anywhere else for that matter. The organisation of that workforce was a monumental task in itself. A celebrated journalist of the day, F. S. Williams, went to Blea Moor during the time of greatest activity, when the immense viaduct was under construction and the notorious Blea Moor tunnel was being driven.

'. . . not a vestige of a habitation could be seen. The grouse and here and there a black-faced mountain sheep, half buried amongst the ling, were the only visible life. Beyond the valley lay the great hill of Blea Moor, an outlying flank of the mighty mountain Whernside, covering 2,000 acres of land, where sundry farmers feed their sheep according to the number of "sheep gaits" they possess. A few months afterwards dwellings had been erected for 2,000 navvies. . . .'

'The town of Batty Wife' he continued – for 'town' it certainly was, temporarily – 'had, when we visited it, a remarkable appearance.'

Top. Ribblehead Viaduct crossing the bleak moorland terrain of the Settle and Carlisle Railway.

Above. Bristol and Exeter Railway: one of James Pearson's strange 4–2–4 tank engines for the broad (7 foot) gauge, as running in 1873. The driving wheels were 9 feet in diameter.

done, for it involved a crossing of the welter of wild and desolate mountain country leading up to the general watershed of northern England, on Ais Ghyll Moor. Compared with the Western Ghats of India, the Blue Mountains of New South Wales, or the Canadian Rockies, Ais Ghyll Moor might be dismissed as little more than a group of rolling uplands. But the Midland had to compete with two existing routes, and this meant ensuring an average

'It resembled the gold diggers' village in the colonies. Potters' carts, drapers' carts, milk carts, greengrocers' carts, butchers' and bakers' carts, brewers' drays and traps and horses for hire, might all be found, besides numerous hawkers who plied their trade from hut to hut. The Company's offices, yards, stables, storeroom and shops occupied a large space of ground. There were also the shops of various tradespeople, the inevitable public houses, a neat-looking hospital, with a covered walk for convalescents, a post office, a public library, a mission house and day and Sunday schools. But despite all these conventionalities the spot was frequently most desolate and bleak. Though many of the men had been engaged in railway making in rough and foreign countries, they seemed to agree that they were in "one of the wildest, windiest, coldest and dreariest localities" in the world.'

The workmen came from many parts, for the 'Settle and Carlisle' was built many years after the halcyon days of the Brassey contracts. There were English, Scots, Irish, and Welsh, veterans of railway building, brought together in these strange and wild communities in the Pennine fastnesses. The viaducts at Batty Moss, Dent Head, Arten Gill, and Smardale are lasting monuments to their skill and fortitude.

At times, we are told, the fury of the wind was such that the bricklayers had to cease work on the viaduct, for fear of their being blown off the scaffolding, while hundreds of other men were toiling in the dank recesses of Blea Moor tunnel, in which water is even now still dripping from chinks in the brickwork lining which is unable to hold back entirely the under-ground streams in the fissures of the limestone.

Even so, Batty Moss viaduct and Blea Moor tunnel were no more than two major works on this extra-ordinary piece of railway. The story of how the line emerged from the northern end of Blea Moor tunnel, and then was carried almost dead level for nearly ten miles, high on mountain sides, across great ravines, through tunnel after tunnel, is an epic of construction in itself. The line was so spendidly aligned through this positive maelstrom of hills and dales that the powerful locomotives of the twentieth century did not need to wait for the downhill stretches to reach 70 miles per hour. They used to attain 70 and often much more on that level 'tableland', 1,100 feet above sea level! The Settle and Carlisle line was opened throughout in 1876, and the Midland Railway was not long in making its presence felt on the Border; for while the London and North Western Railway had its own special partner in Scotland, in the Caledonian Railway, the Midland teamed up with *two* Scottish railways: the North British, to take its trains to Edinburgh, and the Glasgow and South Western. In 1876 the seeds were being sown for some very exciting events on the railways from London to Scotland.

The workmen in the temporary township of Batty Wife who spoke of unexampled hardships were to some extent anticipating conditions that were to arise in the construction of one of the greatest-ever railways of the world, the Canadian Pacific. Following Macdonald's undertaking to build a trans-

A picturesque Currier and Ives print of an American railroad train snowbound. It is curious however that while the locomotive depicted is a typically ornate 'American' type 4–4–0, the rolling stock is not true to type. Squat, flat-roofed cars were characteristic more of the continent of Europe.

Construction workers of the Canadian Pacific Railway re-enacting the driving of the last spike, having missed the actual completion ceremony.

Below. George Stephen, born 1829, the emigrant Scot who became a millionaire in North America. A director of the Bank of Montreal, he became the first President of the Canadian Pacific Railway, in 1881; later he became Baron Mount Stephen.

continental railway from the eastern provinces to the west coast as the price of securing the inclusion of British Columbia within the Dominion, the project was for many years afterwards the shuttlecock of Canadian politics and it was not until 1880 that Macdonald, once again in power, got things really under way, by persuading George Stephen, President of the Bank of Montreal, and R. B. Angus, his general manager, to head a syndicate of Canadian businessmen who would undertake the formation of a company to complete the building of the railway and then run it. Macdonald saw that the only way to do this was to vest responsibility in the hands of a single private company, rather than continue isolated contracts here and there across the entire width of Canada, under government control.

As things turned out, however, it was not only Canadians that played a major role in the great enterprise. A third very powerful member of the syndicate to whom the Act of February 1881 assigned responsibility for building the railway was an American, J. J. Hill, who had partnered Stephen and Angus in restoring the fortunes of the Chicago, Milwaukee and St Paul Railroad. Prior to his temporary eclipse, John A. Macdonald had entrusted Sandford Fleming, engineer of the Intercolonial Railway, with the task of finding a route through the great barrier of the Rocky Mountains. Fleming found to his elation that by going through the Yellowhead Pass, and then using the canyons of the Thompson and Fraser

rivers, he could get through without any exceptionally severe gradients. Blasting a track through the canyons was going to be tough work, but no worse than was to be expected in such a terrain. He recommended the Yellowhead route, and his proposals were accepted by the government. Although some contracts were let for sections of line in British Columbia nothing had been done towards the crossing of the main range of the Rockies when Macdonald's government fell in 1878.

By the time Macdonald was returned to power, doubt was being cast on Sandford Fleming's route. It was realised that the railway would be a strong colonising agent, and the Yellowhead route would run too far to the north, leaving a broadening band of territory between the line of railway and the United States border where American settlers might drive a wedge between Winnipeg and the west. The difficulty lay in the almost complete ignorance of the mountain country south of the Yellowhead Pass. The only known alternative was the Crows Nest Pass, but that lay so close to the U.S. frontier as to be considered strategically dangerous for the new railway. While older and more cautiously-minded men were weighing up the alternatives, J. J. Hill went through all previous agreements like a tornado. He seems to have taken one look at the map, drawn a straight line from Winnipeg to the head of steel marked out for the contracts in British Columbia, at Kamloops on the Thompson river, and decreed

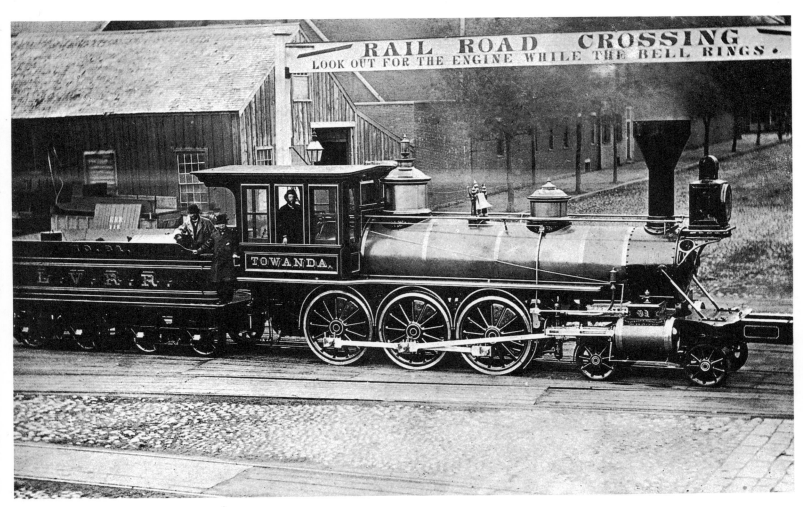

that the C.P.R. should go that way.

Though Hill was every inch the typical 'Yankee' hustler he was equally a very practical man, and in setting such a route and such a target he brought in two men who were to wield immense influence later. A. B. Rogers, a fire-eating railway surveyor, was immediately sent off to the Rockies to find a way through, as near as possible to the imaginary straight line between Winnipeg and Kamloops. The task of William Cornelius Van Horne – destined to become a veritable colossus of North American railroading – was simple enough – to get the railway built! That task fell into three broad sections: the crossing of the Prairies, towards which some work had already been done by the time of his appointment in January 1882; to get through the Rockies, when Rogers had found a way; and to complete the link between the Prairies and the great cities of the St Lawrence basin. In round figures, 2,000 miles of line had to be built, and Van Horne set out to do this in three years.

In the history of railways all over the world there have been many men who became masters of one particular facet of the great complex organism: brilliant engineers, daring projectors, great financiers, men who were past masters in the art of operation. But never surely was there one in whom the talents were mixed and so remarkably combined as in Van Horne. At different stages of his career he displayed the pioneer dash and élan of a Brunel, the sagacity of a Stephenson, the constructional drive and under-standing of a Brassey; in competitive diplomacy he had the intuition of a Hudson – but none of the dishonesty; at the pinnacle of his career he was an administrator second to none. All this, however, lay ahead when he arrived in Winnipeg early in 1882 and began to direct the tremendous drive across the Prairies, setting out to build 500 miles of line before the summer of that year was out. He went into the Rockies, walking for a considerable part of the way to see for himself the almost unbelievable hazards faced by Rogers and those with him in trying to find the shortest way through. But perhaps the greatest mark of his indomitable character was the way in which he forged the link-up between the line on the Prairies and the Eastern Provinces. The route had been settled eastwards from Winnipeg to Fort William at the western end of Lake Superior. Still further east everything was in the air when Van Horne was appointed general manager.

The syndicate to whom Macdonald had entrusted the construction of the C.P.R. had been unanimous in backing J. J. Hill's proposal to go through the Rockies at a point much farther south than the Yellowhead Pass – when Rogers had found a way, that is. There was, however, no such unanimity over the route east of Fort William. Hill wanted to go south of Lake Superior, through United States territory. This not only promised a relatively simple construction job, but it would facilitate connections with American railways in which he had important

Top. The increasing size of locomotives in the U.S.A. is evident from this photograph of the *Towanda* of the Lehigh Valley Railroad, built as early as 1866 at East Boston, Mass., by McKay and Aldus.

Above. Sir William Van Horne, when 39, at the time of his appointment as general manager of the Canadian Pacific Railway, in 1881. One of the greatest railwaymen of all time, he became President of the C.P.R. in 1888 and was knighted in 1894. He died in 1915.

Below. On the Milwaukee: group at Waukesha, Wis., some time between 1863 and 1874.

Bottom. A cartoon of 1870 when the New York Central and its allies were in strong competition with the Erie for the New York–Chicago traffic. The 'Commodore' was the great Commodore Vanderbilt, President of the New York Central.

interests. But George Stephen would have none of it, he demanded an all-Canadian route, on principle, and proposed a route actually along the north shore of Lake Superior, which in his view offered reasonable scope for development. Hill was implacably opposed to this route. Van Horne was quick enough to appreciate the cogency of Stephen's desire to have an all-Canadian route, and despite the loyalty he felt to the man who had given him this great new opportunity, backed his convictions and threw his whole

650 miles from Fort William to North Bay, on Lake Nipissing, were mostly supplied by boat. Special ships had been built to his requirements in Glasgow; gunpowder factories were established along the shores, and Van Horne showed his supreme generalship by ensuring that whatever else the men lacked in these incredibly isolated communities they should be well fed. When cash in the company's coffers at Montreal was well-nigh exhausted he paid the men regularly by cheque, knowing that it would

weight behind the lakeside line, north of Lake Superior. Hill was furious, left the syndicate, and devoted the rest of his life to promoting American railways designed to draw traffic across the Border, away from the C.P.R.

Van Horne had undertaken an immense task. Much of the line had to be blasted from the solid rock. Inland communications simply did not exist, and the working parties spread out at intervals over the

be months before they could attempt to cash them!

Out in the west, the story of the 'explorers' (for such they were) and how they found a way down the precipitous 'Kicking Horse Pass', and the privations Rogers suffered before he eventually found the pass that now bears his name, would fill whole volumes. In the main range of the Rockies, and in the still more confused tangle of the Selkirks, Rogers was among giant peaks soaring to more than 10,000 feet, raging torrents fed from immense glaciers, and mountainsides so densely wooded with pine that it was difficult to gain any vantage point from which an idea of the geography of the region could be grasped. Van Horne, like the good 'general' he was, went to see for himself where the going was toughest through the fearful canyons of the Fraser river, and then from Kamloops eastward made his way on foot, through pouring rain, and the first snows, through the Eagle Pass. The cost of the railway was far exceeding all estimates. The company passed from one financial crisis to another, until at last the Act of Parliament giving the desperately needed monetary aid received the Royal Assent in July 1885.

The end was typical, and characteristic of Canadian Pacific Railway history. George Stephen and Donald A. Smith, who afterwards became the first Lord Strathcona, were both Scots, and in one financial crisis when less stout hearts were wavering Stephen wired Smith in the words of the war-cry of the Clan Grant, 'Stand fast, Craigellachie!' There was nothing

Rogers was holding the sleeper under the final rail. Donald A. Smith drove the last spike. Van Horne spoke no more than a single sentence. There were cheers, and then the train steamed on to Vancouver. A cairn marked the spot, 28 miles west of Revelstoke and 2,529 miles from Montreal.

At first speed was not a consideration on the Canadian Pacific. The line had been carried through places where no means of human transport had previously existed. In the canyons of British Columbia it had followed the old Caribou Trail but elsewhere there had not been even the old Indian tracks as guides. But while Van Horne and his men were toiling beside Lake Superior, and on the forest-clad banks of the Columbia river, a new significance in railway operation was rapidly dawning in Europe, to be followed immediately in the U.S.A. – that of speed. In Great Britain the significance was all the more profound because the most exciting peace-time episode that had so far affected railways anywhere was initiated by a *reduction* in fares. The completion of the Settle and Carlisle line in 1876 and the entry of the Midland Railway into the competition for Anglo-Scottish traffic certainly put the established East Coast and West Coast routes on their mettle. At first the Midland, with its longer mileage, could not compete for speed from London either to Edinburgh or to Glasgow; but even before the Settle and Carlisle line was approaching completion it sowed the seeds of the new competition by deciding to carry third class passengers by all trains. Hitherto in the

Above. The magnificent Garabit Viaduct, just south of Saint-Flour, on the main line from Clermont Ferrand to Béziers. It was designed by the famous Eiffel.

Right. A train of unusually antiquated stock on the Paris–Orleans Railway.

Opposite top. 'The Boat Train, 1865' by Howard Geach. The train is seen ready to leave Dover for London by the South Eastern Railway.

Opposite bottom. 'Across the Continent.' Chinese workers salute a train emerging from snow sheds on the Central Pacific Railroad.

Overleaf. Frith's 'The Railway Station' (Paddington Station, London). A fine panorama of cast iron architecture, broad gauge railway activity and human drama. In the centre, a bewildered foreigner argues with a cab driver; to the right of the bridal party, two Bow Street runners arrest a miscreant. To the left a departing schoolboy, cricket bat in hand, receives a fond farewell from his mother beneath the manly glance of his older brother.

of the Highland Scot about Van Horne, but that telegram fired his imagination, and he determined that the place where the last spike should be driven would be named 'Craigellachie'. There was no question of a 'golden spike'. As Van Horne said, the last spike would be as good an iron spike as any other on the line. In the gloom of 7 November 1885, amid fir trees dripping from all the recent rain, the special from the east approached the place where

United Kingdom Gladstone's Regulation of Railways Act of 1844, which compelled all railways to run at least one train a day calling at all stations and conveying third class passengers in closed-in carriages at the statutory rate of one penny per mile, had been treated by some administrations as an incubus; but from April 1872 on the Midland at any rate, the third class passenger was able to travel on the fastest express trains.

From this start the Midland went one better, to the consternation and annoyance of all other British railway companies. From 1 January 1875 it abolished the second class altogether. Existing second class carriages were made available to third class passengers, and the first class fare was reduced to three-halfpence a mile. The response was astonishing. One could understand the anger and apprehension of other railway companies, who expected serious effects on their own traffic, and threatened ruinous competition and retaliation against the Midland. But some of the leading organs of the British press were strangely critical, irresolute, or hostile. Hardly a word was written in praise of the inestimable boon conferred on the travelling public. One prominent writer remarked 'This is not railway reform, but revolution.' Revolution it certainly was, though reaction through the British railway world was gradual, if none the less profound. Its first effects were felt, somewhat naturally, on the Great Northern and the London and North Western.

Both companies countered the Midland developments with increased speed. The Great Northern admitted third class passengers into their 'Special Scotch Express', the forerunner of the Flying Scotsman, in the summer of 1888, and both East and West Coast routes to Scotland progressively accelerated their 10 a.m. departures from London until Edinburgh was reached at 5.27 p.m. from King's Cross, and at 5.38 p.m. from Euston. It was a sensational speed-up, seeing that the earliest booked arrivals had been

statistical analysis published by two great authorities of the day, Professor Foxwell and Lord Farrer.

Country	Express mileage	Average speed including stops	excluding stops	Inhabitants to 1 express mile per day
Great Britain	62,904	41·6	44·5	525
United States	13,956	41·6	—	4,360
France	11,263	32·8	36·2	920
Holland	8,000	32·5	35·0	540
North Germany	18,637	31·7	34·3	1,250
Belgium	6,919	31·7	33·5	850
Austro-Hungary	6,297	30·0	32·0	2,820
South Germany	2,567	31·2	33·0	1,290
Ireland	1,646	33·0	35·0	1,700
Italy	1,213	29·5	31·2	6,400
Russia (European)	3,060	29·0	31·6	27,700

At that time, as an ultra-patriotic commentator once remarked, it was Britain first, and the rest nowhere. But passing over the above statistics as remarkable evidence of the way railways had developed in this small country, we must nevertheless add that after the 'race' of 1888, which received wide publicity in the world's newspapers, the British lead in respect of maximum scheduled speed was soon overtaken in both France and the U.S.A.

In 1876, that momentous year in the history of the Midland, the International Sleeping Car Company was formed in Europe. The 'Orient Express', running

George Nagelmackers, the founder of the International Sleeping Car Company, photographed in Brussels in January 1898.

Opposite top. Preserved steam in Australia: the 'Puffing Billy' in the Dandenong Hills, near Melbourne.

Opposite bottom. Preserved steam in Britain: the Worth Valley line, near Keighley, Yorkshire.

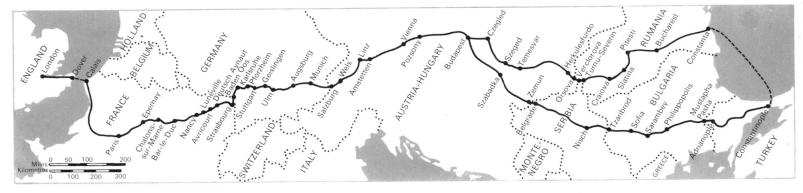

7 p.m. and 8 p.m. respectively. Even these remarkable figures did not tell the whole story. The time had not yet arrived when these trains carried restaurant cars, and a twenty-minute stop had to be included at York on the one route and at Preston on the other, for passengers to obtain lunch. The record times achieved in the height of the 1888 'race' could not well be maintained all the year round, and the standard times from London to Edinburgh became eight-and-a-quarter hours by East Coast, and eight-and-a-half hours by West Coast – a vast improvement on previous standards. The booked average speeds by these two crack trains were 47·7 miles per hour by the East Coast, and 47·3 miles per hour by the West Coast.

Even before this exciting contest passenger train speeds in Great Britain were the fastest in the world. The following table has been compiled from a

daily from Paris to Vienna and once a week over the succeeding 1,020 miles to Constantinople, was one of its first De Luxe trains. The run between Paris and Vienna was inaugurated in 1883, and it was the first train on the European continent to be composed entirely of dining, drawing-room, and sleeping cars. It ran over the tracks of six different railways: the Eastern of France, the Alsace-Lorraine, the Baden, the Württemberg, the Bavarian, and the Austrian State. The distance was 837 miles, and the train leaving Paris at 7.30 p.m. reached Vienna at 10.15 p.m. on the following day – an inclusive average speed of only 32·2 miles per hour. Generally speaking, the railways on the European continent were run at the slowest speeds the administrations chose to provide. The principle in most countries had been to parcel out territories to give each railway a monopoly. Further-

The route of the Orient Express, c. 1890.

Above. Europe's first rack-and-pinion mountain railway: the Vitznau–Rigi, opened in 1871. The first locomotives had vertical boilers, and the chassis was inclined so that the boiler was approximately upright when climbing the gradient. This photograph shows Vitznau station in 1880.

Right. Dining at leisure while waiting for the train: a corner of the dining-room in the London and North Western Railway hotel at Holyhead, Welsh packet station for the Royal Mail route to Dublin.

Opposite top. The morning Anglo-Scottish express from Euston to Edinburgh and Glasgow overtaking a goods train on the water troughs near Bushey, Hertfordshire. The express is double-headed, with a Ramsbottom 2–2–2 of the 'Lady of the Lake' class, a design dating from 1859, and a Webb 'Precedent' class 2–4–0 of 1874 vintage.

Opposite bottom. On the French Riviera: a train on the Paris, Lyons and Mediterranean Railway passing through Monte Carlo. The very primitive coaches will be noticed.

Victoria Station, London, in the 1880s: very ancient rolling stock, and one of William Stroudley's 'DI' class 0–4–2 tank engines of the London, Brighton and South Coast Railway, in the right foreground. These locomotives, painted yellow, were always kept immaculate.

more, in France the government guaranteed a minimum dividend to the companies. The Paris, Lyons and Mediterranean received 11 per cent, and the Nord no less than 13, so that there was little incentive to improve services. Despite the monopoly system, however, a degree of competition arose. In France both the Orléans and the P.L.M. provided services to Spain, in each case reaching the frontier over the tracks of the Midi Railway; and the Orléans,

at any rate, strove to gain a preponderance of the traffic by running some of the best trains in France between Paris and Bordeaux.

On the eastern frontier of France the railway situation had changed profoundly after the end of the war of 1870–1, when the provinces of Alsace and Lorraine had been annexed by Germany, and the railway system, which was formerly part of the French Est system, put under the direct control of Prussia.

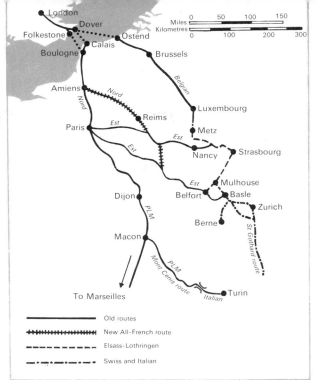

Map to illustrate the strategic importance of the Elsass–Lothringen system, taken by Germany from France at the end of the Franco-Prussian War.

the Imperial Elsass–Lothringen system in relation to traffic eastwards from France, and in particular its controlling situation in relation to through traffic from England to Switzerland and Italy. Except on the old and more roundabout route via the P.L.M., via Dijon, Aix-les-Bains and Modane, the Elsass–Lothringen held a key position.

Taking continental Europe as a whole, one could not, in 1888–9, expect to travel between the capital

Swindon, Great Western Railway of England, in later broad gauge days, showing the complicated layout of mixed-gauge tracks at the junction of the lines to Bristol (left) and South Wales (right), with the entrance to the works beyond.

There was an attempt, after the war, to amalgamate all railways in Germany under one Imperial control; but the states in the south resisted strongly, and those in Bavaria, Saxony, Baden, Oldenburg, Württemberg and the Palatinate, in addition to the newly-acquired Elsass–Lothringen – as it became known – remained outside the general confederation in the north. A glance at the accompanying map is enough to show the immensely strong strategical position of

cities or other important towns at average speeds of much more than 30 miles per hour, and then at first or second class fares only. Nineteenth-century railway travel in Europe was no joy-ride, especially for those who could not afford the excessively high first class fares charged on some routes. The carriages mostly had straight-up-and-down sides, and were as unattractive inside as they were externally drab. Seats, even in the second class, were sometimes cushionless

wall above the yellow-green and white cushions was in brown and white material, with brown wood panelling, and on this wall were the usual two luggage racks and a circular mirror. The clerestory roof (in white material with brown design and dark-brown border) was very high, and from it depended a long gas lamp. Curtains were provided for the two large windows (on the corridor side there were three – one in the door and two at the side). There was also a floor carpet. The corridor had the convenience of a luggage rack along one side of it and portable tables were also supplied there. Lavatory accommodation was good. The first-class compartments were not much better than these admirable seconds, had a square instead of a circular mirror, lincrusta on the ceiling and, usually, velvet cushions.'

In the U.S.A. things were very much better. In the eastern states there was some really fast running on the competitive routes between New York and Philadelphia, with the Pennsylvania having a train covering the 55·7 miles from Jersey City to Trenton in sixty-three minutes, and averaging $48\frac{3}{4}$ miles per hour including stops over the whole journey of $89\frac{3}{4}$ miles. Already, too, the New York Central and the Pennsylvania were in hot competition for the Chicago traffic. The former company had the longer route but much the easier gradients, and covered the 971 miles in exactly twenty-four hours. The Pennsylvania, going through the heart of the Allegheny mountains, took twenty-three-and-three-quarter hours to cover its 911 miles. The average speed on each route was about 40 miles per hour. Both these trains, however, had strictly limited accom-

while in Belgium, although the windows were curtained, the seats were too low for one to look out in comfort. The exceptions were to be found in Germany, where J. P. Pearson, a noted world traveller by train, wrote thus of the *Durchgehende*, or 'D', trains:

'Some of the second-class compartments were open, i.e. the partition wall was not carried right up to the ceiling, but the others, fully closed off, were better. Only three seats were provided each side and these had arm-rests. The partition

modation, and required considerable supplements over the first class fares. It is also interesting to recall how quickly one could then travel right across the American continent. From New York to San Francisco, 3,270 miles, using successively the Pennsylvania, Chicago and North Western, Union Pacific and Central Pacific, the average speed including stops was 25·6 miles per hour. In Canada, by Canadian Pacific throughout, the average speed over the 3,078 miles from Quebec to Vancouver was 21 miles per hour.

In the build-up of the American railway network the service between Washington and New York had an interesting history. An early obstacle lay in the city of Baltimore, where the Patapsco River is about three-quarters of a mile wide. The Baltimore and Ohio, as mentioned earlier, was one of the oldest of the American railways and celebrated its centenary in 1927. But in the 1880s there was no direct track connection through the city of Baltimore. Trains were run for about four miles through railway yards and along the public streets at very slow speed to reach a ferry which crossed the Patapsco River between Locust Point and Canton. By the year 1888, through trains between Washington and Philadelphia were taking a little over three hours, for a run of about 135 miles. These trains usually consisted of four or five cars, and the ferry boat was long enough to take the whole train and its locomotive without any uncoupling. The river crossing took about eight minutes, during which time the tender of the locomotive was filled with water pumped from tanks on the boat. It was good work to maintain an overall average speed of 44½ miles per hour between Washington and Philadelphia, inclusive of the ferry crossing. The locomotives then used were of the 'American' type, with the 4–4–0 wheel arrangement.

In retrospect, the winter of 1888–9, in the aftermath of the Anglo-Scottish 'race to the north', can be seen as the end of an epoch for the railways of the world. The networks in many countries had been extended and multiplied; equipment and working rules had been developed to the stage where it was safe to run regularly at speeds well in excess of 70 miles per hour and there was a growing realisation of the value of railways for speeding up business. At the same time there was an equal realisation that before railways could become generally popular for the promotion of tourist traffic something better than the traditional 'dog-boxes' would have to be provided. It was in England that the twofold movement began towards higher speeds and greater comfort – at *reduced* fares; and as the pioneers of this movement, the names of the Midland Railway and its great general manager James Allport stand high. Although the Midland had not taken any active part in the 'race to the north' its actions in admitting third class passengers to all trains, and then in abolishing the second class, were the catalysts that set the competition going; and during the winter of 1888–9 no two capital cities in the world were connected so rapidly as London and Edinburgh.

Opposite top. The St Paul and Pacific Railroad (later the Great Northern) was fostered by J. J. Hill as the U.S. rival to the Canadian Pacific. In this striking photograph the locomotive *William Crooks* is drawing a train across the Mississippi River bridge between the twin cities of Minneapolis and St Paul.

Opposite bottom. Spectacular bridge construction in Sweden: the first bridge over the river Angermanalven, on the northern main line, photographed in 1887.

Left above. The first British restaurant car: the Pullman-type car *Prince of Wales* introduced on the London–Leeds service of the Great Northern Railway in 1879. The scullery boy peels potatoes on the open rear platform.

Left below. Luxury travel in 1883: in the restaurant car of the Orient Express.

Below. Interior of the first type of coach introduced by the International Sleeping Car Company, showing a daytime compartment transformed for night use, with transverse sleeping berths.

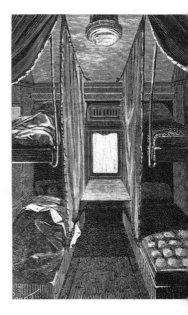

Part 3

Events Around the Turn of the Century

The last years of the nineteenth century witnessed the beginning of many important chains of evolution on the railways of the world. Long past were the days when the value of railways was doubted. In the British Empire long and difficult new lines were being built to further colonial development. Passengers were becoming amenity- as well as speed-conscious; corridor trains with dining and sleeping cars were being introduced, and with the gradual movement towards higher speeds was coming a greater emphasis upon measures to ensure the safety of travel. In remote districts 'light' railways were being built to serve scattered populations with little more than cart tracks for lines of communication; and last of all, in the so-called 'advanced' countries of the world, main line passenger trains were being accelerated to equal, and then to surpass the pre-eminence in speed so far held without question by Great Britain. These various trends had many ramifications of great interest – human as well as technical – and so

Right. Rural Australia in the 1880s: the daily goods arrives at Blacktown, New South Wales.

Below. Natal Government Railway: the spectacular Inchanga Viaduct on the old Durban to Pietermaritzburg line, completed in 1880.

far as colonial development was concerned, the emphasis was at first on southern Africa.

Railway construction in the remote and isolated British colony at the Cape of Good Hope had begun in the 1870s. It was not a very forthright or far-reaching start, and there was ample evidence that the colonists had little desire for expansion beyond the natural geographical boundary to the north, in the mountain barrier that led up to the Great Karroo

desert. How long these attitudes might have prevailed one can only guess, but this situation had been changed dramatically in 1869 by the discovery of the great diamond fields around Kimberley. The towering personality of Cecil Rhodes had come into the business and political life of the Cape, and while on the one hand he was co-ordinating the diamond mining activities at Kimberley, he was equally the moving spirit in pushing forward railway develop-

ment to connect this suddenly rich area with established seaports. At the back of Rhodes's mind was a great imperial vision of a railway running the entire length of Africa, from the Cape to Cairo. 'The railway is my right hand, and the telegraph my voice' was his famous remark.

Then at the end of 1886 gold was discovered on the Witwatersrand in the Transvaal, one of the republics to the north settled by the Dutch Boers of the Great Trek, which Rhodes had planned to skirt round. Johannesburg, which had scarcely existed until then, became a magnet for innumerable investors and speculators, and Cecil Rhodes immediately began making plans to extend the Cape Government Railway line from Kimberley forwards to the gold fields. But the Transvaal was hostile to Britain, and President Kruger projected an independent railway to connect his new-found treasure trove with the sea by a route eastwards from Pretoria to the frontier of Portuguese East Africa, and so to Lourenço Marques.

Kruger tried his level best to block Rhodes's advance from the south until his own line was completed to Delagoa Bay, but his funds ran out long before his line was completed. Rhodes, with a characteristic stroke of diplomacy, persuaded the Cape Parliament to lend him £600,000 to finish the work, and the gesture was enough to make Kruger relent. In fact Rhodes was confident of his own ability to reach Johannesburg before the line from Delagoa Bay did. So it eventuated. The first train from the south steamed into the little shack that was the first Johannesburg station on 15 September 1892—a full two years ahead of the all-Dutch rival. It was a great triumph for Rhodes, but naturally one that did not receive much public recognition in the Transvaal.

There was little in the way of speed in the working of railways in South Africa at that time; it was simply a case of opening lines of communication. But in Europe and in the U.S.A. the accelerators were definitely on the move. In both France and the U.S.A. it was competition between two rival routes between major cities that led to the speeding up, just as it had been in Great Britain in 1888, between London and Edinburgh. In 1893 there was a great international exhibition in Chicago, and one of the competing routes from New York, that taking the so-called 'water-level' route via Albany, Buffalo and the level country to the west, made a dramatic acceleration in putting on a new train, the Exposition Flyer. Hitherto the New York Central line, which paid for its easy gradients by having a much longer route, had run on equality with the Pennsylvania. The Pennsylvania's route, running through the Allegheny Mountains, was 60 miles shorter. Both had timed their crack trains to make the journey in twenty-four hours, involving overall running averages of 40·7 and 38 miles per hour. The Exposition Flyer was booked to make the run in the level twenty hours—a very fine average of 49 miles per hour. The Pennsylvania made no response to this obvious challenge, and

Crossing the Vaal River: President Kruger (hand on chest) and President Reitz of the Orange Free State at the official opening of the temporary bridge at Viljoensdrif, May 1892.

The Pennsylvania Special–the crack train between New York and Chicago–leaving Jersey City on its inaugural run, 15 June 1902. The train was later renamed the Broadway Limited.

it seemed that the timing was a little too hot to sustain. Once the exhibition was over the train was withdrawn, and the 24-hour timing was resumed, until 1902.

In that year of 1893, however, speed fever had certainly gripped the New York Central and its associates, and even before the Exposition Flyer started running some startling speed records had been claimed for the Empire State Express, put on in October 1891. This train was being run by some very speedy examples of the characteristic American outside-cylindered 4–4–0, and the claim was made that on 9 May 1893 a maximum speed of 102·8 miles per hour was attained near Grimesville, between Syracuse and Buffalo. Only two days later the amazing speed of 112·5 miles per hour was claimed for the same locomotive, the *999*. While there is no doubt that some fast running was being made on these trains the claims for these exceptional speeds were not supported by the kind of corroborative detail that would be considered essential today to substantiate the claims. Indeed, a few years later, when the veracity of this claim was strongly challenged from outside the U.S.A., the railway company replied that the speed had been 'about 81 miles per hour'. These claims were enough to show, however, that the value of high speed as a commercial proposition was becoming fully appreciated in the U.S.A., and in 1902 both the principal rivals on the New York–Chicago service cut the time to the level twenty hours.

The city of Chicago is probably the greatest centre of railway activity to be found anywhere in the world. At one time, at the height of American development, it was served by no fewer than twenty-two different main line railways, with through trains to every part of the U.S.A., and including two that were subsidiaries of the two great Canadian systems. In the 1950s the number had reduced no more than slightly, to twenty; but since then the financial difficulties affecting American railways generally has led to further groupings and amalgamations.

It is interesting to work round the compass and trace the routes of the lines that converge on Chicago like the spokes of a wheel. Sweeping round the most southerly part of Lake Michigan and coming in from the east are the Baltimore and Ohio; the Chesapeake and Ohio; the two components in this area of the New York Central, namely the Michigan Central, and the Cleveland, Cincinnati, Chicago and St Louis (the 'Big Four'); the Wabash; the Erie; the mighty Pennsylvania; and the Grand Trunk Western–a subsidiary of the Canadian National. All converge on a group of lines running close to the lakeside in the final approaches to the city.

Then from the south, keeping to the west of the state boundary between Illinois and Indiana, come the lines of the Chicago and Eastern Illinois, the Illinois Central, the Wabash again, and the Gulf, Mobile and Ohio. The next spokes in the wheel begin to take us a little west of south, to the great lines providing the services to the west coast. First comes the Atchison, Topeka and Santa Fe, then the Chicago, Rock Island and Pacific, followed by the Chicago, Burlington and Quincy. Of these only the Santa Fe goes through to California on its own metals. By this time the spokes are pointing nearly due west, and we meet the Chicago and North Western, the Chicago Great Western, the Chicago, Milwaukee, St Paul and Pacific, and another line of the Illinois Central. Railways like the Chicago and

Railway Company was founded. Thirteen of the principal railways serving the city combined in the setting up of this enterprise, and by 1929 it was dealing with 6,000 wagons a day. When the motive power was almost entirely stream, a stud of seventy-five locomotives was needed to operate the traffic exchanging between the various main line railways. The 'Belt' had twenty-two miles of its own, and running powers over a further twenty-five miles, while in its extensive siding and marshalling yard

Central Station, Chicago, at the turn of the century, used by the Illinois Central Railroad.

North Western, the Milwaukee, and the 'Burlington' are not confined to one route; they too have spokes of their own. Then, finally, jostling each other as it were, there are the closely-grouped lines heading due north, parallel to the western shore of Lake Michigan, nearly all making for the city of Milwaukee before beginning to fan out to the north and west. Here are the lines of the Chicago and North Western, the 'Milwaukee' itself, and the Minneapolis, St Paul and Sault Ste Marie. This latter, always known as the 'SOO' line, is a subsidiary of the Canadian Pacific.

Around the city there grew up an extensive series of freight transfer railways, extending in arcs of circles connecting with all the spokes of the wheel, and providing a diversity of facilities for interchange of traffic. These had been enterprised by individual companies, among which may be mentioned the Chicago Junction, the Indiana Harbor Belt, and the Chicago Union Transfer. At one time some of these operated suburban passenger services, while Chicago also owned an 'Elevated' modelled on that of New York.

There were at one time six stations in Chicago dealing with main line terminal traffic, but until the year 1946 there were no through-carriage facilities between east and west of the city. In many cases passengers had not only to change trains but also to change stations, and lengthy waits for continuing trains were often involved. For freight such a situation would have been intolerable and in 1882 the Belt

accommodation, it had a further 300 miles of track.

Railways made Chicago, and Chicago's growth was a reflection in turn of the opening up of the Middle West during the third quarter of the nineteenth century. At the heart of Chicago the famous Union Stock Yards – estimated in the year of 1889 to have handled three million head of cattle, three million sheep and six million pigs – symbolised the mutual relationship between the three.

Chicago's railway history began about 1850. In 1854, a property dealer recorded with delight the benefits the railways were bringing to his business, in a booklet entitled *The Rail-Roads, History and Commerce of America*, and could already see the railway future that lay in store for the city.

'A careful perusal of these facts [of the growth of railway activity in the city in the last year] will, we think, satisfy the most skeptical, whether at home or abroad, that Chicago is soon to take rank among the greatest cities upon the American Continent . . . These facts, if carefully pondered, become more interesting and, we might add, more astonishing than the wildest visions of the most vagrant imagination.'

After listing the fourteen principal routes now coming into Chicago, the writer reminds his readers of the pace at which the railways have been growing and reflects on the implications for present and future.

'. . . Less than two years ago we had only one railroad entering the city – the Galena and Chicago Union – and that was finished only a few miles. Can it be wondered at that our city has doubled its population within the same time, and that the price of real estate and business of all kinds have increased in a corresponding ratio?

But will some cautious wiseacre ask "Are these things to continue?" We will not stop to answer the question, but will simply say, on the first of January next we shall have 3,000 *miles* of railroad, and by a year from that time it will be entirely safe to add another thousand.'

A comparison between the map in this booklet and one from a guide published in 1893, the year of the Columbian World's Fair, tells its own story. The web of lines coming into the city from all quarters has almost doubled in density, the stockyards are built, and the enormous complex of the Chicago Union Transfer Railway Yards stands out as a prominent feature. The population was now one and a half million. Chicago was in its heyday as the railway freight capital of the U.S.A.

Let us leave Chicago with a contemporary account of the intense activity to be viewed from a vantage point on the viaduct over the North Western Railroad tracks at Halsted Street and Chicago Avenue.

'The broad yard of the North Western road underneath the viaduct contains hundreds of freight cars from all parts of the country in seeming confusion, while darting to and fro are speedy locomotives busy taking a car out here, adding another there, and generally bringing order out of chaos. Moving across the viaduct to Chicago Avenue we come upon the round house of this great railroad. Radiating from a moveable track platform are about twenty-five tracks leading to as many doors in the circular building. A score of steaming locomotives, puffing and hissing, ready for action, await orders on the tracks between the platform and the building, while within the doors two or three more can be seen on each track, all coaled and wooded, ready for the torch.'

It was the question of speed that brought us to Chicago. In France, curiously enough, some of the speeding up arose from the rivalry of two *steamer* routes, on the journey from London to Paris. In the 1890s, on the English side of the English Channel, the South Eastern Railway and the London, Chatham and Dover were still in deadly rivalry. The South Eastern worked its principal Paris service via Folkestone and Boulogne, while the Chatham steamers went from Dover to Calais. Both services were continued to Paris by fast express trains of the Northern Railway of France. The Folkestone route, which achieved the journey in seven-and-a-half hours to its rival's eight, despite a longer sea crossing, involved some fast running in France, and began to bring into prominence the celebrated four-cylinder compound locomotives built on the principles worked out by Alfred de Glehn. He was in close collaboration with M. du Bousquet, the locomotive engineer of the Northern Railway of France, and produced at his works of the Société Alsacienne, in Belfort, a design of locomotive that was to prove the prototype of many hundreds of French express engines, of steadily increasing size and power, for more than thirty years.

Crossing the English Channel, 1900. At Dover the boat trains ran alongside the packet steamers on the open wharf of the Admiralty Pier. In rough weather the sea often broke over the parapet and crashed on to the roofs of standing trains. The locomotive in the right foreground is one of James Stirling's 'F' class (South Eastern Railway).

It was de Glehn's engines, just as much as the flying Americans of the New York Central, that began to steal much of the British thunder in express train speed.

In the U.S.A. it was not only on the New York Central that there was a pronounced speed-up in the last years of the nineteenth century. The Chicago and North Western Railroad put on their celebrated Fast Mail, running through the night over the miles between Chicago and Omaha on the Missouri, in 1899. The journey time was ten hours, but punctuality was considered a veritable point of honour, and there are tales of very fast running to make up time when delays had occurred. I am afraid that these, like those told about the Empire State Express in 1893, must be taken as enthusiastic exaggerations, such as that of one gentleman who had an engine pass, and wrote in the English *Railway Magazine*:

'Through Denison we passed at one mile for every minute and out into the open to Siding X, and here with the dawn crowding her very tender, 592 outdid all known records of the world for fast speeding with the mail – and your letter. From Siding X to Arion is just two-and-four-tenths miles by the measurement of engineers. Over this distance 592 ran in one minute and twenty seconds or two miles per minute. Pity it was that she did not have a speed recorder attached, in order that the record thus made should become official. Nevertheless John and I know that she did it, and so does 592, so that everybody ought to be content . . .'

The summer of 1895 saw the climax of the century's rivalry between the East Coast and West Coast routes to Scotland, and it was undoubtedly the construction of the Forth Bridge that precipitated that amazing contest. But before coming to the race, we must give more than a passing mention to the great bridge itself.

Before its construction, the wide estuary of the Firth of Forth, like that of the river Tay another forty miles to the north, had presented a major obstruction to the building of a reasonably direct line of railway from Edinburgh to the north. The Forth was crossed first at Stirling, where it had narrowed from a wide estuary to a river, and a long detour was necessary in the journey from Edinburgh to Perth, Dundee or Aberdeen. The great viaduct across the Firth of Tay bringing the North British line directly into Dundee had been the first step in shortening the way north, but a terrible disaster befell the first Tay Bridge. It must be said that the bridge was not very skilfully designed; but worse than that was the way in which it was actually constructed. It stands unique among the great railway civil engineering works of Great Britain in suffering from slipshod and makeshift workmanship; and where this might have been detected and stopped with proper supervision, of this, one regrets to add, there was virtually none. The first Tay Bridge was completed in May 1878. Just over a year later Queen Victoria travelled over it on her way to Balmoral, and shortly afterwards she knighted its designer, Thomas Bouch. On 28 December 1879, at the height of a storm of wind and rain, it collapsed just as a train was crossing, and every one of the eighty passengers

on the train was drowned. Before this catastrophe Bouch had been entrusted with the design of an even greater bridge, across the Firth of Forth; but with his reputation in as great a ruin as the first Tay Bridge itself, those promoting the crossing of the Forth turned elsewhere.

The Forth Bridge was a colossal project, so big that no one railway company could bear the total expense, and a separate company was formed in which the investors were the four railway companies mainly interested. The partners in the East Coast route from London to Scotland were the Great Northern, the North Eastern, and the North British, with boundary points at Shaftholme Junction, four miles north of Doncaster, and at Berwick-upon-Tweed. But in addition to the East Coast partners the Midland Railway had no small interest. The Midland and North British together ran the third competitive service from London to Edinburgh, following the very beautiful Waverley route north of Carlisle. By that route the Midland sought to run through-carriages from London to Aberdeen, to Perth, and to Inverness, when the Forth Bridge was completed; and although its earliest ambitions were not for entire through-trains of its own, the Midland Railway actually became the biggest guarantor in the Forth Bridge Company, backing the payment of a perpetual dividend of 4 per cent per annum. The proportions were North British 30 per cent, Midland $32\frac{1}{2}$ per cent, and Great Northern and North Eastern $18\frac{3}{4}$ per cent each. The magnificent

Alfred de Glehn, famous the world over as a designer of four-cylinder compound locomotives. He was chief engineer of the Société Alsacienne de Constructions Mécaniques, of Belfort, Alsace.

Below. One of de Glehn's most famous engines, a Nord 'Atlantic', waiting on the quayside at Boulogne ready to take a boat train at high speed to Paris.

Bottom. The simplicity of Dutch locomotives: two highly ornate British-built 4–4–0s of the Netherlands State Railway.

bridge was opened in March 1890 by the Prince of Wales, later King Edward VII. The beauty of the basic design was to some extent overshadowed by its tremendous size. Use of the cantilever principle made possible a structure of great elegance, but an important feature which contributed to its slenderness was the use of steel throughout, instead of wrought iron. It was a time when structural methods were changing considerably, and not many years

were to pass before a new railway in the West Highlands of Scotland was to have its viaducts constructed in reinforced concrete, instead of brick or stone.

So events moved towards the amazing August of 1895. There were many points in which this later race differed from that of 1888, chiefly in the great change in managerial policy that had taken place on the London and North Western Railway in the intervening years. In 1891 Sir Richard Moon had retired from the chairmanship, and all ideas of keeping speeds down to the minimum to save operating expense vanished overnight. The North Western was to be 'the premier line' in speed and efficiency as well as in its princely revenue, and it was the summer tourist traffic to the Highlands of Scotland that became the focal point of rivalry with the East Coast route, and in particular with the age-old competitor, the Great Northern.

Queen Victoria's annual sojourn at Balmoral invested with royal patronage a touring fashion that had begun even before the first construction of railways in the Highlands of Scotland. Rereading them today it is perhaps difficult to imagine the tremendous impact the Waverley Novels had upon what might be called the 'educated' public of the day. It was by no mere catch-phrase that Sir Walter Scott was called the 'Wizard of the North'. No modern travel agent ever did more to publicise his native land. Tourists flocked to Scotland to visit the scenes described in *The Lady of the Lake*, *Waverley* or *The*

Fair Maid of Perth. The latest Waverley Novel, whether set in Scotland or not, would be an essential item in everyone's luggage, and it only needed the residence of the Court on Deeside to bring visitors to Aboyne, Banchory, Ballater, and Braemar. To get there they all had to travel by train via Aberdeen.

Since the completion of the Forth Bridge, the East Coast route from London had enjoyed the advantage of being sixteen miles shorter than the West Coast, and there is little doubt that they relied on this to

Opposite top. An imposing view of the majestic Forth Bridge, a railway landmark in engineering design with its revolutionary use of giant cantilever trusses.

Opposite bottom. Scottish disaster: late on 31 December 1879 the first Tay Bridge collapsed while a train was crossing. Next morning with the storm but little abated, launches went out from Dundee to search for survivors, but there were none. Eighty lives were lost.

Left. The dining room at York during the twenty-minute luncheon stop of the Flying Scotsman *c.* 1892, before the introduction of restaurant cars.

some dramatic cloak-and-dagger game of espionage. Scouts were sent to the rival stations to try and procure scraps of information; but the East Coast 'spies' did not, apparently, venture into the exclusively West Coast strongholds of Crewe and Carlisle, or they would have found out quickly enough. The West Coast special was being worked through as quickly as possible. There was no waiting for the booked times at intermediate stations; the train left as soon as it was ready. Engine crews and everyone else

provide them with superiority in running times in perpetuity. But a vital factor in the operation of the London–Aberdeen train service under the new conditions created by the completion of the Forth Bridge was that although the East Coast had secured a route which was shorter by sixteen miles, the concluding thirty-eight miles of the journey still had to be made with running powers over the Caledonian line, from Kinnaber Junction, where the two routes converged, about three miles north of Montrose. Both routes ran a special summer tourist express leaving the respective London terminal stations of King's Cross and Euston at the same time, 8 p.m., and the arrival times at Aberdeen were 7.35 a.m. East Coast, and 7.50 a.m. West Coast – a difference in almost exact relation to the difference in length of run. Both connected, on paper, with the 8.5 a.m. departure on the G.N.S. line to Ballater.

As the tourist season of 1895 approached, the West Coast companies felt it desirable to increase the time margin at Aberdeen, because for passengers having much luggage for a long stay in the Highlands fifteen minutes was not a great deal of time for changing trains, particularly as at that time the Scottish railway stations were not famed for their speed or efficiency in dealing with passengers and their luggage.

Then there began a month the like of which has never been known since, in which the two sides watched or tried to watch each other's moves as in

concerned entered fully into the spirit of the race.

Then during the heaviest period of the tourist season, leading up the twelfth (of August), both sides let the competition simmer down a little. But once this traffic was over the managements of the East Coast companies felt they must really assert the potential superiority of their shorter distance. They had come to realise that their opponents were disregarding timetables, and decided that for the sake of prestige they must briefly do the same, and from 19 August it was to be an all-out race. By that time the contest was becoming front page news in the papers; partisan feeling was running high, with all the national love of a sporting event centred on the running of these two sleeping car expresses that were going to race through the night for the little signal box on the hillside above Montrose, where their routes converged. At first the West Coast retained its supremacy, but then on the night of 20–21 August there came the closest-run thing of all, when the two trains converging upon Kinnaber Junction actually saw each other across the waters of Montrose Basin, and the West Coast secured preference by *less than a minute.* Thereafter they led the way to break all previous records by arriving in Aberdeen at 4.58 a.m. – an overall average of 60 miles per hour throughout from London – and nearly *three hours* earlier than the time booked only two months before. On the following night the East Coast made a supreme effort and got into Aberdeen easily first, at 4.40 a.m.

But the times to Kinnaber Junction were in almost exact correspondence with the distances from London, thus:

	East Coast	West Coast
Distance from London to Kinnaber Junction, *miles*	485·7	501·7
Total time, *minutes*	482½	497
Average speed, *miles per hour*	60·3	60·7

London and North Western locomotive type that took part in the great railway race of 1895: a Webb three-cylinder compound of the 'Teutonic' class.

Nothing like it had been seen, anywhere in the world; but after this the East Coast companies felt they had done enough to assert their superiority on distance, and that the risks undoubtedly taken, particularly on the line north of Edinburgh, did not justify any attempt to press things further. There is no doubt that passengers by the East Coast train generally had a very rough ride. The coaches were all six-wheelers, and rode very 'hard', whereas the West Coast was using close-coupled bogie stock. There were several bad shake-ups – passing through Berwick, taking the S-curve at Portobello, just outside Edinburgh, and at Inverkeithing, Burntisland and other places in Fife. So normal running was resumed by the 8 p.m. from King's Cross on the night of 22 August. Not so that from Euston, however! The West Coast train was taken north like the progress of a thunderbolt, and each successive engine crew, first North Western and then Caledonian, sustained the pressure from start to finish, with the result that Aberdeen was reached at 4.32 a.m. – a further cut of eight minutes. The journey had been covered in 512 minutes, at an average speed of 63.3 miles per hour, a London–Aberdeen record that has not been surpassed to this day.

The revival of British superiority in speed was, however, short-lived. In the following summer the very West Coast train that had been involved in the races of 1895 crashed in spectacular fashion on a curve just north of Preston. Hauled by two engines,

manned by drivers who knew the road but were inexperienced in this particular duty, it ran through Preston at greatly excessive speed, and the whole train except for the rearmost brake van was wrecked. Fortunately, because of the massive construction of the bogie carriages, there was only one person killed; but the accident raised again all the fears and scaremongering that had been rife at the height of the race a year earlier, and public opinion virtually put an end to further acceleration. It did even worse: it compelled the deceleration of some of the fastest trains. Generally speaking one imagines that the railway managements were glad of this since it was a time when more luxurious rolling stock was being introduced. The dead weight to be hauled for each passenger was steadily increasing, and if the speeds of 1895 had been maintained and become general on all express trains, a most serious problem would have been presented to the locomotive engineers. To take a single example: on the last night of the race to Aberdeen the train from Euston weighed no more than 72 tons. At the same period in time the afternoon corridor dining car express from Euston to Glasgow and Edinburgh was never less than about 270 tons, and often over 300.

The introduction of dining cars in Great Britain came in a variety of ways, and in describing some of these a farewell tribute must also be paid to the era of refreshment stops at certain major stations on the main lines. One of the earliest of these to be instituted was at Wolverton, the appropriate half-way house between London and Birmingham in 1840, and for some few years afterwards. A contemporary account tells how

'very early in the morning–in cold winter long before sunrise–"the old man" wakens the two housemaids, to one of whom is entrusted the confidential duty of awakening the seven very young ladies who wait upon the passengers. They must be called at exactly seven o'clock in order that their *première toilette* be concluded in time for them to receive the passengers of the first train, which reaches Wolverton at 7.30 a.m.
'As these useful handmaidens stand in a row behind bright silver urns, silver coffee pots, silver teapots, cups, saucers, cakes, sugar, milk, with other delicacies over which they preside, the confused crowd of passengers simultaneously liberated from the train, hurry towards them with a velocity exactly proportional to their appetites. Considering that the row of young persons have among them only seven right hands with but very little fingers at the end of each, it is really astonishing how, with such slender assistance, they can in the short space of a few minutes manage to extend and withdraw them so often; sometimes to give a cup of tea, sometimes to receive half-a-crown, part of which they have to return, then to give an old gentleman a plate of warm soup, then to drop another lump of sugar into his nephew's coffee cup, then to receive a penny for a bun, and then again threepence for four "lady's fingers".'

The great Brunel once told the manager of the famous station dining room at Swindon that he did not believe they ever served coffee. He thought the beverage was merely 'badly-roasted corn'. But the

urns, tea pots, and coffee pots really *were* silver, and today surviving specimens, especially if they carry the coat of arms of the railway company, are highly prized collector's pieces. So are the cutlery and glassware from the earliest dining cars. These were very exclusive vehicles, on some railways separate, and not connected with the rest of the train. Passengers taking lunch or dinner travelled throughout in the dining car, to which other passengers had no access. The first of such vehicles was introduced in 1879 by the Great Northern Railway on the London–Leeds service. It was a most ornate affair, very tall, with a clerestory roof, and looked most incongruous in a train of small, flat-roofed six-wheelers. Passengers were charged half-a-crown over and above the cost of the meal for the pleasure of travelling in the car. The kitchen was fitted with a coke-burning range, and the scullery boy peeled potatoes and did other menial tasks on an open platform at the rear. The first all-corridor trains, with connections to the dining cars from every carriage, were the afternoon Anglo-Scottish expresses to and from Euston, with through portions to both Glasgow and Edinburgh.

By the turn of the century prestige trains in many parts of the world were becoming more luxurious; but on the continent of Europe in particular much of the coaching stock was cramped and uncomfortable inside and dingy-looking outside. Nevertheless, there were certain railways which even in their cramped and spartan equipment had an undoubted fascination,

and those were the narrow-gauge lines built to open up remote districts, where money was scarce and where the railway was a social necessity rather than a promising business investment. There were some fascinating little narrow-gauge lines built into the deep mountain recesses of the Colorado Rockies, of which the Denver and Rio Grande was perhaps one of the most famous. The spirit of the men who ran these remote and difficult lines was the living

Top. A busy scene on the narrow gauge in Colorado: the roundhouse at Salida, on the Denver and Rio Grande Railroad, in 1906.

Above. On the Georgetown Loop of the Colorado Central.

101

embodiment of all that goes to make up the image of an old-time steam railwayman, whether the scene is laid in Colorado, the South African veldt, running the West Coast 'corridor' express from Euston, or working the Orient Express through many countries of continental Europe. Pictures speak louder than words, and the sight of those little Rio Grande 'Moguls' with their 'balloon' stacks, and the tough old 'boomers' who drove them, in their own mountainous country, is certainly enough to stir the blood of anyone with a feeling for railways.

One did not, however, need to travel as far as Colorado to experience the remoteness and charm of the narrow gauge. The little railways of Ireland were built, as it were, to dodge the engineering. They snaked their way up mountain sides with so little in the way of earthworks that their tracks were often almost invisible from the valleys below. They followed old water courses; they wriggled their ways through deep glens, where it was sometimes difficult indeed to find a foothold even for their narrow-gauge 'right of way'.

But while narrow-gauge railway construction in Ireland was entering on its period of greatest activity an immense project was launched on the continent

of Europe, the construction of the Simplon Tunnel. This was initiated in 1898, and to appreciate its profound importance we must take the story back nearly thirty years to trace the pioneering of railway communication through the High Alps. 'Through' is certainly the operative word. There was no question of avoiding difficult or expensive engineering tasks here: the Alps constituted a tremendous natural barrier between north and south in Europe. When the first project was launched, in 1857, there were dire forebodings over the folly of tampering within 'the bosom of the mighty fortress', as one English newspaper put it. But the Mont Cenis tunnel, between France and Italy, was successfully completed in 1871.

With France first in the field strong pressure naturally arose for a direct route from Germany through Switzerland and into Italy, and this was naturally projected along the line of the historic St Gothard pass, over which the coaches and mail carts had made their hazardous way. The call for engineering ingenuity on this second Alpine epic came as much in conquering the problems of the approach valleys as in the driving of the great tunnel itself. Thanks to glacial action in prehistoric times there are pronounced 'steps' in the levels of the

Mountain railroading in Europe: on the Gothard line in Switzerland – an engraving showing the great viaduct over the entrance to the Maderaner valley near Amsteg.

Swedish State Railways: construction work in a cutting near Umeå in the north of the country, 1895.

approaches, which would have involved an ordinary railway in quite impossible gradients. It was here that the exciting principle of the spiral tunnel was first postulated. To gain height, without resorting to impracticable gradients, or the inconvenience and slowness of changing over to a rack-and-pinion drive, the line was carried into the mountain side, climbing all the time on a gradient of 1 in 38, and spiralling in tunnel to emerge almost immediately above the entering portal but at a much higher level. To drive a spiral tunnel into the solid rock of the mountains and emerge at the correct place was something that required consummate skill in surveying.

In ascending from Erstfeld to Goschenen, however, not one but *three* spiral tunnels were needed to gain the necessary height, and then, once Goschenen was reached, there was the job of driving more than nine miles clean under one of the highest ridges of the Alps to reach Airolo. Here again the utmost precision was needed in the instrumentation, because the St Gothard tunnel, like the Mont Cenis, was driven from both ends simultaneously. To secure bearings for the direction of the bores, from Modane and Bardonnechia in the case of Mont Cenis, and from Goschenen and Airolo for the St Gothard, it was necessary to use the process known in surveying as 'indirect triangulation'. A geometrical link-up had to be obtained between the lines of entry at either portal, and this could be done only by a succession of bearings taken up the approach valleys, and then over the mountain passes to the far sides. The surveys for both the Mont Cenis and the St Gothard tunnels were done with marvellous accuracy, and the parties working from either end met in the middle with no more deviation from course than a few inches.

From the year 1882, when the St Gothard line was

opened, it carried all the international traffic that came into Switzerland through Basle, which included that from Germany and from the Eastern Railway of France. But more was needed: another important line from France tunnelled under the Jura mountains to reach Vallorbe to make an easy connection into Lausanne. From there a relatively fast route existed beside Lake Geneva, past Montreux and into the heart of the Valais, but it stopped short at Brigue, beneath another formidable *bloc*. From Brigue there had existed for centuries a mountain pass, over which a 'diligence' road had been constructed in 1805 by order of Napoleon. This was the Simplon, and in 1898 contracts were placed for the construction of a railway tunnel beneath the pass, to provide a much shorter and more direct route to Milan. It was to be the longest-ever railway tunnel in the world, and unlike the Mont Cenis and the St Gothard was to have two independent bores instead of one double-line tunnel. Before referring to the traffic developments that followed the completion of the tunnel, some comparative statistics of the great Alpine tunnels will be interesting.

Alpine tunnels

Name	Year opened	Length, *miles*	Summit level of tracks
Mont Cenis	1871	8·53	—
St Gothard	1882	9·35	3786
Simplon I	1906	12·33	2312
Simplon II	1922	12·05	2312

From its opening in 1882 the St Gothard line was worked with steam locomotives, and it was assumed that at first it would be the same with the Simplon.

103

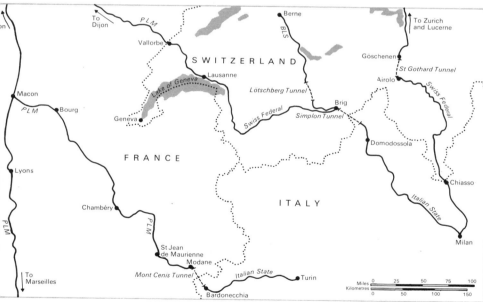

Rail routes through the Alps
in 1914, after the completion
of the Lötschberg line.

current French practice and did a great job in the
mountains. Because of the gradients, however, the
maximum load they could haul was only four coaches,
and anything more meant using a pair of locomotives.
Fortunately, all the spiral tunnels were built for
double track so that there was clearance to provide
some air movement and ventilation when two of these
engines were pounding up the 1 in 38 gradients with
a heavy train. The main St Gothard tunnel was built
on fairly easy gradients, as the line had practically
reached the maximum altitude necessary when
Goschenen was reached.

The opening of the Simplon Tunnel in 1906 put
two of the French railways into direct competition
for the Italian traffic. It was originally intended that
each of the major French railway systems should
operate in a definite area, with a minimum of parallel
or competitive services. This situation still prevailed
in France itself; but from 1906 there was the Eastern
running to Belfort and entering Switzerland at Basle,
thence connecting with the St Gothard route, while
the Paris, Lyons and Mediterranean, by its subsidiary main line from Dijon to the Swiss frontier at
Vallorbe and connection with the Simplon route,
had a definitely competitive route from Paris to Milan,
not to mention the second route that left the main line
at Macon, and ran through Aix-les-Bains to the
Mont Cenis Tunnel, and so to Turin. The relative
positions of these lines are shown on the accompanying map, and between them they made possible an

But electric haulage was used during the construction
work and, although some goods trains were at
first hauled by steam, the passenger traffic through
the Simplon Tunnel was electric from the start.
Steam working on the St Gothard line, with its
severe gradients and spiral tunnels, was a tremendous
job. Some very powerful four-cylinder compound
4–6–0 locomotives were built specially for the job
and first introduced in 1894. They were based on

admirable series of tourist services. That the Swiss sections of the journey lay through magnificent scenery goes almost without saying, though it is to be feared that few of the passengers would be in a mood to appreciate it. The principal expresses from Paris to the south left in the late evening, and despite the liberal provision of sleeping cars, French railways in the early years of the twentieth century were not exactly famed for smooth running. It was said amongst experienced travellers that the drivers used to put on their biggest spurts where there were sharp curves or a difficult junction on the line! A famous author, travelling from Paris to Marseilles, once began a book of Mediterranean journeys with the sentence, 'The French train went mad in the night.' Pale and shattered, passengers for Italy might therefore be dozing thankfully while the train continued at a more leisurely pace through the mountains of Switzerland.

The sleeping car, on all railways on the continent of Europe, has always been a curiously inconvenient affair. The two-tier bunks in the first class cars would be awkward in any case; but space inside is so cramped that it is usually necessary for one person to take a sojourn in the corridor while his or her companion prepares for bed, and the ladders by which the top bunk is attained are likely to be hazardous if the driver should be putting on one of the traditional spurts. Even from the earliest days of sleeping cars, however, the British traveller had been rather spoilt by the spaciousness and privacy of the accommodation at

The British style of first class sleeping car was used on certain overseas railways where the British influence was strong, as in South Africa. This leads me on to another great epic of railway construction, the progress through Rhodesia of what Cecil Rhodes himself hoped would be the 'Cape to Cairo' railway. The line had been opened as far as Bulawayo in November 1897 and progressed north-eastwards, at first continuing on a high plateau around 4,000 feet

Opposite top. Construction of the Simplon Tunnel: a group of the men who worked on this great task, 1899.

Left. The Liverpool and Manchester at turn of century. The dramatic Olive Mount Cutting, near Liverpool, with trains from the Manchester direction approaching. The express on the right is hauled by one of the 'Lady of the Lake' class 2–2–2s.

Below left. Swiss Federal Railways: checking the overhead wires for electrification on the Simplon route. The steam locomotive is propelling the electric.

home. No doubt space on the continental night trains has always been at a premium, and single private berths, as on British trains, could not be afforded. But in any case, sharing a two-berth cabin in a *wagon-lit* on the continent was better than the communal atmosphere of contemporary American sleepers, where the only seclusion was obtained by drawing the curtains which shielded the 'beds' from the central gangway.

above sea level, where even today the bush is as lonely and untamed as when the line was first built. Those who today join wild life safaris in tropical Africa can have little conception of the kind of opposition encountered by the railway builders who ventured into northern parts of Rhodesia and built the amazing line into the heart of Uganda. Lions were everywhere. George Pauling, the intrepid English contractor, tells of one particular encounter:

Luxurious travel in the U.S.A. Interior of a parlour car about the turn of the century.

'We were creeping along at about four miles an hour, taking no particular heed of our surroundings, when suddenly the engine-driver discovered ahead a herd of lions, lionesses and cubs, resting in the side cutting which ran alongside the railway bank. It was an awe-inspiring sight, and the driver was for a moment nonplussed. He knew that he dare not increase speed and run the risk of derailment. There was not a gun on the train. Few men are valiant in the immediate presence of wild lions, and we three "passengers" deemed it expedient to scramble out of the truck and on to the side of the engine away from the herd. With a view to making as much noise as possible the driver opened his whistle and cylinder cocks and commenced to creep past the place where the lions were resting. The noise was too much for them, for they all bolted with the exception of one stately old lioness, who stood her ground, and snarled at us as we passed. Had we remained in the truck it is not improbable that she would have made a jump at one of us, but she funked the engine and its steam and noise. Having reached a position of security we counted in all thirty-two lions, lionesses and cubs.'

106

Left. A postal car in the U.S.A., with sorters hard at work.

Below. 'Cape to Cairo': high hopes in Rhodesia. Locomotive of the first train from Umtali to Salisbury, carrying the slogan 'Now we shan't be long to Cairo'.

Below. South Africa, 1906:
the Cape Mail at
Potchefstroom, on the run
from Cape Town to
Johannesburg via Kimberley.

Bottom. Group at the
ceremonial opening of the
Gold Coast Railway in 1905.

Wild life hazards on the line still remain today, chiefly from elephants, who have been known to charge trains and derail box-cars and passenger coaches.

Heavy earthworks and other constructional problems were generally avoided on the Cape–Cairo railway, but the mighty Zambesi river had somehow to be crossed. It is rather extraordinary to recall that the stupendous Victoria Falls had remained unknown to civilisation until 1855, when David Livingstone

The result was one of the most spectacular railway locations imaginable. The rock on each side of that tremendous cleft through which the tumultuous river flows away from the base of the Falls was so hard that the bridge was designed to fit the profile of the gorge with as little expenditure on excavation as possible. The centre span was 500 feet long, consisting of what is known technically as a two-hinged spandrel-braced arch. It was designed to spring from the rock walls of the gorge, and to be erected cantilever-wise, member by member, from both sides of the gorge simultaneously. By this means it could be erected without the need to erect scaffolding, which would have been virtually impossible in such a location. One of the great problems in construction was to get all the heavy girders and materials over to the north side. Such was the drive and determination being put into the building of the Cape to Cairo line that it was decided early on that matters could not wait on the north side until the bridge was finished, and some means had to be found of getting not only the bridge members across, so that construction could proceed, but rails, sleepers and track laying equipment – sufficient to lay at least one mile per day! To meet this need a cable-way was erected across the gorge, capable of carrying a ten-ton load. The work went ahead remarkably well, continuing through all seasons, tropical heat and rain alike. Rarely can there have been a great engineering work executed with so few casualties. Through the rainy season in the early months of 1905 the cantilever arms extended uniformly from either side, and on 1 April 1905 they met in mid-air. The link-up was perfect. Rhodes himself never saw the bridge; he died in 1902, three years before its completion.

If carrying the track of the Cape to Cairo line northwards from Bulawayo was a hazardous business at times, how should one describe the beginnings of the Uganda Railway, the line that was taken from the East African coast at Mombasa towards Uganda? The distance was roughly 550 miles, through country that alternated between waterless desert, impenetrable thorny jungle, and an area like that of the Athi plains, of which an early report included these words: 'Progress has been seriously impeded by man-eating lions. Twenty-eight men have been killed by lions.' The fortitude and resource of the young pioneer who led a party of 500 Swahilis on this amazing trek is beyond belief. Messages were sent back by native runners; the party lived off the countryside as best they could. In such manner was the way paved for the regular railway construction parties who followed the trail that had been hacked through the virtually unknown country, relying on the camps that had been set up by the survey parties. In due course the Kenya and Uganda railway – now the East African Railways – became one of the most efficient of lines. But anyone travelling on its mail trains today, or riding, as I have done, its huge Beyer-Garratt locomotives, cannot be other than mindful of the 'blood and toil, tears and sweat' that went into its construction. It was opened for traffic throughout in October 1903.

Opposite. Balloon-stacked
Finnish 'Tk3' 2–8–0 wood-
burner at snowbound dawn.
It bears a strong resemblance
to its American-built
ancestor, the Baldwin 'Tk1'
of 1900.

described how 'creeping with awe to the verge I peered down into a large rent which had been made from bank to bank of the broad Zambesi.' Cecil Rhodes had never seen the Falls himself but the description of them gripped his imagination and he decreed that the railway should cross the Zambesi, not only within sight of the Falls, but near enough for the trains to be wetted by the curtain of spray which he was told was ever-present.

This is essentially a book of contrasts and mention of the years 1903 and 1904, when so much invaluable pioneer work was being done in opening up remote areas of the world, brings me to some remarkable events in the west of England. In 1892 the Great Western Railway had finally eliminated the broad gauge, not without many feelings of regret, sentimentally, that a feature once of immense prestige had had to be yielded up to *force majeure*. But a tremendous spirit of new enterprise permeated every facet of operation of the company, and the locomotive department at Swindon was engaged in a drive to increase the efficiency of engine performance, needed to cope with the longer non-stop runs that the management was striving to achieve. At this stage that great engineer George Jackson Churchward enters the picture. In 1902 he had succeeded William Dean as locomotive, carriage and wagon superintendent of the Great Western Railway, and the technical development that was eventually to have almost worldwide repercussions had scarcely begun in 1903. But by then he had already produced one new locomotive design that was very quickly to take the railway world by storm.

In the early months of 1903 the first engine of a new class was completed at Swindon; this was No. 3433, the *City of Bath*. It was of the 4-4-0 type, traditionally G.W.R. in its use of outside frames, but unconventional in the coned shape of its boiler barrel. The capabilities of this new design were to be strikingly demonstrated in a year's time.

Competition between various shipping lines on the North Atlantic run was increasing, for both passenger and mail traffic, and there was a growing tendency for the German steamers to land passengers and mails at Plymouth. This not only saved almost a day, compared to the service provided by the British steamers operating from Liverpool, but was attractive to passengers bound for the continent of Europe, who could travel by train from Plymouth to London, and then take one of the short sea routes, to Calais,

Above. On the Metropolitan Railway, part of London's Underground, before electrification. A train from the suburbs at West Hampstead station hauled by one of the famous cabless 4-4-0 tank engines.

Left. Early days on the Great Central. The ticket examiner at Leicester included in his duties the setting of the train indicators and the departure indicating clocks. He seems very happy in his work.

Opposite. Steam and sunrise on the German railways. *Top.* An '038' class 4-6-0 puffs away from Horb with a train bound for Stuttgart. *Bottom.* Class '044' 2-10-0 heading south along the Mosel valley.

Boulogne or Ostend, thus saving a good deal of time over the alternative of staying on the trans-Atlantic liner till it berthed at Hamburg or Bremen. Both the London and South Western and the Great Western were alive to the importance of this traffic, which was being patronised mainly by American travellers, and a competition began to develop for the Plymouth–London stage of the journey. By an unwritten 'gentlemen's agreement' the London and South Western Railway took the passengers, and the Great Western took the mails.

What had begun thus, however, developed into an all-out race, to see whether the passengers or the mails would be delivered first in London, leading up to the achievement of what was referred to for many years afterwards as the 'record of records' on 9 May 1904. Two engines were involved in the record-breaking run. *City of Truro*, one of Churchward's new class, was the engine from Plymouth, and it was once through Exeter, with the sharply curved sections of the South Devon Line behind them, that the men on the *City of Truro* really began to pile it on. The twenty-mile rise to Whiteball Tunnel was covered at an average of 60 miles per hour, and then down the Wellington bank the engine was 'given her head'. Speeds leaped up until one very experienced recorder clocked a quarter-mile at 102·3 miles per hour; but then, shades of George Pauling and his pride of lions on the track, some platelayers were working on the line, and did not seem to realise how fast this 100-miles-per-hour thunderbolt was bearing down on them. To a screaming fanfare on the whistle the brakes were applied, and all chance of increasing speed or corroborating the record already secured was lost. That 102·3 will always be a point of controversy. The build-up towards it was rapid and continuous, with successive quarter-mile timings registering 81·8, 84·9, 88·2, 90·0, 91·8, 95·7, and 97·8 miles per hour. As an engineer I have analysed all the evidence and, although I too have doubts about the 102·3 for the final quarter, I would certainly

Germany's idea of a commuter railway, the Berlin elevated monorail.

Opposite top. A luxurious saloon of the International Sleeping Car Company on the Trans-Siberian Railway in 1900. The beautiful appointments included a white piano.

Opposite left. Wreck of the Leeds and Newcastle Express which crashed at Felling on 26 March 1907. The toll of casualties was not as bad as the picture suggests: two were killed and six injured.

accept 100 miles per hour and perhaps a little over.

At Pylle Hill Junction – the engine changing point in Bristol – the *City of Truro* was exchanged for the single-wheeler *Duke of Connaught*, and in the course of the run on to London the 70·3 miles from Shrivenham to Westbourne Park were covered in 52¾ minutes, an average of exactly *eighty miles per hour*. Never previously had a train run at such speed continuously, over so long a distance, and it was truly

said at the time that the men who rode in that train had travelled faster than man had ever done before, by any form of transport.

After this the fever of competition slackened somewhat, though the rival trains continued to be run very smartly. It is sad to recall, however, that high speed on these American specials came to an end when a terrible accident befell the South Western train, in the early hours of 1 July 1906, at Salisbury.

Above. The race with the Ocean Mails from Plymouth to London in 1904: two of the Dean 7 foot 8 inch single driving wheel 4–2–2 locomotives, which hauled the racing trains of the Great Western Railway from Bristol to London. The two engines pictured are hauling the Flying Dutchman through Uphill station, Somerset.

113

Japanese National Railways: the impressive Central Station exterior at Tokyo.

For some reason that was never explained the boat train, which had changed engines at Templecombe as usual, approached Salisbury at high speed, and instead of slackening to take the curve at the eastern end of the station, where there were also some awkwardly-aligned points, ran through at practically full speed. The result was a frightful smash. There were forty-three passengers on board, mostly American tourists, and no fewer than twenty-four were killed. The dead also included the driver and fireman, and the fireman and guard of another train with which the express collided as its engine turned over. The shock to public opinion in Great Britain was overwhelming. It certainly brought to a full stop any plans that were maturing for faster trains.

In the meantime, while this brilliant period in British speed prowess was brought so abruptly to a close, some interesting developments were taking place in the Far East. From its quaint and leisurely beginnings, the railway system of Japan was developing rapidly. Many new railway companies had been formed. The Tokaido Line, between Tokyo and Osaka, was being changed to double track throughout, and station layouts and travelling facilities were being generally improved. Furthermore, the Japanese locomotive building industry was developing. The early work of W. M. Smith on the Imperial Government Railways has already been referred to. When that great engineer returned to England to begin his notable work of locomotive designing on the North

Eastern Railway he was succeeded in Japan by Richard Francis Trevithick, grandson of the great Cornish pioneer and eldest son of Francis Trevithick, who was locomotive engineer of the Northern Division of the London and North Western Railway, with his headquarters at Crewe.

The locomotives imported during the earlier part of R. F. Trevithick's time on the Japanese railways were variously of British and American manufacture, and the former, coming from Neilson's and from Kitsons of Leeds, had a distinctive Scottish air about them, rather than any resemblance to the earlier Crewe locomotives built in such quantities in his father's time. But Japanese rolling stock and locomotives were developing rapidly in the early years of the twentieth century, though all railway operations in that country were to a considerable extent governed by the demands of the never-ending contest with nature. Hardly a year passes without parts of the system being devastated by avalanches, floods, typhoons, volcanic eruptions or tidal waves, and over the years the organisation of maintenance work on the line has been developed with great skill, drawing deeply on the experience of each disruption of service as it occurs. In the early years of the twentieth century the complexity of the railway network was rapidly increasing, with the provision of many alternative routes for use in case of occasional obstruction. At the same time the government of the day felt that all this proliferating was taking place

114

in a rather haphazard manner. It is true that practically all railway development was taking place along the coastal strips on the main island of Honshu. There was good reason for this, because between the shores of the Pacific Ocean and the Sea of Japan lay a continuous and virtually impenetrable chain of high mountains. The spread of population was almost entirely along the coasts, and particularly along the Pacific.

By the year 1899 there were more than thirty

The new century opened with evidence of many notable developments in locomotive design in the advanced countries of the world, and these can be classified into three distinct groups, relating respectively to Great Britain, continental Europe, and North America. At that time coal was still the staple diet of the steam locomotive nearly everywhere in the world, and it was the varying quality of coal available that was the basic influence on design. By far the best coal in the world for locomotive purposes

private railways in Japan, in addition to those operated by the imperial government, and it was at this time that the question of nationalisation came to be considered. As a result of much investigation, the Railway Nationalisation Law was passed in 1906, enabling the Government to purchase the private railways. During 1906 and 1907 a total of seventeen of the leading privately-owned lines were purchased. The mileage of the Government-owned railways thereby increased to 4,371, which was almost three times what it had been previously; but not all the private railways were absorbed, and records taken some fifteen years later revealed a total railway mileage of 7,900 in Japan, of which about 1,700 were still privately owned. From these figures it will be appreciated that although Japan as a country was developing rapidly its railway system, in relation to the size of the country, was still not very large, since the total extent of the government-owned system, 6,200 miles, was just about equal to the mileage worked in England by the locomotives of the London and North Western and Great Western added together – 3,000 and 3,160 respectively. But in Japan the enlargement of the national system following the Act of 1906 allowed a great measure of co-ordination and standardisation to begin, and in that Act can be seen the genesis of the astonishing line of development which is only gathering its full momentum today in the vast extension of the Shinkansen network of super high speed lines.

was that mined in Great Britain, and the output of the industry in the years before World War One was such that supplies were not only ample for all the home railways, but ample also for large-scale exports to the Baltic states (in exchange for which Britain imported the excellent Baltic pine for railway sleepers) and to South America, while the Paris, Lyons and Mediterranean Railway, with much of its system many hundreds of miles from the coalfields of northern France, used Welsh coal, shipped from Cardiff to Marseilles in its own colliers. In the U.S.A. the quality of coal available for locomotive use was much below that mined in England and Wales, and it was this factor that had a strong influence on twentieth-century American locomotive design.

To burn the lower-grade 'brown' coal effectively a firebox with a very large grate area was necessary, and development of the characteristic 'American' type – the 4–4–0 with outside cylinders – had already begun by the turn of the century. The presence of a pair of large-diameter coupled wheels under the rear end of the locomotive restricted the size of the grate, and the designers turned to the 'Atlantic' type, which was, in effect, an 'American' but with a pair of trailing wheels at the rear end. Over the smaller, non-powered wheels the grate of the firebox could be spread out and a high steam-raising capacity built in. There had, in fact, been one or two attempts to provide a wide firebox while still retaining an eight-wheeled locomotive, by changing from the 4–4–0 to the 2–4–2

R. F. Trevithick, grandson of the great Cornish pioneer, locomotive engineer of the Japanese National Railways.

Left. Japan, country station at the turn of the century. The locomotive was built by Neilson and Co. of Glasgow.

115

wheel arrangement. This involved moving the coupled wheels forward, and having a single pair of leading wheels instead of a bogie and a pair of trailing wheels under the grate, as in the 'Atlantic' type. A very elegant-looking example of the 2–4–2 express type, called the 'Colombia', had been introduced on the Chicago, Burlington and Quincy Railroad in 1895, having coupled wheels no less than 7 feet 6 inches in diameter, and a grate area, enormous for that period, of 44·4 square feet. There were few British locomotives at that time with as much as 20 square feet of grate area. But the 2–4–2 did not prove very satisfactory as a fast-running express passenger type, because of unsteady riding, and future development centred upon locomotives fitted with a leading bogie.

The upsurge in booked speed that had so marked the final decade of the nineteenth century on American railways continued and, with the introduction of still heavier rolling stock and an increase in passenger business, the era of the 'big' locomotive was at hand. The 4–6–0 type, which eventually came to achieve such popularity in Great Britain, was never greatly favoured in the U.S.A., and development proceeded almost directly from the 'Atlantic' (4–4–2) to the 'Pacific' (4–6–2). The latter first began to be adopted as a standard express type as early as 1903, and a very powerful example was in service on the Union Pacific Railroad in 1904. This large engine weighed almost 100 tons without its tender, and it was significant of the advantage taken of space at the rear end that the grate area was no less than 49½ square

feet. The boiler was very long, and had what appeared to be two steam domes. The forward mounting, however, was that containing the sand for applying beneath the driving wheels to improve adhesion when necessary. This locomotive had one of the earlier examples of the Vanderbilt type of tender. The conventional form, in all countries, had hitherto been a rectangular box, which contained the water tank and space for the coal. The Vanderbilt type had a water tank of cylindrical form, on which was mounted a coal hopper at the front end. It was a distinctive and functional form but was not universally adopted in later years.

If the size of the passenger locomotives in the U.S.A. showed a very marked increase in the early 1900s, this trend was even more pronounced in the case of freight locomotives. In contrast to current British practice, all freight trains in North America were fitted with the continuous automatic air brake, and it was thus possible to control safely trains of great length on steep descending gradients. The fact that many of the main lines in North America consisted of long stretches of single track, with passing loops often scores of miles apart, meant that relatively few trains were run, but these were made up to a tremendous size. So, again in contrast to what was happening in Great Britain at the same time, construction of some extremely large and heavy freight locomotives took place in the U.S.A. In 1903 the first of what was claimed to be the heaviest locomotive class in the world was built by the Baldwin Loco-

The station at Elkhart, Indiana, on the Cincinnati, Wabash and Michigan Railroad (later part of the New York Central), about 1906.

motive Company of Philadelphia, for the Atchison, Topeka and Santa Fe Railroad. An order for no less than seventy was placed, and they were of the 2–10–2 type, henceforth known in the U.S.A. as the 'Santa Fe'. The engine alone weighed 128 tons, and with tender fully loaded with coal and water the total weight was 200¾ tons. These locomotives were indeed so heavy that it was found necessary to re-lay parts of the track before it was safe for them to run.

There was, however, a major point about these

of locomotive, with ever-increasing cylinder size to provide the enhanced tractive power demanded.

An incidental problem that was causing some concern in the U.S.A. at this time was the difficulty in sighting signals experienced by a driver ensconced in a cab at the rear end of a lengthy boiler that was getting progressively larger in diameter. The view ahead was no longer over the top of the boiler, as in the early 'Americans', but only round the side; and when the blast was soft and steam was drifting down

The 'Atlantic' type locomotive (4–4–2): a high-speed example on the Chicago and North Western Railway, built by Schenectady. This was a development of the famous 'Fast Mail' 4–4–0 of 1899.

engines, other than mere size and weight, which requires some emphasis because it was an important feature of a phase in locomotive development all over the world that had some interesting repercussions. The giant 'Santa Fe' freight engines were of the tandem compound type. Compounding was a means of increasing the range of expansion of the steam so as to maximise its utilisation, without resorting to the costly expedient of building boilers to carry a very high working pressure. In North America, from the turn of the century, the earlier practice of using outside cylinders only led to several different systems of compounding that distinguished them greatly from contemporary British and continental systems, which also used four cylinders, two high pressure and two low pressure. In the tandem system the high and low pressure cylinders were placed literally in tandem, one behind the other, with their centrelines coincident, and the pistons of both carried on a common piston rod. Another American system of compounding was the Vauclain. In this the high pressure cylinder was mounted vertically above the low pressure. Each had its own piston rod, but both drove on to a common crosshead. But Stephenson's link motion was still the favourite form of valve gear in North America, and this was mounted between the frames. There was a degree of logic in this since motion did not need such constant attention as the cross-head, connecting rod, crank pins and big ends; and with the motion inside one could take a big end down without disturbing any of the members affecting the valve setting. Nevertheless, while some railways used tandem, and others Vauclain, compounds, others remained faithful to the simple two-cylinder single-expansion type

117

Right. A typical North American signal cabin of the early 1900s, showing an interlocking frame of Saxby and Farmer design, known as the 'rocker and grid' type.

Below. Improving the driver's view ahead: a 4–4–2 for the Atlantic City Railroad, built by Baldwin in 1896, with the 'Mother Hubbard' cab half way along the boiler.

Bottom. An early example of a Mallet compound articulated freight locomotive, on the Denver and Rio Grande. The wheel arrangement is 2–8–8–2; the high pressure cylinders drive the rearward group, and the very large low pressure cylinders are just behind the pilot. This locomotive was built by ALCO in 1913.

from the chimney the view ahead could be completely obscured. It was then that some genius decided to erect a cab specially for the driver, halfway along the boiler, but leaving the fireman on his own, on a somewhat exposed footplate at the rear end of the boiler. Engines with cabs arranged thus were humorously named 'Mother Hubbards' – the driver being placed in a separate 'cupboard'. The vogue for Mother Hubbards did not last very long. Many locomotives on the Central Railroad of New Jersey were built to this design, and it was also used on the 4–4–2 engines of the 'Atlantic City Flyers', working from Philadelphia to Atlantic City. But the co-ordination between driver and fireman, which is so essential in working a steam locomotive, especially in times of difficulty, must have been next to impossible on a Mother Hubbard.

One of the most interesting applications of compounding in the U.S.A., which led, some thirty years later, to one of the most remarkable groups of really high-power steam locomotives, lay in the development of articulated units of the 'Mallet' type. The principle originated in a design built to deal with the combination of steep gradients and almost continuous curvature on the St Gothard line by the Frenchman Anatole Mallet, who also designed the earliest form of compounding in 1875. Mallet's St Gothard engine had two six-wheeled bogies, the rear one being driven by the high pressure cylinders and the forward one by the low pressure, and the steam pipes being made with articulated

connections. The Mallet arrangement (which was not popular in Europe) took a rather modified form as introduced into the U.S.A. in 1903–4. Unlike the St Gothard engine, practically all the American examples were tender engines, and they had a different arrangement of the suspension. Mallet's tank engine on the St Gothard line was carried on two bogies. In all the American articulated locomotives the rear engine, driven by the high pressure cylinders, was on the rigid frame that carried the boiler; the front engine was on a pivoting truck.

The first locomotive to be constructed on this principle was a powerful 0–6–6–0, by the American Locomotive Company, for the Baltimore and Ohio. It was shown at the St Louis Exhibition in 1904, and created immense interest by virtue of its novel features, great size, and high tractive power of 71,500 pounds. It was essentially a slow-speed, heavy freight job, and it was followed two years later by a still larger and heavier articulated Mallet on the Great Northern Railway of the U.S.A., having a 2–6–6–2 wheel arrangement. The inclusion of a pair of leading wheels on the pivoting low pressure engine unit, and a pair of trailing wheels on the main frame beneath the firebox, made a much steadier-riding locomotive than the original Baltimore and Ohio 0–6–6–0, and formed the starting point of a long succession of American Mallet compound articulated freight locomotives. The Great Northern 2–6–6–2 of 1906 weighed 158 tons without its tender, which weighed another sixty-six tons. There then ensued a race for the honour of building the longest and heaviest locomotive ever; but without stepping too far beyond the period at present under discussion, we must mention the construction at the end of 1908 of an enormous 2–8–8–2 by Baldwins for the Southern Pacific. This locomotive weighed 190 tons without its tender, and another eighty tons with it. Other than these huge freight engines, in the period 1904–7 the 'Atlantic' was the most popular American passenger locomotive, with 'Pacifics' coming into use on a few railways.

The extent to which the American locomotive builders influenced design was greater than in any other country in the world. In Europe, and more

Matthews Vauclain. In 1872, when he was sixteen, he became an apprentice in the Altoona shops of the Pennsylvania Railroad and on completion of his training he joined Baldwins. The way he rose from shop foreman to be President of the Baldwin Locomotive Works, directly connected during his association with the company with the construction of more than *sixty thousand* locomotives, is one of the greatest success stories of the entire railway world; but he was equally a success as an engine designer, a production expert, an administrator, and above all as a businessman who by participating directly in every facet of the job of designing and building locomotives was able to keep his company in the forefront of the trade. He retired from the

Left. An Italian cab-in-front type, by Signor Plancher, of Florence. A four-cylinder compound of 1900 for the Southern Railway of Italy. The coal was carried in the bunkers adjacent to the cab; water was carried in a tender coupled at the rear end.

Below. The American 'accommodation', the train that will stop anywhere on request. An Illinois Central train stops at Denison, Iowa, drawn by a ten-wheeler (4–6–0), No. 2025.

recently in Australia, South Africa and elsewhere, railway mechanical engineers specified their requirements, but in America to a marked degree the manufacturer continued to call the tune, even after the pioneer days were far gone. This was shown with redoubled emphasis when the time came for the introduction of diesel traction. In what could be called the 'middle ages' of American steam traction there was perhaps no greater personality than Samuel

office of President in 1929, and continued as chairman of the board until his death in 1940. As an engine designer he will always be remembered by his ingenious solution to the problem of having a four-cylinder compound with all cylinders outside the frames, to provide that accessibility that was such a cherished precept of American locomotive practice.

It was in 1868 that the American Railway Master Mechanics Association was founded. In the U.S.A.

Another well-known figure on the American railroads before the advent of CTC: the general despatcher directing the movements of all traffic with hand-written 'train orders' posted to train crews.

the Master Mechanic on a railway was broadly speaking the equivalent of the Locomotive Superintendent in Britain, and the A.R.M.M.A could be likened to the British Association of Railway Locomotive Engineers. This latter was a rather exclusive little 'club', membership of which was by invitation only, and confined to the most senior men on each railway and, in some cases only, to their chief assistants. In the U.S.A. railways grew to be a 'calling', and if not enjoying at every level the status of the older professions, became something to which men became completely dedicated. Sons of railwaymen had no thoughts but to follow in their fathers' footsteps. This was understandable in a country that was almost as new as the railways themselves. There was not, as in England, generation after generation of men who had worked in other professions or trades, and where younger sons, or those whose school results were poor, were sent into railway service as a kind of last hope, as an alternative to the law, the Church, or the army! In the U.S.A. one found instances like that of F. Stewart Graham, on the Delaware, Lackawanna and Western, whose father and grandfather had been Master Mechanics on that railway.

Lower down the hierarchy of railway employees, the brakemen were the embodiment of all the characteristics and virtues of the American railroad man. They were among the more numerous categories of railway staff, as the highest proportion of American railway traffic was freight, and every freight train had several brakemen. The brakeman had to regulate the brakes on each of the cars he was responsible for by means of an independent control-wheel mounted on the top of each car. Though he spent some of the time relaxing in the sunshine admiring the passing view – perhaps the breath-taking scenery of the Rockies or the Rio Grande – at other times he would have to operate without protection on top of the speeding train in an Arctic blizzard, dashing from car to car to stop the brake-wheel from freezing solid. Whatever the weather, his job was dangerous, as he leapt the gap between swaying, bouncing cars to keep the train under control. A writer referring to conditions before the end of the nineteenth century described a particular hazard the brakeman had to guard against: the possibility that a long, heavily-laden freight train might break in half as it passed over the summit of an incline and began to descend on the other side.

'To avoid this breaking-in-two the brakemen must be wide awake on the instant and see that their brakes are tightened before the speed even begins to elude control. As soon as the whole train has got beyond the summit, and the speed is reduced to a proper rate by the application of the brakes on, say, one-third or one-half the cars, it will perhaps be found that one or two brakes too many have been put on and that the train is running too slowly. Some of them must then be loosened. Or perhaps some are set so tightly that the friction heats the wheels unduly or causes them to slide along the track instead of rolling; then those brakes must be released and some on other cars applied instead.'

These particular hazards were of course eliminated by the introduction of continuous automatic air brakes, the invention of George Westinghouse, after which the brakeman no longer had to adjust brakes on individual cars, but was only responsible for seeing that cars were running smoothly, that brake blocks were not overheating, and so on. Today every American freight train carries a front and a rear brakeman.

On the continent of Europe in the same period interest was centred mainly on France, Germany and Austria. In France the work of Alfred de Glehn, of the Société Alsacienne in Belfort, in collaboration with M. du Bousquet, the locomotive engineer of the Northern Railway, had produced the world-famous de Glehn four-cylinder compound. The features which contributed to its great success were the independent controls of the valve gears for the high and low pressure cylinders, the facility for admitting a limited amount of high pressure steam direct to the low pressure cylinders, to give something of a boost when climbing a heavy gradient, and above all a very successful proportioning of the cylinder dimensions and valves, equalising as far as possible the amount of work done in the high pressure and low pressure engines. The result, as applied to the 'Atlantic' locomotives of the Nord, was an extremely powerful machine. Exceptional speed was not called for, because maximum speed on all French railways was limited by law to 120 kilometres per hour

(74·5 miles per hour). The Nord practice of the du Bousquet–de Glehn partnership was followed on the Orléans Railway, but a somewhat different and independent development took place on the Paris, Lyons and Mediterranean Railway.

In Germany there were two quite separate developments in progress. One concerned Dr Wilhelm Schmidt on the Prussian State Railways, the other the firm of Maffei at Munich, Bavaria. Schmidt was a consultant, at first concerned almost entirely with stationary engines and steam plants; but his work in connection with the 'superheating' of steam attracted the attention of the Prussian railway authorities. In the normal way the boiling point of water takes place at a temperature dependent on the pressure in the boiler. Thus if the working pressure of a boiler is 150 pounds per square inch, the temperature of formation of steam is 382°F, while if the pressure is 225 pounds per square inch the temperature is 392°F. If, after its formation, the steam is further heated, or 'superheated', its total energy, or capacity for doing work, is considerably increased, and its volume is increased by expansion. Schmidt showed how this fundamental feature could be used to increase the power and efficiency of locomotives. Of course the fitting of superheaters increased the first cost of locomotives; but it was considered that the increased work to be got out of them, and the reduced coal consumption resulting from their increased efficiency, would more than pay for the extra cost of putting on superheaters. The Prussian State Railways took up

this proposition with avidity, and other continental railway systems followed suit, including the Belgian, Swedish, Swiss, Austrian, French and other German states, the railways of which were then independent. By the year 1907 the Canadian Pacific had fitted many locomotives, and it had also been tried on the Cape Government Railway in South Africa. In Great Britain, chiefly because of the high quality of coal so liberally available, only a single locomotive had been fitted experimentally – one of Churchward's large

Austrian State Railways: one of the celebrated four-cylinder compound locomotives of Karl Gölsdorf, here shown at the Vienna West Station.

Left. An animated scene at the junction at Borås, in Sweden, 1900. The locomotives are heading trains from Gothenburg and Varberg, and both have spark-arresting devices in their chimneys. Much of the Swedish railway network passes through forest land, and precautions have to be taken against fires.

new 4–6–0s, on the Great Western.

The work of Maffei, in Bavaria, was very important in respect of engine layout. He also was building compound locomotives as a means of maximising efficiency and minimising coal consumption. Like Alfred de Glehn on the French railways and the engineers of the Prussian State Railways, and unlike the Americans, Maffei had no inhibitions about mounting some of the cylinders inside the frames; but whereas de Glehn had taken advantage of having four cylinders to divide the drive, making the inside pair of cylinders drive the leading pair of coupled wheels, and the outside cylinders drive the second pair, Maffei arranged all the cylinders in line, and drove entirely on to the one axle. There was considerable difference of opinion over this. De Glehn's method distributed the driving force between two axles, and the forces transmitted to the frames through the axleboxes were lessened. Maffei applied the driving force all in one place, as it were. Both types were very successful as locomotives, but the significance of Maffei's layout was not appreciated until several years later, and then in a different way.

In Great Britain at this time, developments were coming rather slowly. While the need for larger boilers was generally appreciated, there was no positively explosive growth like that evident in America, and there was equally a reluctance to indulge in the 'scientific' advances of continental Europe. On the Great Western, Churchward, one of the most far-sighted of British locomotive engineers, was certainly impressed with de Glehn's work to the extent of persuading his management to buy three compound 'Atlantics' for trial; but having got them, and assessed their work, he set out to produce a single expansion locomotive that would do the same job. Some railways built a few large 'Atlantic' and 4–6–0 locomotives for special duties; but for the most part the well-run express trains of Great Britain were pulled by the traditional, neat 4–4–0 locomotives with inside cylinders, fired with carefully selected grades of high-quality coal. In the year 1906 one could move around the main line railways of Great Britain and on fifteen of them see this remarkable medium-powered passenger type in a variety of lineaments, in a far greater variety of liveries, but all roughly within the 50 to 60 ton range. All were little masterpieces of artistic symmetry; all were the pride and joy of the men who ran them. But with very few exceptions they were leading the locomotive practice of their owners into a blind alley, from which the vastly changed economic circumstances of the 1920s were to block nearly every single road of escape. The Great Western was the only British railway on which a really far-sighted plan of development was evolving in the first decade of the twentieth century. Churchward was planning for the future, and always considered that the boiler constituted the principal problem of the steam locomotive, and in 1908, furthering all the features he had so far developed, he built a huge engine, the first British 'Pacific', which in respect of weight and power was a close competitor to anything constructed up to that time in the U.S.A. and France, excepting perhaps the colossal 'Pacific' of the Pennsylvania, built in 1907. But Churchward's engine, *The Great Bear*, was vastly in advance of its time so far as Great Britain was concerned, and his much smaller four-cylinder 4–6–0s of the 'Star' class, weighing no more than 75·6 tons, and having a grate area of 27 square feet, proved amply adequate for the most severe demands of everyday traffic, until the year 1923. The four-cylinder 'Star' was a single expansion engine, but had the machinery arranged as in the de Glehn compound, with the drive divided between two axles.

We must now switch the story from the huge main line express passenger locomotives to the less spectacular sides of railway operation, first to the unglamorous and often tiresome business of commuter travel, and then to the country stations. Commuter railways were revolutionising life in big cities all over the world, making possible huge increases in working populations while greatly reducing the numbers of people living at the centre. Even before the turn of the century the process was well under way and the railways threading their several ways into the central areas were becoming ever more congested with traffic in the peak hours. In London, the lines coming in from south of the Thames, and the Great Eastern, with its terminus in the heart of the City at Liverpool Street, daily conveyed an almost incredible number of passengers in the little four-wheeled coaches – sometimes unkindly referred to as 'dog-boxes' – and hauled by diminutive, but highly picturesque little steam tank engines. Although there were such swarms of trains, following each other at close intervals and intersecting each other's paths at numerous junctions, the safety record was impeccably high. The discipline and sense of responsibility shown by every man concerned with operating was beyond praise, and never more so than when fog descended, and required the additional task and anxiety of fog signalling. In the cities of the U.S.A. the pressures were hardly less intense, while in Australia similar problems were rapidly developing in Sydney and Melbourne.

The thoughts of many people turned to ideas of relieving the ordinary railways, which also had their main line traffic to operate, of the burden of commuter business. Tram cars running in the streets were introduced in many cities and large towns, while underground and overhead railway systems were constructed running beneath and above the streets. The famous London Underground system, the first underground railway in the world, was inaugurated with the opening of the Metropolitan Railway in 1863. One of the most remarkable examples of an overhead railway was that built in New York, extending from its first opening in 1872 until it included a route network of thirty-six miles by the turn of the century. The line was constructed on high elevated galleries running along the middle of the main streets, and the trains followed each other, at sight, at about one minute intervals all day long. The noise of passing trains was continuous, and was made much worse by the clatter of the viaducts as trains passed over them, the confined space that separated the tracks from the buildings on either side, and the sharp exhausts of the steam locomotives accelerating from the frequent station stops. The New York Elevated had no less than 326 steam locomotives working on its thirty-six miles of track, and 1,116 bogie cars. Porters rode on the platforms between the cars and shouted the name of the station they were

approaching and, although the cars were built in the American style with doors only at each end, passengers were disciplined into a continuous flow system, entering the cars at one end and leaving at the other. The station stops lasted no more than ten seconds, and in that time passengers poured in and out in a positive torrent.

By the early 1900s thoughts were turning to electrification of these suburban lines, not only to provide more rapid acceleration but also to eliminate

Below. This unusual picture, taken in 1892, shows the arrival in Chicago of the first consignment of locomotives for the Chicago and South Side Rapid Transit Company.

Right. This spectacular location on the Ceylon Government Railway occurs on the climb from the plains of Colombo to Kandy. It was known as 'Sensation Rock'.

the smoke and dirt of steam traction. It is incredible, perhaps, to recall that until the year 1906 the Inner Circle in London was worked entirely by steam locomotives. But the financial situation of the railways was giving rise to some anxiety and, with competition developing on the streets from horse-drawn buses and electric trams, railway managements were naturally disinclined to indulge in large schemes of capital investment. The protagonists of electric traction became highly skilled in their publicity and were not

the pre-eminent means of transport in every sphere it could be called the 'pastoral' of the 1900–20 period. Much has been written of the vagaries and idiosyncrasies of the British branch line, but one did not need to move from the main lines to see the comedy and drama of the old-time country station played out to the full. In those far-off days everything that the village required came by train. Apart from the station platforms there would be a small goods yard, a shed, a coal stack, and simple equipment to deal

New railway construction in England, 1905. The King Edward Bridge of the North Eastern Railway across the Tyne at Newcastle. It provided a valuable relief to Robert Stephenson's High Level Bridge, opened in 1849.

Opposite top. A country station on the Ceylon Government Railway, showing a typically British type of 4–4–0 locomotive in tropical surroundings.

Opposite. An English country station of 1899 vintage. Calvert is in Buckinghamshire on the Great Central main line, and the station consists of a single island platform with through roads on either side. Goods were unloaded at the side 'table', and collected by local traders.

backward in telling the world that they could do certain things that steam just could not equal. The yardstick of argument became the attainment of a speed of 30 miles per hour in thirty seconds from rest. One British locomotive engineer, James Holden, of the Great Eastern, took up this challenge on behalf of steam. The outcome was the celebrated 'Decapod' – a massive three-cylinder tank engine of the 0–10–0 wheel arrangement, which did the job alright, but proved far too damaging to the track to be used regularly. But Holden had laid low for more than thirty years the idea that steam could not do the job, and no more was heard of electrifying the Great Eastern line until the later 1930s.

Altogether in contrast to the rush and intensity of commuter travel was the atmosphere of the country station. It is a feature of the railway scene that has practically disappeared in Great Britain; but it is still very much in evidence in other parts of the world and as a 'period piece' of that era when railways were

with any special local traffic. The station master and all his men would be well-known personalities in the village, and in those days it was a prestige job to be on the railway, in however humble a capacity. The long-distance passenger trains might roar through without stopping; no one except the signalman might apparently take any notice of the passing of the crack express; but there would be plenty of activity all the same. A trader's cart is at the goods shed; a local coal merchant is at the stack; one of the porters is carefully tending the flower beds on the platform, because they are entered for the 'best-kept station' competition and last year they came near to winning the prize. But now things are happening. It is past five o'clock and the local train from town is due in less than half an hour. A coachman-driven carriage and pair comes into the station yard; the squire and his lady are expected. A superannuated trap powered by a fiery little Exmoor pony brings one of the local traders to collect his week's supply of goods from town. The station bus rattles into the yard, with seats for about ten inside and two on the box with the driver. There is not a petrol-driven vehicle among all those foregathering to meet the train. It is high summer. The station master, in his immaculate array of gold braid, has a rose in his buttonhole; the veteran ticket-collector, unofficial head gardener of the station, sports a carnation. The train when it comes may have a vintage locomotive, long since demoted from main line express work, but it is the living embodiment of 'spit and polish', and the carriages, probably nothing grander than non-corridor six-wheelers, bid fair to out-do the engine in the cleanliness of their paintwork and the beauty of the company's coat of arms carried on each one of them. As the train steams

Right. A horse-drawn survival, in north-west Cumberland: the 'Dandy', on the branch of the North British Railway from Drumburgh to Port Carlisle–a photograph taken about 1900.

Below. A small town station on the Welsh border: Llangollen, on the Great Western Railway. The signals and points are fully interlocked; passengers cross from one platform to the other by the footbridge, *never* across the tracks. The locomotive is a 2–4–0.

Opposite top. Yugoslavia. A tank engine built in Hungary and taken over from the Austrian Empire in 1918 heads for Jesenice through the Slovenian countryside.

Opposite bottom. Finland. 1920s Helsinki suburban tank engine, relegated to shunting duties at Pieksämäki, on a dark winter's morning.

away a single phrase comes to mind to describe it all, and to epitomise British railway working in the early 1900s: 'pride in the job'.

Few railways outside Europe could afford to equip even their main lines to the state of completeness that was required by law in Great Britain and Ireland. All signals and points on lines used by passenger trains were interlocked, and train movements along the line were regulated by the block system, which did not permit a second train to pass a 'block post' until advice had been received on the block telegraph instruments that the preceding train had passed the block post ahead. On the busiest English main lines, like that of the London and North Western, the block posts were about two miles apart. The signals were

the driver's sole authority to proceed, once the guard had given the 'right away' from the station platform. It was very different in North America. There train working was regulated by train orders. The driver was given a slip of paper telling him to proceed to a certain station, where perhaps a further order would be awaiting him. On the lengthy stretches of single line, which are still the bulk of the railway mileage in the Middle West and the western states, a driver would be advised to proceed to a certain place where there was a passing loop, and there to await train No. so-and-so, which would be coming in the opposite direction. Sad to recall, there were times when orders were faulty or misunderstood and two trains met in head-on collision in mid-section.

There was a striking and terrible example of how the absence of interlocking could lead to disaster in July 1905, with no less celebrated a train than the Twentieth Century Limited, running between New York and Chicago. The train was running on the Lake Shore line, following roughly half-an-hour behind another express and travelling at about 60 miles per hour. At Mentor station there was a siding leading into a freight shed, and the switch for this had been correctly set for the main line when the previous train passed. But in some way that was never subsequently explained, the switch had become reversed by the time the Twentieth Century Limited approached. There was no signal or any other indication that the points were wrong and, while

running at full speed, the express was turned into the siding and crashed into the freight shed. The shed caught fire, and it and the wrecked leading coaches of the train were burned out. The casualty list was a grievously long one.

It was a time of considerable anxiety in railway operation in many parts of the world. In Great Britain, despite all the safety precautions built into the regulations, there were times when, by force of circumstances, even the most responsible of men could make mistakes, or commit acts of simple forgetfulness. Inventors were busy trying to devise means whereby these errors could be avoided. They lay in two broad categories: those of signalmen making errors in carrying out the rules of block signalling, and those of drivers in misreading signals, or misjudging their distance in braking, and over-running. What could have been a climax, possibly leading to some additional clauses in the regulations, occurred in the early hours of 2 September 1913 on a lonely and mountainous section of the Midland Railway, near Kirkby Stephen, Westmorland. Two south-bound sleeping car expresses were following each other from Carlisle. Both locomotives had been loaded with coal of indifferent quality, and the first train got into such difficulties that it stalled, for lack of steam, on a heavy gradient approaching the summit of the line at Ais Ghyll Moor. It was, of course, protected by the block signalling, and the signalman at Mallerstang box, some three miles behind the train,

not having received clearance from Aisgill – as the name was rendered by the Midland Railway on the signal box – had all his signals at danger.

The second train was not so heavily loaded as the first, and had a less powerful locomotive. But the poor coal was giving this driver and his fireman much anxiety as they got on to the heaviest part of the climb, south of Appleby. So concerned was the driver that he gave the steaming of the engine practically his entire attention, supervising the work of his fireman and in so doing making the fatal mistake of misreading one of the Mallerstang signals. Wrongly reassured that the line was clear, he did not trouble to observe any of the other signals and went on to crash into the rear of the first train, which was still standing

Above. A great British station: Manchester Central, shared by the Midland, the Great Central, and the Cheshire Lines system. This photograph shows a Midland express departing for London, hauled by one of the famous Deeley three-cylinder compounds.

Left. An unusual scene at another great station: in 1912 the royal garden party was held at Windsor Castle, and to convey guests from London the Great Western Railway ran special trains from its Paddington Station. The locomotives in the foreground are of the latest four-cylinder 4–6–0 class; they had drawn in the empty coaches, and were allocated to take following specials to Windsor.

Opposite top. Austria. 1890 rack/adhesion tank engine struggles with an iron ore train for Präbichl amid breathtaking mountain scenery.

Opposite bottom. Yugoslav Railways Class '25' 2–8–0 silhouetted against the sunrise on the bridge at Maribor.

Top. A remarkable German viaduct near Kehl, in 1900. The heavily-latticed girders are functional rather than artistic, but the gateways at each end are astonishing neo-Gothic.

Above. Another ornamental piece of German railway engineering: the bridge across the Rhine, between Mainz and Wiesbaden, seen in a photograph of 1904. As at Kehl, only the driver of the train enjoyed the full experience.

Opposite. Temporary bridge on the Ceylon Government Railway, with steel girders supported on a series of timber grillages. Heavy masonry work for the permanent piers is being put in place.

while its crew were trying to raise steam. The collision was a bad one, and many lives were lost. Inventors redoubled their efforts to try and find some mechanical or electrical means of preventing a train from ignoring the warning given by the signalling system. There was great difference of opinion as to how far such 'control' should go. Railway engineers, as well as many freelance inventors, all had their own ideas; while the infinitely higher accident rate in the U.S.A. was leading public concern to the point of virtually demanding legislation. So far as Great Britain was concerned, active interest was brought to an abrupt halt in August 1914 by the outbreak of war in Europe. Railways in all the belligerent countries were immediately called upon for a new and vital rôle, and the burning question of automatic train control was pigeon-holed, in Europe at any rate, for more than a dozen years.

Part 4

Stress and Strain

Dr Wilhelm Schmidt, designer of the Schmidt superheater, which increased the thermal efficiency of steam locomotives by more than 25 per cent.

High railway bridge over the Kiel Canal. Kaiser Wilhelm II inspecting the works on board the royal yacht *Hohenzollern* in 1911.

By the time the nations of Europe became involved in the fearful conflict that was eventually to engulf much of the world, there were signs on every hand that railways were beginning to pass beyond that age of elegance and pre-eminence that they had enjoyed for many years previously. One could single out the year 1910 as one starting point for the beginning of a new age, though others might not discern much difference until that fateful 4 August of 1914. An Englishman naturally tends to think first of British affairs, and from 1910 there was much social and political unrest in Great Britain in which the railways collectively, as among the largest employers of labour, were inevitably much involved. There was movement in other directions too. Rising costs, in raw materials, fuel supplies and labour, were causing most railway administrations to seek economies in operating. There was no lack of first-rate locomotive coal in Britain; the trouble was it was always getting more expensive.

bridled at the prospective increases in capital costs, and serious differences of opinion developed within certain individual companies, when larger locomotives were actually authorised. One case, which rather typified the parochial attitude obtaining in certain departments, is important in the bearing it had on developments in the post-war years.

The situation occurred on no less a railway than the London and North Western. C. J. Bowen-Cooke, who was appointed chief mechanical engineer in 1909, was planning a design for some large new express passenger engines of the 4–6–0 type that would haul far heavier loads over the mountain gradients of the north country than had previously been taken by a single engine. They were to have been much heavier in themselves; but there was more to it than dead weight on the axles. In locomotives with only two cylinders, where the cranks were necessarily arranged at right angles, there was a degree of unbalance inherent in the machinery, which had been

The onus of finding means of improvement centred on the locomotive engineers. The British tradition of running trains with the smallest locomotives possible had bitten deeply into the souls of many who carried major responsibility for running the railways. Yet many locomotive engineers saw clearly enough that if heavier trains were to be conveyed economically, larger and more powerful locomotives were essential. Yet those who controlled the purse-strings

compensated by putting balance weights into the driving wheels. This gave a good workable compromise so far as the engine itself was concerned, and provided a steady ride at high speed. But as the speed rose the balance weights, cast into the wheels, set up what was known as the 'hammer blow' effect on the track, and a locomotive that had no more than 19 tons dead weight on its driving axle could have a combined load of something like 30 tons when running at 80 miles per hour – adding together the dead load and the hammer blow.

On the continent of Europe the answer to this situation had been found by constructing locomotives with four cylinders, all driving on to the leading coupled axle. This eliminated 'hammer blow' altogether and, in Holland particularly, where axle loading had to be restricted in view of the spongy nature of the ground, the civil engineers permitted the use of these heavier locomotives, so perfectly balanced dynamically. Bowen-Cooke adopted that arrangement for his big new 4–6–0s being designed at Crewe in 1911. They had a heavier dead weight on their driving axles, but this was not augmented in any way at speed, so that they would have been considerably easier on the track and the bridges than many existing L.N.W.R. locomotives.

Unfortunately the civil engineer could not be convinced; dead weight per axle was the sole criterion so far as he was concerned. Bowen-Cooke, rather than precipitate a crisis between himself and a colleague of equally high status, set the Crewe drawing office to work on a revised design, using a smaller boiler. The first of the new engines was completed at Crewe early in 1913, and named after the chairman of the company, *Sir Gilbert Claughton*. The engines of this class were soon doing some remarkable work on the line, but one can nevertheless reflect how much better they might have been had not the original proposals been vetoed – quite unjustifiably.

The name of Trevithick will always be associated with the London and North Western Railway and with Crewe works, thanks to Francis, the son of the great early pioneer, who was the first locomotive chief of the Northern Division at Crewe. Three of his sons attained positions of eminence in the railway engineering world. In 1910 A. R. Trevithick was wagon superintendent of the L.N.W.R., while mention has already been made of the work of R. F. Trevithick, in Japan. The third of these three brothers, Frederick Harvey Trevithick, was chief mechanical engineer

Below. London and North Western Railway: a four-cylinder 4–6–0 'Claughton' engine making a fast ascent of the Grayrigg Bank, Westmorland – speed about 45 miles per hour on a gradient of 1 in 31.

Bottom. On the Milwaukee in 1912: the 'Olympian' crossing Hull Creek Bridge near Garcia, Washington.

of the Egyptian State Railways, and in the period before World War One he carried out a series of important experiments to improve working efficiency and reduce fuel consumption on a railway that was then dependent almost entirely on imported fuel. Although in one respect the Egyptian State Railways were easy to operate, in that there were no gradients at all, either in the Nile delta or on the long single-tracked line that ran for more than 300 miles beside the Nile from Cairo to Luxor, they had their own

A unique locomotive event: in 1914 a series of 4–4–0s for the South Eastern and Chatham Railway, of England, was built by A. Borsig and Co. of Berlin. The contract was awarded to Germany because no British builder could meet the required delivery date. The locomotives were delivered only just before the outbreak of war in August 1914, and ironically were immediately put to work on military traffic between London and Dover! This photograph was taken outside the ornate entrance to Borsig's works at Tegel, Berlin.

on the Great Western Railway, and left us this account of some of the special difficulties faced by the British management, written in 1903.

'The district superintendents in charge of the running sheds are as a rule Englishmen, and their position is no sinecure. Some of the native drivers are excellent men, but others are truly Oriental in their ideas of punctuality. It is not uncommon to have several goods trains ready to start and only half the engine crews at hand for them.

'The engine cleaner is another trying individual. When not engaged in saying his prayers in some remote corner of the running shed, the dim religious light of which renders it eminently adapted for temporary conversion into a mosque, he may perhaps bring his mind to the consideration of wiping down locomotives from an academic point of view. He reasons that if engine No. 74 has to be cleaned by somebody, and if he, the cleaner, does not do it at once, it is evidently the will of heaven that it may be left until "tomorrow", unless of course somebody else does it in the meantime. Having duly thought this out, he possibly proceeds down the sidings for a quiet smoke, if he can do so without being discovered . . .'

It was against these kinds of human problems that Frederick Harvey Trevithick embarked upon his experiments to improve the technical efficiency of locomotives. I should add that very little evidence of difficulties with personnel would be apparent to the traveller by 'express' passenger trains. The relatively few express drivers were mostly Englishmen and the locomotives themselves, in their crimson livery with much polished brasswork, were kept looking very smart. Trevithick sought to utilise the waste heat in the exhaust steam, and the waste heat in the furnace gases, and this he did by diverting a portion of the exhaust steam, with which of course the furnace gases were mixed in the smokebox, and using it for heating the feed water entering the boiler, or superheating the steam. This involved the installation of special equipment in the smokebox, and sometimes queer-looking excrescences on the sides. The standard 4–4–0 express locomotives used on the Cairo–Alexandria run had exceptionally long extended smokeboxes, to contain the special apparatus. While these experiments were in progress Trevithick arranged for the purchase of three French-built de Glehn compound 'Atlantics' of the design so successfully in use on the Northern Railway of France, for comparative purposes, just as Churchward had done on the Great Western Railway of England. But while the French compound engines proved more economical than the standard Egyptian express engines, before any of Trevithick's improvements had been added to them, these large 'Atlantics' were surpassed in haulage capacity by the modified 4–4–0s which did the work on roughly two-thirds the amount of coal.

The outcome of Trevithick's experiments was the adoption by his successor of a very high degree of superheat in the steam, in some large new 'Atlantic' engines built towards the end of 1913, not in Great Britain or France, but by the Berlin Locomotive Works. This was not a sign of increasing international competition on a railway where British influence was

peculiar difficulties. The only trains which could be called expresses ran between Cairo and Alexandria, a distance of 130 miles, and the fastest timing before World War One was a level three hours. In the Nile delta the wind is almost constantly from the north, and in the summer particularly it is of considerable strength. Statistics showed that the coal consumption required to keep the three-hour schedule was 30 per cent greater on the northbound than on the southbound journey.

The problems of running the Egyptian Railways of the time were not only technical ones. The great locomotive historian E. L. Ahrons joined the staff of the railway not long after completing his training still supreme, but reflected the fact that at that time the British locomotive building industry was so busy that it could not take any more orders. At about the same time the South Eastern and Chatham Railway ordered some new 4-4-0 express locomotives from A. Borsig of Berlin! The German railways, even in the days of the independent state systems, were always impressive to the visitor. Rolling stock, if not excessively luxurious, was always clean, and often made a contrast to the trains of some neighbouring countries. In 1913, for example, J. P. Pearson referred to the 'marvellous railway system of Germany', though his multitudinous notes do not reveal any outstanding features of train operation. What was immensely impressive, and remained even more so in the period between the two World Wars, was the grandeur of the principal stations. It was surprising that in the straitened economic circumstances of the 1930s so much attention should be devoted to station reconstruction, and on such a magnificent scale.

Germany's 'Iron Chancellor', the legendary Bismarck, attempted to amalgamate all the railways of the country under imperial control; but the influence of the individual states was too strong and his great project failed. At the same time, however, the dominating position of Prussia in all German affairs made the other states increasingly dependent for traffic on the encircling Prussian lines. After the dismissal of Bismarck by Kaiser Wilhelm II, the prospect of railway unification in Germany receded still further, though a degree of co-ordination was

Left. South Eastern and Chatham Railway: the great landslip in the Folkestone Warren in December 1915, which blocked the line between Folkestone and Dover for nearly four years. The train shown in the picture was caught in the subsidence, but there were no casualties. The rolling stock was drawn back to Folkestone through the Martello Tunnel, seen in the background. All wartime traffic to Dover was worked over the alternative route via Canterbury.

Below. A pre-war scene at Dieppe, as the boat train for the packet from Newhaven leaves for Paris, on the State Railway of France.

Toronto in wartime: a view looking west towards the old Union Station, used jointly by the Canadian Pacific and the Grand Trunk Railways. Photograph taken late in August 1914.

imposed by the imperial government for strategic purposes. Within the central administration of the Prussian State Railways there was a marked degree of decentralisation in actual working – the system being divided into no fewer than eleven regional administrations, such as Berlin, Magdeburg, Left Rhine, Right Rhine, and so on.

But even before the year 1913 the shadows of impending international crisis were beginning to slant across Europe, and these cut short a French development of exceptional promise. In 1911 du Bousquet, of the Nord, who in collaboration with de Glehn had made history with his famous compound 'Atlantics', produced two enormous compound engines of the 4–6–4 type. They were by far the largest and most powerful locomotives in Europe at the time, and were almost transatlantic in their size and proportions. He bequeathed them to his successor M. Georges Asselin at a time when political tension was mounting in the face of the aggressive tactics of Imperial Germany. While these huge 4–6–4 compound engines showed great promise in their early tests, it was obvious that a considerable amount of development work would be necessary before the design was ready for 'batch production'. The development would take time, and in any forthcoming international crisis it could not be continued. The Nord needed new engines, of greater capacity than the 'Atlantics', and since M. de Glehn's firm, the Société Alsacienne, of Belfort, had recently supplied

some new compound 'Pacifics' to the Alsace-Lorraine Railways, then extensively Germanised, the Nord decided to adopt this design with little modification, to obtain reasonably quick delivery. Twenty of these fine engines were delivered in 1912, and English travellers soon became aware of their capabilities in the excellent running of the boat trains between Calais, Boulogne and Paris. That they were an expedient rather than a considered development was, at the time, incidental.

The onset of war, in 1914, had many repercussions on railway working, apart from nipping in the bud a promising French technical development; and two programmes of new railway construction in the British Empire, far removed from the actual areas of conflict, must next be considered. I have told earlier in this book how the Canadian Pacific Railway was built from coast to coast. The great prosperity it came to enjoy in the early years of the twentieth century led to the projection of further routes across Canada; these were actively supported by the federal government, which was anxious that there should not be a monopoly of transport across the country. The activity that led eventually to a critical situation in 1914 began logically enough out of the astonishing trade boom that had developed in the prairie provinces, when two one-time Ontario farm boys, William Mackenzie and Donald Mann, set to work to tap the grain-producing areas and convey the golden traffic from Winnipeg southwards to the

United States border, and south-eastwards to Port Arthur, on Lake Superior. Having worked on the construction of the Canadian Pacific, Mackenzie and Mann knew their business and the Canadian Northern, as their enterprise was named, was a success from the outset. At the same time the fact that traffic was being fed into the U.S.A. for conveyance eastward was unacceptable to many Canadians, and with the Grand Trunk wishing to share in the prosperity of the prairies and the Canadian Northern seeking an outlet to the east other than through the U.S.A., an alliance seemed the natural outcome. But the two companies could not come to terms, with the astonishing result that both embarked on the colossal task of expanding their existing lines into complete transcontinental systems. This amazing situation developed in the spirit of boundless optimism that characterised the early years of the twentieth century in Canada. Both projects aimed at reaching Pacific tidewater, and while Mackenzie and Mann took up for their 'Canadian Northern' the precise route that Sandford Fleming had originally recommended for the Canadian Pacific (through the Yellowhead Pass, and heading afterwards for the canyons of the Fraser river), the Grand Trunk in applying for government aid to build the Grand Trunk Pacific proposed to run roughly parallel to the Canadian Pacific, but somewhat to the north as far as Winnipeg, and from there also to make for the Yellowhead Pass. There they planned to continue northwards into the virtually uncharted wilds of British Columbia, to reach salt water at Prince Rupert.

There would then have been three routes across Canada. The Grand Trunk, and its protégé the Grand Trunk Pacific, would connect Montreal and Toronto and all the earlier Grand Trunk interests in south-west Ontario and the U.S.A. with Winnipeg, Edmonton and Prince Rupert. The enlarged Canadian Northern would pass from Port Arthur through Winnipeg and Edmonton and, after negotiating the Yellowhead Pass, drop down to Kamloops and run within sight of the historic Canadian Pacific main line for the rest of the way to Vancouver. Then to crown it all there was launched in 1903 a proposal for a 'National Transcontinental Railway' that would start at Moncton, New Brunswick, cross the St Lawrence at Quebec, and then make an almost straight line across virgin country, disregarding all the existing centres of population, until it reached Winnipeg. It was a grandiose scheme, which the Government hoped would stimulate colonisation. The accompanying map shows the vast extent of these projects. Progress was slow and in spite of government aid the construction costs were proving crippling. The Grand Trunk must have many times wished it had never embarked on the 'Pacific' project which, when it was completed, could not even cover its operating expenses. By the year 1914 the Canadian Northern had no money left to complete its line through the canyons to Vancouver. As for the National Transcontinental, the traffic was just not there. But the Government had encouraged the building of all these lines, and with the outbreak of war they became vital lifelines, whether they paid or not. The National Transcontinental in particular which, as a straight commercial proposition, had looked like becoming such an incubus, became of immense importance in its direct route to the Atlantic ports, avoiding all the congested eastern areas of Sudbury, Toronto, Ottawa and Montreal. The outcome of the acute financial difficulties of the Grand Trunk Pacific, Canadian Northern and National Transcontinental was that these three railways were brought under federal control for the duration of the war.

Meanwhile another great national project was being pushed forward to completion in Australia. It was in 1901 that all the formerly independent colonies of Australia joined together to form the Commonwealth of Australia; but when this great federation was first proposed Western Australia showed no desire to be included. That beautiful and wildly extensive land of the black swans was almost completely cut off from the rest of Australia, and the colonist out in the west saw no advantage in having any federal ties. Between them and South Australia lay the immense barrier of the Nullabor Plain – treeless, waterless and as devoid of wild life as it was of any human population. The attitude originally shown towards federation by the people of Western Australia was strikingly parallel to that of British Columbia towards the Confederation of Canada. Western Australia's barrier separating it from the rest of the country was the Nullabor Plain; British

Canadian transcontinental lines prior to 1922.

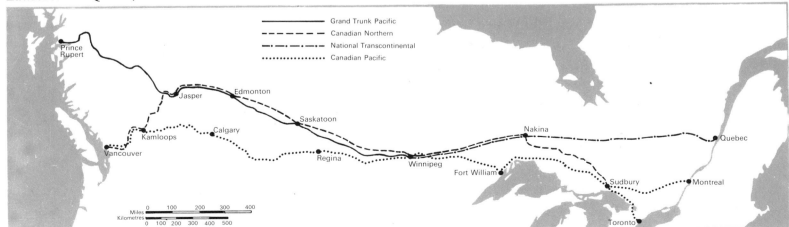

Columbia had the mighty chain of the Rockies. And both colonies were won over by the promise of a transcontinental railway.

In Australia the 'Trans', as it is familiarly known among railwaymen, was a Commonwealth project; it was enterprised with funds provided by the federal government to link up the most westerly extent of the railways of South Australia and the Western Australian railways at Kalgoorlie. The 'link' was a small matter of 1,085 miles long, and it formed the

One of the New South Wales type 4–6–0 locomotives adopted as a standard for working the Trans-Australian line of the Commonwealth Railways.

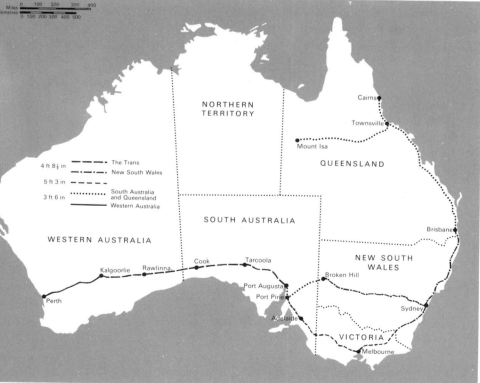

Australia, principal railways in 1917. (The 4 foot 8½ inch gauge line from Sydney to Brisbane, built in 1930, has also been included.)

first part of the Commonwealth Railway system. It has to this day remained independent of the State systems that were previously in existence. It was also sharply divided from them in another vital matter.

Earlier in this book I have described the different rail gauges prevailing in Australia, and the way they originated. Part of the South Australian Railways was laid to the 5 foot 3 inch gauge, and part to the 3 foot 6 inch; the Western Australian lines were uniformly 3 feet 6 inches. As the furthest west link in South Australia, at Port Augusta, was 3 foot 6 inches it would have been an easy way out to have settled for 3 foot 6 inches for the 'Trans'; but the federal government had, by the turn of the century, become very conscious of the inconvenience of the various breaks of gauge, and with a rare touch of far-sightedness looked forward to a time when there should be a national network on a common, standard gauge. After lengthy discussion the British gauge was decided upon, even though only one Australian state was then using it. So the 'Trans' was made to 4 feet 8½ inches and on its completion it involved breaks of gauge at both ends.

Because of its immense potential value in wartime its construction was pushed vigorously ahead. The job was unlike any of the other great pioneer works that have been described earlier in this book. There were no great rivers to bridge, no mountain passes to scale, no red Indians to attack the working parties, no lions to eat the coolies. There was simply nothing—nothing except the blazing heat of inland Australia! The construction gangs had to take everything with them—food, water, equipment, everything. Camels were used as draught animals, and the camps that were set up along the line became the 'stations', where the surface men eventually lived and where locomotives were serviced and re-manned. In the middle of the war locomotives could have been a serious problem, especially since engines from the contiguous systems could not be used because of the break of gauge; so the Commonwealth Railways adopted two well-tried New South Wales types, and had a small number of each built in Great Britain. Because of their strategic importance, the requirements of the Commonwealth Railways claimed high priority; the 2–8–0 goods engines were built in Glasgow by the North British Locomotive Company. The 4–6–0s, twenty-six of the famous N.S.W. 'P6' class, were built by the same celebrated company. The line was completed in 1917, and the first through train left Kalgoorlie for the east on 25 October. After the workings had become established on a regular basis three changes of locomotive were involved in the journey. The four sections were:

Kalgoorlie to Rawlinna	235 miles
Rawlinna to Cook	303 miles
Cook to Tarcoola	256 miles
Tarcoola to Port Augusta	257 miles

On reaching a staging point, the locomotive came off the train and was coaled, watered and serviced before proceeding further on the long run by a succeeding train. The engine crews worked over shorter distances than the locomotives, and intermediate staging points were set up, with sleeping accommodation and canteen facilities for men who had been relieved. It is certainly significant of the difficulties that were faced in working this line in its early days that a stud of twenty-six locomotives was needed to operate a service of three passenger trains *a week* in each direction.

For those who do not know the Nullabor Plain it is perhaps difficult to imagine the utter isolation of the divisional staging points on the line. From the engine cab one looks ahead over an absolutely straight track laid over the natural surface of the ground. There is no vegetation save the low scrubby salt bush, blue-grey in colour, against the prevailing orange-brown of the soil. The land is flat in every direction. Days of hot, cloudless sunshine produce mirages, and as one goes pedalling along – speeds never exceeded 50 miles per hour in the early days – the first sight of an approaching station comes like the first sight of islands or a ship on the horizon on a sea journey. One's first glimpse is of the tops of water towers, sheds, and the one-storey houses appearing over the curve of the earth. The 'station' will consist of nothing more than a passing loop, or perhaps a siding where locomotives can be 'rested' and serviced, while the 'town' is no more than a group of hutments depending entirely for its supplies on what comes along the railway. The completion of the 'Trans' in 1917 was a major step forward.

An old driver who worked on the line has written:

'I started off on the construction of the east–west line in 1914, shovelling sand for 10s 6d a day on stale bread, oily butter, salt beef and a bit of rice.

'It was a tough job. I doubt if we will ever again see men work under the conditions the men on the Trans-Australia did with horses, camels, shovels and picks. Remember that on this 900 miles not one stream of water was crossed, no man lived and the land was so flat no tunnel had to be built, no bridge across gulches. We lived in tent-houses – sometimes wood part way up with a canvas top, sometimes a cutting in the earth with a tent above that. Willy-willies when they came swept in and blew the top off these houses. I saw a man near our tent-house left standing among his furniture with his roof gone in the wind of the willy-willy.

'Even as the line was built we had to use sand scoops fastened on to the front of a slow-moving train to clear the sand off the line.

'When we couldn't make bread we had damper and brownies. We kept flour, baking powder, pepper and salt on hand in case we were cut off and of course vinegar and onions for turkeys. We used to get about two wild turkeys a week. We'd rub them with vinegar and put an onion inside them and hang them for a bit, then cook them in a kerosene tin. They were very good eating. We caught most of them up Wirripa way near where the rocket range is today. We kept our food cool by digging a hole in the ground, lining it with clinkers from the engine around a kerosene tin. We made jellies and ice-cream in that out there in the above-century temperatures.

'Port Augusta just before the beginning of the 1914 war got to be a busy town as the men started to come for the construction jobs. There weren't enough houses and the men who brought their families home-built their own camps out on the sand hills a mile out of town. The single men lived in tents.'

Before the terribly prolonged period of trench warfare began on the western front in Europe, there were various rapid military and naval movements that strained the resource and adaptability of railway managements almost to breaking point. In front of the headlong advance of the German armies through Belgium and into northern France a fair number of locomotives had been withdrawn in time, and the Allied countries in the west wanted to use them. But while the locomotives themselves had been saved, all the equipment and parts for servicing them had been lost, and the Belgian locomotives in particular had no features that were standard, with either British or French practice. To help out, the British Government undertook to manufacture the necessary items of consumable spares at the Ashford works of the South Eastern and Chatham Railway; but before this could be done, of course, a large number of drawings had to be made by the laborious process of measuring up actual articles. Then there was the vast deployment of the Royal Navy, as dramatic as it was secret, and begun on Winston Churchill's orders *before* war had actually been declared. It was, however, one thing to decide to base the Grand Fleet at Scapa Flow, but quite another to furnish that great fleet with the necessary supplies. One thing that put an immense burden on the railways was the supply of coal. All our warships were then coal-fired, and they needed coal of the same first-rate quality as an express locomotive required. From the very beginning of the war the enormous tonnage of coal needed by the fleet had to be hauled up to the very north of Scotland. These trains used to be known as the 'Jellicoe Specials'.

The existence of German colonies in southern Africa, and the aggressive colonial tactics of Imperial Germany even before war had broken out, placed in some danger a new railway that was under construction in the Portuguese colony of Angola. The enterprising of the Benguela Railway, as it was named, was to provide the shortest route from Europe to the copper belt in the Belgian Congo and northern Rhodesia. In 1902 an Englishman, Robert Williams by name, had obtained a concession from the Portuguese government to build a railway from the virgin haven of Lobito Bay, across Angola, to the frontier of the Congo. The distance was 830 miles, and the country was tropical throughout, with all that that entailed in hardship and disease among the construction forces. Progress was slow, and by 1908 the line had advanced inland to no more than 130 miles from Lobito Bay. One after another the contractors failed. Progress, or more correctly the lack of it, was being closely watched in Berlin, and the relative proximity of the line to the frontier of German South-West Africa made those on the spot fear a German coup. Fortunately Robert Williams was well enough aware of the danger, and he was able to arrange the necessary finance to enable new contracts to be placed with a British firm, the celebrated Pauling's, whose founder, the redoubtable George Pauling, had built much of the railway network in South Africa and practically all of what then existed in Rhodesia.

The experience and resource of Pauling's soon-extended the Benguela Railway, and although the fears of a German coup were intensified in 1914, a skilfully-planned attack on South-West Africa from the south and the rapid overrunning of the German forces there removed all danger from Angola, and construction of the Benguela Railway went smoothly ahead. It was, however, not until August 1928 that the frontier of the Congo was eventually reached. As completed and operated ever since, the Benguela Railway provided a remarkable and probably unique example of the use of indigenous fuel supplies existing almost over the whole of its length. Its steam locomotives are fired with wood cut from eucalyptus trees grown specially by the company in thick parallel belts, one on each side of the line for hundreds of miles. A system of rotational cropping is in operation, so as to ensure a regular supply. Wood is used to fire the largest locomotives of the present day, as efficiently as with the smaller units employed when the line was first opened. On the large articulated locomotives of the Beyer-Garratt type, which will be described in detail later, an engine crew of four is employed; two men riding in the fuel bunker feed the logs forward to the fireman, who works alongside the driver in the usual way.

In Britain, alone among the belligerents in the first two years of war, the speed of passenger train service remained unaltered. It is true that many trains were withdrawn, but others hitherto run in separate sections were combined into enormous tonnages;

Hazards of wartime operating in France: a Great Central type 2–8–0 of the Railway Operating Division of the British Army (R.O.D.) damaged and derailed by enemy action.

and in these circumstances the capacity of British locomotives, and the spirit and skill of the drivers and firemen, were never displayed to better advantage. Coal shortage was not the only difficulty faced by those responsible for running the railways in Britain during the war. The railway workshops with their magnificent equipment were well suited to production of specialised items of war munitions. This of course lessened their capacity for building and repairing

locomotives, and the consequent need to run locomotives for mileages considerably longer than the normal span between periodic overhauls made it essential to reduce wear and tear in service by lessening the actual haulage tasks when out on the line. There was no chance of reducing loads; it would be done only by reducing speeds, and from January 1917 there was general deceleration all over Great Britain.

Great Britain was of course not alone in having serious problems with wartime transport. Beyond the ordinary network of the French railway system was the remarkable organisation of the Railway Operating Division of the British Army. It was under the command of Cecil W. Paget, in peace time general superintendent of the Midland Railway. He was one of the most original and unorthodox of operating officers, always in the thick of things, and no matter how large his command grew, steadfastly refusing promotion from the rank of Lieutenant-Colonel with which he first went to France. He could eventually have become a full General, such was the magnitude of his command; but that would have involved moving to General Headquarters and giving up the train which he cherished for the mobility it gave him. Paget's mobile headquarters was no ordinary train. It took him, often at a moment's notice, to areas behind the main battle fronts wherever there were transport problems. The locomotives of the R.O.D. were many and various, borrowed from the British railways, but also including some Belgian and Dutch types. In administration paper-work did not exist; instructions to senior officers were given by word of mouth, usually by highly detailed telephone calls. In the mobile headquarters the day started with Paget sprinting the length of the train twice, to keep fit, and then cooking breakfast for his officers! An epicure himself, he was also a *cordon bleu*. To provide track for the main special lines required by the R.O.D., tracks in England and Scotland for which there was no wartime use were lifted and shipped overseas.

Rationing had never been known before in railway history. In many ways at this time the state was intervening in the lives of individuals on a quite new scale, and now, for the first time in railway history in Great Britain, a form of travel rationing was imposed – not in the amount of travelling an individual might do, but in the routes and trains he must use. This applied particularly to the Anglo-Scottish services from London. In pre-war days, if a man wanted to travel from London to Edinburgh, or to Glasgow, there were three routes available to him for either Scottish city, morning, midday, and night: Euston, via the West Coast route; St Pancras, via the Midland; and King's Cross via the East Coast route. From 1917 onwards, for Glasgow in the morning it was St Pancras, and no other station; for Edinburgh, King's Cross. There was a morning Scotch express from Euston but passengers from London were not allowed to use it. On every line except the Great Central there was a complete withdrawal of dining cars, and to carry more people for the same dead weight of rolling stock non-corridor carriages were substituted for corridor vehicles on certain routes. There was little joy in travelling anywhere in Europe in the years 1917–18, while in England the increasing incidence of Zeppelin raids made it necessary to run with the blinds down at night.

In the later stages of the war the railways of Switzerland assumed a strategic significance that was repeated in 1940–5. As a neutral country completely surrounded by belligerents of both sides, it became a kind of clearing house, and the town of Constance, a German enclave in Swiss territory on the south of Lake Constance, became the principal point of exchange for prisoners of war. Nationals of countries then at war with Germany had to watch their step when travelling by Swiss trains calling at Constance. If they stayed in the carriage, all was well; but the story is told of two Englishmen who got down on the platform to stretch their legs, and were immediately arrested by the Germans and interned for the rest of the war! The very important north to south route

Railroad and highway rub shoulders in the U.S.A. Parkersburg, West Virginia, a divisional point on the one-time Pittsburgh and West Virginia Railroad, later part of the Norfolk and Western Railway.

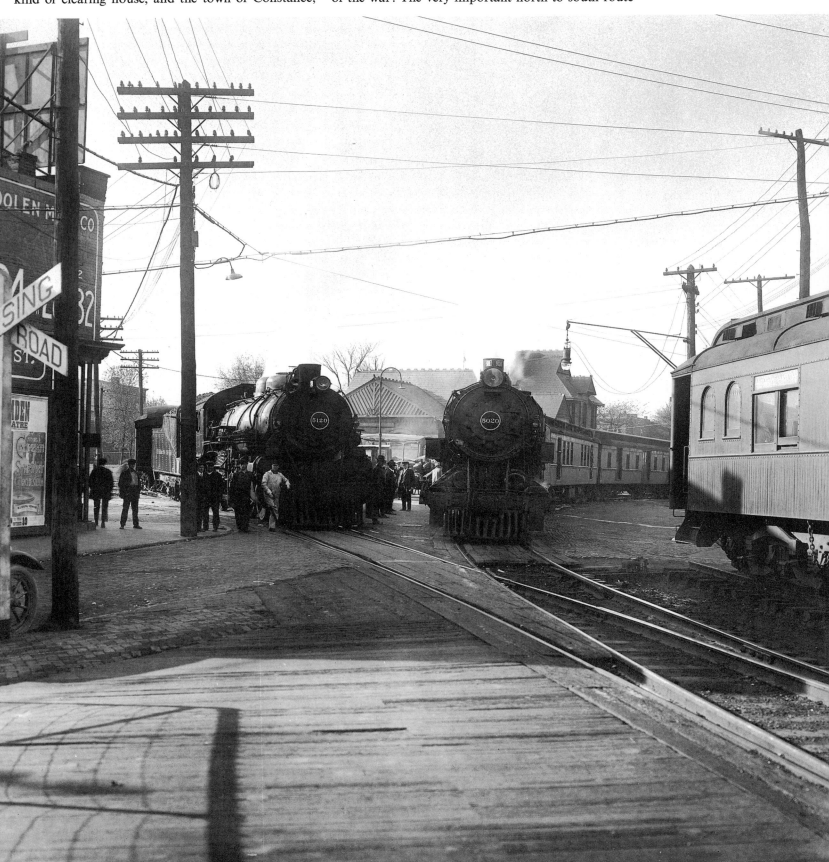

through Switzerland via the St Gothard tunnel had, in 1914–18, countries that were at war with each other at each end. It was still worked entirely by steam and, as the largest passenger locomotives in use could not take a load of more than 150 tons single-handed up the lengthy 1 in 38 gradients, there was a great deal of double-heading. Fortunately for the comfort of the enginemen the line was double-tracked throughout; otherwise the exhausts from two hard-worked locomotives climbing through the

Bern–Lötschberg–Simplon Railway, Switzerland: a photograph inside the great Lötschberg Tunnel, driven for nine-and-three-quarter miles under some of the greatest mountains of the Bernese Oberland. The tunnel was opened in 1913.

to enjoy the scenery, particularly if travelling in some of the older, cramped, non-corridor carriages that were such a feature of continental railway journeys in the years before World War One. When electrification did come to the St Gothard line, it did not immediately attain to the standards of speed and efficiency that we enjoy today, when the great international express trains are taken up the 'ramps' to the St Gothard tunnel at sustained speeds of more than double those of steam days.

Another great and superbly scenic Alpine route had scarcely become known to foreign travellers when war came in 1914. This was the magnificent Lötschberg line – to name it in full, the Bern–Lötschberg–Simplon – striking south from Spiez on the Lake of Thun, through the heart of the Bernese Oberland, to reach the Rhône valley and link up with the main line of the Swiss Federal Railways at Brigue, at the northern end of the Simplon tunnel. The Lötschberg line, which was opened throughout in 1913, was electric from the outset, and it was indeed a trail-blazer. Although most of the railways of Switzerland were then being taken over by the federal government, the Lötschberg was privately promoted, with the strong backing, however, of the Canton of Bern. It was this private railway, with a main line only fifty-three miles long, which made the decision, not only to electrify from the start, but also to use a system of electrification that was eventually to become standard throughout Switzerland. Technicalities apart, the Lötschberg is one of the most grandly picturesque mountain lines in Switzerland. It begins with the vista down the Lake of Thun to the giant mountains lying to the south of Interlaken – the Eiger, the Mönch and the Jungfrau – and then climbs into the Kander valley on a continuous gradient of 1 in 37.

No word-picture can convey the utter magnificence of the mountain scenery of Felsenberg, Blausee-Mitholz and Kandersteg, through which the line ascends by a series of spirals, open loops and tunnels. At one stage three successive levels of the line can be seen on the same mountain side. The summit tunnel, from Kandersteg to Goppenstein, is nine miles long and the contrast on emerging at the southern end is astonishing. From the picture-postcard beauty of the Bernese Oberland the railway leaves the tunnel to continue into the truly forbidding terrain of the Lonza Gorge. Running on a track blasted out of bare, solid rock walls, crossing deep clefts worn by mountain torrents and avalanches, the line is protected at frequent intervals by avalanche shelters of the most massive kind. Although the line itself is on a steep descending gradient the valley falls still more rapidly, and there is an ever-increasing sheer drop from the railway to the valley floor. Then comes a long tunnel and, if the traveller is fortunate enough to have a seat on the right-hand side of the carriage, the exit from the tunnel brings the surprise of a lifetime. Instead of the savage, desolate Lonza Gorge, there spreads out far below the smiling, green valley of the Rhône. In another ten miles the Lötschberg line is down to

succession of spiral tunnels could have been asphyxiating. The locomotives used were German-built four-cylinder compound 4–6–0s, of a design originated by the celebrated Bavarian firm of Maffei. During the war however plans for the electrification of the mountain section of the line, between Erstfeld and Bellinzona, were developed and the first trials were run in 1918. While electrification, when it did come, ended the early picturesque era of the St Gothard route, with its never-ending fascination of seeing and hearing hard-worked steam locomotives pounding their way up severe gradients in sublime mountain scenery, the rate of progress was tedious to the majority of passengers, rarely exceeding 22 or 23 miles per hour. Not all of them would be in the mood

river level and swinging alongside the Swiss Federal main line to enter Brigue. Because of the war the Lötschberg line remained largely unknown as a tourist route, but with the return of peace its glories and engineering interest soon became famous. Not for the last time had this relatively small railway proved a mighty pioneer of engineering and operating practice, as we shall see later in this book.

One of the few British passenger train services that retained a semblance of its pre-war speed during the war was the Irish Mail, then providing the principal means of communication between London and Dublin. This was long before the days of air mails, and the link was a vital one, particularly in view of the political troubles that had so sadly affected Ireland from the tragic Easter of 1916. In the conveyance of the Irish Mail there persisted then, and for many years after, a survival of the earliest days of Anglo-Irish communication. Each evening the 'King's Time' was sent out from London to the Irish capital in a picturesque little ceremony that was enacted night after night on the platform at Euston. I last saw it myself in 1938. It was on 1 August 1848 that the Irish Mail train made its inaugural journey. The departure time was 8.45 p.m. and it remained so for upwards of a hundred years. About 8.30 p.m. a postman from St-Martins-le-Grand Post Office would come down the Euston platform carrying a leather pouch; it contained a watch, and he handed it over to the postmaster of the travelling post office on the train, who signed a receipt for it. It was carried to Holyhead, thence by the mail steamer, and so to the chief Post Office in Dublin. After the war, with the coming of wireless time-signals, the watch was not conveyed beyond Holyhead, but the fact that so picturesque a custom was continued right down to the time of World War Two serves to emphasise the traditions and romance behind the conveyance of the Irish Mail.

I have written earlier of the immense problem of fuel supply created by the basing of the Grand Fleet at Scapa Flow, in the Orkney Islands. There was equally the problem of personnel. While the attenuated wartime train services of the London and North Western and Caledonian Railways could, with additional overcrowding, have coped with the flow of sailors going on and returning from leave, it would have been an entirely different matter north of Edinburgh or Perth, where the resources of the Scottish railways were already strained to the utmost.

To meet this situation a 'Daily Naval Special' was run from Euston to Thurso, all the year round except on Sundays, leaving London at 3 p.m. and reaching Thurso at 12.45 p.m. the next day. While the main battle fleet was at Scapa Flow the battle cruiser squadrons were based at Rosyth, and in consequence of this the Naval Special took the North British rather than the Caledonian route from Carlisle, made a twenty-minute stop in Edinburgh, and then stopped also at Inverkeithing, just north of the Forth Bridge, for the benefit of men whose ships were based at Rosyth. Thence the train continued over the North British line to Perth, where the Highland Railway took

over, for the long haul to Thurso. While there were several other intermediate stops for locomotive purposes the only booked passenger stops were at Inverness (for breakfast), Alness, and Invergordon – both of the latter being adjacent to naval bases. The train was confined to naval passengers and Admiralty officials; civilians, except those possessing special permits, were debarred from using this train at any point, or the corresponding southbound train which left Thurso at 11.45 p.m. and reached Euston at

10.5 a.m. the next morning. The official name for the service might have been the Daily Naval Special, but men of the fleet had a much more picturesque name for it. To them it was always 'The Misery'!

I have written much of how railways were constructed and developed to assist the war effort during the years 1914–18, but there was one country in which the failure of railway transport, due partly to misplaced pre-war strategic planning, and still more

Dramatic scenery on the Bern–Lötschberg–Simplon Railway: the line is single tracked except through the nine-and-three-quarter miles of the Lötschberg Tunnel, and it was electrically operated from the outset.

so to lack of governmental understanding once the war had started, was a major factor in the complete collapse of the country itself. That country was, of course, Czarist Russia. Prior to 1914 Russian expectations of war had been mainly in the Far East, and towards the northern frontiers of British India. Long, expensive, and completely unviable lines had been built across the eastern wastes of Siberia, and into Central Asia, and had put the railways in a difficult financial position. When war did come, in 1914, these 'strategic' lines were of no avail in the propagation of campaigns against Germany and Austria. Lines leading to the western battle fronts were immediately overloaded, though they at first did a mammoth and successful job. But the railways received no help from the government. No priority was given to essential railway supplies; key men were drafted into the army, and naturally the whole edifice

Above. Revolt in the Desert: a train destroyed in the historic desert campaign of T. E. Lawrence–'Lawrence of Arabia'–still standing fifty years later where it was immobilised and abandoned.

Right. Colonel Lawrence, called by the Arabs 'destroyer of engines', visits the place where they were made after the war–at the North British Locomotive Company's headquarters at Springburn, Glasgow, accompanying King Feisal. Standing on the left in front is Walter M. N. Reid, a director of the company, and on the right, Hugh Reid, deputy chairman and chief managing director.

Opposite top. India. Animated scene by the trackside on the Futwah–Islampur Railway, one of the 2 foot 6 inch gauge lines.

Opposite bottom. South African Railways Class '23' 4–8–2 heads north from Bloemfontein with a seventeen-coach passenger train.

of railway operation began to totter. When at last it was realised in 1916 that military operations were being impeded by the failure of transport to maintain the necessary flow of supplies, panic measures were attempted, and by then it was too late.

A cartel of railway manufacturers attempted to profit from the desperate situation by demanding greatly increased prices. The government refused to be intimidated, and ordered instead from the U.S.A. 1,000 locomotives and 30,000 wagons, while American railwaymen were imported to reorganise the workings. But these proved to be measures of despair. Before much in the way of new equipment could arrive the Russian armies were being defeated on all hands; there was famine in the cities, which ample stocks of grain in the country districts could not relieve because the railways could not move it. In October 1917 came the revolution that placed the Bolsheviks in power. During the civil war which followed, fought inevitably along the principal railway lines, the situation deteriorated to the point of almost complete collapse of railway operation. Coal supplies were held up; locomotives were fired on freshly-cut timber, and for a time a complete embargo was imposed on the running of passenger trains in order that the only locomotives and stock in a usable condition might be employed in transporting grain to the starving cities. Railwaymen left their posts to search for food; trains were abandoned in open country, with their bunkers completely denuded of any kind of fuel. No supplies were forthcoming to repair or service locomotives and, by the year 1921, when the civil war ended, some *two-thirds* of the nominal locomotive stock of 19,000 was rusting away in engine graveyards! Not until nearly ten further years had elapsed were the railways of Russia firmly on their feet again.

The case of Russia was but an extreme instance of the extent to which railways had now become an integral part of national economics, politics and defence. Of this there was perhaps no more dramatic example than the revolt in the desert so skilfully fostered, and brilliantly sustained, by T. E. Lawrence. Ingeniously avoiding major battles he, and the tribesmen he led, caused immense embarrassment, amounting to major tactical defeats, for the Turkish armies by destruction of trains on the Medina and Hejaz railways. Among his followers Lawrence in fact became known as 'destroyer of engines'.

To victors and vanquished alike the end of World War One brought little satisfaction in the field of railways. Germany was required to hand over large quantities of rolling stock to the continental allies by way of reparations. France and Belgium had immense leeway to make up in restoring their tracks and equipment, while in Canada the financial plight of the Grand Trunk, Grand Trunk Pacific, and Canadian Northern led to the formation of the Canadian National Railways, which merger did not, however, include the highly successful Canadian Pacific. In Great Britain the armistice of November 1918 had scarcely been signed before there were ominous signs of labour unrest, while the wage

concessions that had been made during the war on a national basis made almost inevitable some re-grouping of the old companies so that the inflated wage bill could be shared more or less equitably. At the same time one of the most disquieting factors in the post-war railway situation in Great Britain was the passing from the scene, either by death, retirement, or movement to other fields, of some of the most able and eminent men, whose counsels would have been of inestimable value in the time of re-organisation that was so close at hand. There was Sir Guy Calthrop, general manager of the London and North Western, who died a victim of the terrible epidemic of influenza that swept the country at the end of 1918; Sir Cecil Paget, the brilliant commander of the R.O.D. in France, went into industry rather than returning to railway service; while Sir Henry Thornton, another of the outstanding railway managers of the day, left England to become the first President of the newly-formed Canadian National Railways. That consummate statesman among railway magnates, Sir Gilbert Claughton, the chairman of the L.N.W.R., respected and admired by railwaymen of every grade from the highest to the lowest, retired in 1921.

In the technical field some of the most interesting immediate developments in both Britain and the U.S.A. were in signalling and train control. The need for some safeguard against the inadvertent errors of signalmen and engine drivers was as pressing as it had been in 1914, when war conditions had temporarily held up development. But in England argument ranged around the form that the signal of the future should take. In America the upper-quadrant signal was in common, if not exclusive, use. In contrast to the traditional British lower-quadrant, which was inclined downwards in the clear position, the American went upwards, and it was developed to provide a third position, pointing vertically upwards. This was 'all clear'; inclined upwards was 'caution'; and horizontally outwards was 'stop'.

In the meantime an entirely new type of signal had made its appearance on the Liverpool Overhead Railway, that fascinating line which used to run just inshore from the Mersey river waterfront, and give a bird's eye view of operations in the Liverpool docks. This was the daylight colour-light signal which, by use of an ingenious and powerful lens combination, enabled light signals of such strength and con-centration to be displayed that they could be seen easily in strong sunlight from distances of up to one mile. The new signals on the Liverpool Overhead Railway were brought into service in 1920, though at that time the main line managements in Great Britain were still thinking entirely in terms of sema-phores – whether upper- or lower-quadrant did not then matter. In 1922, however, the Institution of Railway Signal Engineers decided to set up a com-mittee, whose remit was to make recommendations as to how three-position signalling might be applied to the future benefit of the railways of Great Britain. The deliberations of the committee lasted for two

years, and when its recommendations eventually came they proved to be the most historic, epoch-making, and decisive set of directives in the entire field of railway signalling.

With only one dissenting member the committee solidly recommended the use of colour-light, rather than semaphore, signals using the colours now familiar to every motorist in traffic lights: red for 'stop', yellow for 'caution' and green for 'proceed'. That was in 1924 – just fifty years ago. But the committee looked much farther ahead than the simple stop–caution–go formula. The yellow was not like its counterpart on the roads. It signified 'be prepared to stop at the next signal ahead'. They recommended an additional aspect – two yellows – which would provide a pre-liminary warning for a fast express train. The driver of one of these, sighting a 'double yellow', would understand that he was expected to stop at the next signal but one, and would have ample distance in which to slow down.

Its simplicity and its immense significance were certainly not appreciated at the time, and applications of the principles were at first slow in coming; but it has stood the test of time so well that today, with the far higher speed of trains, it is the standard system of signalling on the principal main lines of Great Britain, providing safe transit for diesel and electric trains

following each other at five-minute intervals, at 100 miles per hour. Even in Great Britain, however, not all railway engineers and operating men accepted the principle at first, but the divergencies were small compared to those that existed in the 1920s in the U.S.A. Up to that time the American railways had had a bad accident record. Quite apart from the many thousands of miles of track that had no sig-nalling at all, and where train movement was regulated by the issue to drivers of written 'train orders', there were frequent accidents in interlocked and automatically-signalled areas and the Interstate Commerce Commission began issuing mandatory recommendations for additional safety equipment to be installed on sections of line carrying a dense traffic. Before we enter into a discussion on the complicated business of automatic train control (A.T.C.) the varying forms of signalling to be seen in the U.S.A. must be mentioned. There were semaphore signals working in both the lower and the upper quadrant, some two-position and others three-, and three distinct forms of daylight light-only signals.

The ordinary three-aspect colours, red, yellow and green, were being adopted on certain lines, though the ingenious British development of the fourth aspect – the double yellow – never found favour

in America. As an alternative to the ordinary colour light, the so-called 'position light' was introduced. This consisted of a series of white lights displayed against a large black circular target. Three white lights in a horizontal line meant 'stop'; three similar lights inclined upwards was 'caution'; and three white lights vertically was the 'all clear'. This form of signal was adopted as standard on one of the greatest of American railways, the Pennsylvania.

Some railways were not content with this relatively simple display and used *colour* position-light signals. On the target the same configuration of lights was used as on the Pennsylvania, but the horizontal 'stop' line was displayed in red, the inclined 'caution' in yellow, and the vertical 'proceed' in green. As if this did not provide enough diversity, however, there developed in the U.S.A. two distinct schools of thought as to how the approach to a junction should be indicated to a driver: should he be told the route he was to follow, and left to regulate his speed accordingly, or should he be given a speed indication only? The controversy spread to Great Britain and other countries, and it was not until some years after the period of which I am now writing that it was finally resolved.

In the U.S.A., with the requirements of the Interstate Commerce Commission stated in mandatory terms, inventors and manufacturers produced a variety of systems under the general heading of automatic train control. The basic principle underlying all was the provision of apparatus which would act as an immediate reminder and corrective if a driver ignored or misinterpreted the indications given by the line-side signals. Without going into the technical details of how each effect was produced, it can be said that there were three broad systems developed and installed to a considerable extent on the eastern railways of the U.S.A., namely:

1. Continuous cab signalling, without any form of speed control.

2. An intermittent system of automatic control, which applied the train brakes if necessary.

3. A system of continuous automatic control, with visual indicators in the locomotive cabs indicating 'high', 'medium' and 'low' speed, according to the state of the line ahead.

With the third system the limits of 'high', 'medium' and 'low' speed were defined for the routes concerned, and if the speed exceeded those limits, the brakes were automatically applied. In Great Britain, with the experience of accidents in pre-war years still clearly in mind, these American developments were closely watched, but the general feeling was that the requirements of the Interstate Commerce Commission were demanding equipment that was unnecessarily elaborate and expensive. A committee was set up to examine the whole situation, from both signalling and locomotive operating points of view, and it was some time before any conclusions were reached and recommendations made.

On the continent of Europe, in the rehabilitation of railways after the war interest at first centred on France. No changes were made in the administrative structure of the various companies, though there was considerable pressure for a time to evolve standard types of locomotive which would be adopted by all. But from the outset the Nord stood out against any such proposals. The company had been disappointed in having to abandon development of the great du Bousquet 4–6–4 in pre-war years, and to accept as an expedient an improvised version of the

Alsace-Lorraine 4–6–2. After the war its management and engineers were anxious to resume their own highly individual practice. This stand against unification of design set the pace for others, and both the Orléans and the P.L.M. continued to go their several ways. So in 1923 under the direction of Monsieur Bréville the Nord introduced a splendid new 'Pacific' design, while in 1925 there came the gigantic P.L.M. 4–8–2s, designed specially for the hilly section that came in the middle of an otherwise level main line from Paris to Marseilles. The 4–8–2s were used on the 92-mile length through the Côte d'Or mountains, between Laroche and Dijon. The immediate post-war development on the Orléans was slower in coming; but when it did, by the hand of André Chapelon, it was to shake the entire steam locomotive world to its foundations. In the meantime it was the

of the war about railway unification in Britain, but what was actually decreed by Parliament was the 'grouping' scheme, in which all except a few joint and local railways were merged into four large administrations. It was a grouping by companies, rather than a rationalisation by territories, and it had some rather odd results geographically. Outstanding among these oddities was the case of the West Highland line. Prior to 1923 it had been part of the North British Railway. In the grouping scheme this company became part of the London and North Eastern Railway which thus became possessed, at Arisaig in Inverness-shire, of the most *westerly* station in Great Britain! But so far as administration and engineering were concerned all the groups, except the Great Western, took some little time to settle down after the inevitable upheaval of amalgamation, inter-

London and North Eastern Railway: the great crossing at the east end of Newcastle Central.

'Pacifics' of Bréville that 'hit the headlines', and their performance on the boat trains between Calais and Paris was used by certain English commentators as a stick with which to scourge the backs of British locomotive designers who outside commentators thought were rather dragging their feet.

It was really not surprising that British locomotive development was moving rather slowly in the early 1920s. There had been much talk in the later months

changes of personnel between the various constituents and clashes of personality at high, medium and low levels. The Great Western was scarcely affected, because amalgamation in its case concerned only certain of the local lines in Wales, and the absorption of others. So the Great Western had something of a start on the other groups in that facet of railway operation most appealing to enthusiastic onlookers – the steam locomotive. At first the others continued to rely on pre-grouping types, with little in the way of detail modification.

The London and North Eastern was in the most fortunate position of the three, for only a few months before the grouping H.N. (later Sir Nigel) Gresley had built two very large 'Pacific' engines for the Great Northern Railway, and the design was subsequently accepted as an L.N.E.R. standard. The L.N.E.R. came very prominently into the public eye in 1925 with the celebration of the Railway Centenary in

Japanese National Railways: one of the celebrated 'C51' class of 3 foot 6 inch gauge 'Pacific' locomotives of 1923. This one was allocated to working the Imperial train.

September of that year. It was a hundred years since the momentous opening of the Stockton and Darlington Railway, and all the magnificent pageantry of the celebration took place at Darlington, in the heart of L.N.E.R. territory. All the British railways co-operated wholeheartedly, in what proved to be a wonderful display of past and present. George Stephenson's *Locomotion*, with which the Stockton and Darlington Railway was opened, was made to run once again and haul a train of chaldron wagons carrying a highly picturesque load of 'period' passengers. *Locomotion* did not, however, run under her own steam. A petrol engine, cleverly concealed in her works, provided the power; but equally ingenious was the way in which the old engine was made to 'smoke' realistically from the chimney.

The year 1925 was not only one of pageantry and celebration. It was one of acute controversy in locomotive design between the practices of the Great Western Railway, continued from the precepts of Churchward into the new and highly successful 'Castle' class 4–6–0s, and the Great Northern, as exemplified in the new Gresley 'Pacifics'. An interchange trial was arranged in the spring of 1925, in which a 'Castle' worked for a fortnight between King's Cross and Doncaster, while a Gresley 'Pacific' worked on the G.W.R. – during the second week on the severe duty of the Cornish Riviera Express between Paddington and Plymouth. The results, while outwardly favouring the 'Castle', included so many

modifying circumstances as to be technically inconclusive. It was the L.N.E.R. that was the beneficiary, since some important changes were subsequently made to the valve gear design of the Gresley 'Pacifics' which greatly improved their performance, and so reduced their coal consumption as to make possible the spectacular non-stop running between King's Cross and Edinburgh inaugurated in 1928. It was indeed remarkable that this run of $392\frac{3}{4}$ miles, the longest ever made regularly without stoppage anywhere in the world, should have been accomplished in this small country. But before we trace out the crescendo of British development which came as the London Midland and Scottish, the London and North Eastern, and the Southern Railways got into their respective strides, there are some important overseas matters to be noted.

There was first of all Japan. In September 1923 the whole world was shocked to learn of an earthquake of unprecedented violence, which in the very first shock practically destroyed the cities of Yokohama, Ofuna, Kamakura, Hiratsuka and Odawara. It was followed immediately by an enormous tidal wave, and a terrible fire swept across the capital city of Tokyo. The death toll was apocalyptic. On the railways nearly fifty stations were completely destroyed, while thirty-three locomotives, nearly 500 carriages and more than 1,000 wagons were heavily damaged. On the railways alone more than 200 people were killed, while the damage to track, bridges, tunnels and other structures was incalculable. Quite apart from the human tragedy, the setback to the railways in terms of both material and financial loss was indeed a grievous one; for although the annual budget of the administration provided a considerable sum for putting to rights the devastating effects of avalanches, floods, typhoons and volcanic eruptions, they had not previously been experienced on such a colossal scale as in September 1923. The Japanese railways had by that time developed tremendously from the primitive system described earlier in this book, although the speed of travel on the 3 foot 6 inch gauge could not then compare with contemporary European and American standards.

Discerning travellers, with wide experience of railways in most parts of the world, frequently expressed the view that the standard of passenger accommodation on Japanese railways was second to none east of Suez, and its maintenance first class. The Tokyo–Shimonoseki Limited train, running the 705 miles between the capital and the southernmost point of the main island of Honshu, was perhaps exceptional, as it was built to *train de-luxe* standards; but other long-distance trains also included dining and sleeping cars. At the prevailing speeds the journeys were long. Even the Shimonoseki Limited did not average more than 28 miles per hour overall, and its speed on level stretches of track did not much exceed 40 miles per hour. The imperial government railways had, by 1923, developed some handsome and workmanlike modern 'Pacifics' for passenger service and 2–8–0s for mixed traffic and heavy goods.

It is a mark of their quality that the last of the 2–8–0s have been taken out of operation only within the last twelve months; even so they are still in evidence at the sidings of some running sheds. In 1923 the total mileage of railways in Japan was about 7,900, of which about 6,200 came under the imperial government administration. This latter figure is roughly the same as those of the larger 'grouped' railways in Great Britain at that time.

Moving still farther afield, there were some important developments on the Australian railways in the 1920s. Inter-state connections were not a major consideration when the first railways were pioneered in Australia; and although I have told earlier how the Transcontinental line came to be built, between Port Augusta and Kalgoorlie, there remained a rather primitive means of communication between the adjacent state capitals of Sydney and Brisbane until the year 1930. Up till that time the journey was made by a roundabout inland route of 715 miles. The section in New South Wales from Sydney to the border station of Wallan-garra was 492 miles long, and took seventeen hours (29 miles per hour). There one had to change from the 4 foot 8½ inch gauge N.S.W. train to the 3 foot 6 inch Queenslander, to cover the remaining 223 miles; and that took almost another ten hours. With about half an hour changing from one train to the other, and all the trans-shipment of luggage and mails, the journey between Sydney and Brisbane took nearly twenty-eight hours. (There was then no alternative of going by air. It must have been almost as quick to go by sea!) The construction of the north coast line, and the continuation on the 4 foot 8½ inch gauge for seventy miles into Queensland territory to South Brisbane, made possible a tremendous speed-up on the journey, which now takes only fifteen-and-a-half hours – an average speed of almost 40 miles per hour by the shortened route. The north coast line was opened in 1930.

Until the year 1922 Australian locomotive power was inclined to be on the small side, partly because of the moderate speeds demanded on the passenger services, and thanks to the physical nature of many of the routes which precluded running at sustained speeds such as those customary in Europe and America. This trait was especially noticeable in South Australia. Although there were some exceedingly heavy gradients to be surmounted in crossing the Mount Lofty range, it had been the practice to double-head the heaviest trains with a pair of the small but efficient 'RX' class of 4–6–0 locomotives. The chief mechanical engineer who had held office during the war years had been asked to provide larger locomotives, to avoid this duplication of men and machines, but eventually gave his opinion that it could not be done. The conditions certainly were tough. The gradients at their worst were as steep as 1 in 45 – not much easier than the Swiss Alpine slopes – and the curvature in the mountain ranges made the going even more severe. But in 1922 the government of South Australia appointed a new Commissioner of Railways, an American named W. A. Webb, and he was the kind of dynamic leader who was not prepared to take 'no' for an answer. But he was equally a diplomatist, who knew that the way to get results was not to criticise everything and everybody, and what they had done up to then. Fortunately by that time there was a new chief mechanical engineer in the person of F. J. Shea, and he took as a challenge the problem of providing new power to conquer the curves and gradients of

Panama Canal Railroad: a striking and picturesque view of the running sheds and workshops at Paraiso, taken about 1911.

the Mount Lofty range. The result was a series of locomotives that were positively gigantic by previous Australian standards, and larger and heavier than anything then running in Great Britain, rivalling the largest contemporary passenger locomotives in the U.S.A. Thirty new engines – ten each of the 4–8–2, 2–8–2, and 4–6–2 types – were built by Sir W. G. Armstrong-Whitworth and Co. of Newcastle-upon-Tyne, England, and when the first of them arrived in Australia they created a sensation. Never in all railway history had there been such a stunning step-up in power. The smart little 'RX' 4–6–0s had an all-up weight of eighty-nine tons, and a tractive effort of 22,000 pounds. Shea's 4–8–2s for hauling the Overland Express over the Mount Lofty ranges, single-handed, had a total weight of 213 tons, and a tractive effort of 51,000 pounds. No wonder the South Australians, railwaymen and general public alike, were staggered! The step-up all round was roughly two-and-a-half times – at one swoop. What is more, the great engines fulfilled every expectation, and their further development, in the 1930s, continued this amazing success story on the South Australian railways.

In South Africa, the amalgamation of railways that had followed the establishment of the Union in 1910 had been wholly successful and the South African railways were firmly set on the course that was to make them, in a remarkably short time, one of the greatest national railway systems of the world.

In building his great engines F. J. Shea had the advantage of the South Australian 5 foot 3 inch gauge. No such facility favoured his contemporaries on the South African railways where the 3 foot 6 inch gauge prevailed. But while the gauge itself was narrow the loading gauge allowed the use of locomotives and carriages wider and taller than on the 4 foot 8½ inch gauge of Great Britain. In 1925 delivery was taken from the Baldwin Locomotive Co., U.S.A., of some handsome 'Pacific' engines for the increasingly heavy express trains between Cape Town and the cities of the Transvaal; but the formidable gradients of the Hex River Pass, where the line climbs from the coastal valleys to the high tableland of the Great Karoo desert, required something different from a 'Pacific', and in the following year the first of a notable series of really big engines was introduced in the shape of the '15 CA' class 4–8–2s. These huge machines ended for ever the conception that the South African Railways were restricted in the size or power of their locomotives. The '15 CA', the first examples of which were built in Glasgow by the North British Locomotive Co., weighed, with its large bogie tender, no less than 173 tons in working order. The tractive effort was 42,000 pounds – again greater than that of any British passenger locomotive built up to that time. Although they extended considerably beyond the gauge of the rails these great engines rode very steadily up to speeds of around

One of the celebrated Great Western 'King' class 4–6–0s of 1927, of which the first, the *King George V*, represented Great Britain at the centenary celebrations of the Baltimore and Ohio Railroad in 1927. In this picture the *King William IV* is shown hauling the Cornish Riviera Express near Reading, Berkshire.

50 miles per hour, which was then about the maximum run by South African passenger trains.

Some years before the introduction of these large, but quite conventional, locomotives one of the great classic events of world railway history had taken place on one of the most severe stretches of line in South Africa, the Natal main line between Durban and Ladysmith. I have referred earlier to the Mallet articulated type of locomotive, which was being currently developed to enormous proportions in the U.S.A. The South African railways had purchased some large engines of the 2–6–6–2 type from the North British Locomotive Co. and were using these in heavy freight haulage in Natal. Then in 1921 the management was persuaded to try an articulated locomotive of the Garratt type. It was as far back as June 1908 that a consulting engineer named H. W. Garratt had taken out a patent for an articulated locomotive of novel design. It consisted of two entirely separate engine units, with a central cradle slung between them and pivotally mounted to them at each end. On this cradle was carried a single large boiler supplying steam to both engine units. Within a very short time Garratt's patent was taken up by Beyer, Peacock & Co., who realised the immense potentialities of this new form of locomotive. Not only was it a much better tracking unit, on a sharply curved road, than the Mallet, more importantly it permitted the use of a boiler of ideal dimensions – short barrel of maximum diameter, and a wide firebox, completely unencumbered by wheels underneath, giving the possibility of infinite expansion. Railway engineers in various parts of the world were interested, though rather slow to take up the new design, but Beyer, Peacock's saw its great potentialities for overseas railways running through difficult country, and it was through their advocacy that the South African railways were persuaded to try a large locomotive of the 2–6–0+0–6–2 type, and to test it against a huge four-cylinder compound Mallet. The latter had a nominal tractive effort of 65,000 pounds and weighed 179½ tons in working order; the Garratt had a tractive effort of 47,385 pounds and weighed 133½ tons. At the outset it seemed that the Garratt did not stand a chance over the twenty-seven-mile ascent at 1 in 58 from South Coast Junction, just outside Durban, to Botha's Hill.

From the very start of the trials, however, the Garratt showed powers of haulage far beyond her nominal capacity, while the huge Mallet disappointed. One thing immediately noted – which could have been seen from a study of the respective boiler designs – was that the Garratt steamed much more freely. Had the Mallet always been assured of an ample supply of steam she might have been better. But interested parties were incredulous, and to put the trials on a longer term basis, a three-month trial was arranged in the spring of 1922 between Ladysmith and Glencoe Junction. Both engines made fifty-eight round trips, of eighty-eight miles each, with roughly equal loads of about 825 tons. Detailed timings were taken on the three worst inclines, and the aggregate time on the fifty-eight trips was 5,358 minutes by the Mallet, but only 4,130 minutes by the Garratt. Furthermore, the latter engine was much more economical, and used roughly three-quarters of a ton less coal on each round trip than the Mallet. It was a triumph for the Garratt principle, and from this time onwards the Beyer-Garratt type of locomotive, as it became known, developed into one of the finest export items of the British heavy engineering industry. Beyer-Garratt locomotives, from small units for light narrow-gauge lines to monsters like the South African 'GL' class, were exported to many parts of the world and became the standard 'heavy power' on some African railways. The last chapter refers to the later successes of these superb locomotives in widely varying locations all over the world.

The Beyer-Garratt was never developed into a high-speed main line job, and while British industry was gearing itself to the needs of many developing countries overseas, a great upsurge in speed was evident in France, Great Britain and the U.S.A. Britain was at first in the lead, and in the year 1923 was the only country in the world to have any trains making average speeds of more than 60 miles per hour from start to stop.

But when the new Bréville 'Pacifics' on the Northern Railway of France began to get into their stride times almost as fast as the fastest English expresses began to be made with more than double the loads, and it was evident that in the realm of maximum power output British achievements were being left behind. The Great Western 'Castle' class, with 31,625 pounds tractive effort, was slightly surpassed in 1926 by the Southern *Lord Nelson* (33,500 pounds); but thanks to the vigorous intervention of its dynamic general manager, Sir Felix Pole, the Great Western was not long in replying. There were, however, considerations other than those of locomotive prestige alone which influenced the introduction of the ever-

famous *King George V* in the summer of 1927, when the centenary of another great railway was to be celebrated, that of the Baltimore and Ohio Railroad. It was to be celebrated in no ordinary style. A noted connoisseur of railway history, Ed Hungerford, was sent to England in 1925 to see the Railway Centenary celebrations at Darlington, and in the course of that visit he met Sir Felix Pole. Hungerford explained that the B. & O. wished to pay tribute, in its celebrations, to the British origin of railways, and would like to have a British locomotive in its pageant and exhibition. Sir Felix Pole welcomed the suggestion, and, since to him a 'British' locomotive could not be anything but one from the Great Western, immediately

Below. Pennsylvania Railroad: crack express freight train No. LCL-1, with merchandise from the New York and Philadelphia areas, nearing Pittsburgh in the early morning. The locomotive is one of the large 4–8–2 type, No. 6846.

Bottom. Delaware and Hudson Railroad: an old 'Mother Hubbard' type switcher is involved in the installation of a large new turntable at Colonil shops in 1928.

Right. A dramatic location on the Western Pacific Railroad. showing a heavy express train hauled by 4–8–2 No. 172 on a steel trestle with a Y-junction.

Below. London Midland and Scottish Railway: the 'Royal Scot' class of three-cylinder 4–6–0 designed in 1927 to run the London–Carlisle stretch of 299 miles non-stop. This photograph shows one of the class on arrival in Euston Station, London.

offered to send one of the new 'super Castles' then not beyond the design stage. The work at Swindon thereupon became a tremendous race against time, for the exhibition engine had to be in the U.S.A. by August 1927. So emerged the *King George V*, recapturing in no uncertain style the honour of being Britain's most powerful passenger locomotive, for

the tractive effort was no less than 40,300 pounds – a mighty step ahead of the *Lord Nelson*.

To say that the engine created a sensation in the U.S.A. is an understatement. The fine colouring and immaculate finish attracted immediate attention. In its name, *King George V*, it was the very embodiment of Great Britain, while in a rare touch of pageantry, arrangements were made for a young lady of regal presence, Miss Lilian Schueler, daughter of one of the B. & O. directors, to personate Britannia, and form part of the British exhibit. The assembly at Baltimore was a real *concours d'élégance* of railway rolling stock. In size the *King George V* was dwarfed by huge Canadian and American locomotives. While Britain, except in the case of the Gresley 'Pacifics' of the L.N.E.R., had remained faithful to the 4–6–0 for the heaviest express traffic, America was no longer content with 'Pacifics'. At Baltimore, both the New York Central and the Canadian Pacific were represented by 'Hudsons' – 4–6–4 type; the Baltimore and Ohio itself had a 4–8–2 which was claimed to be the heaviest passenger locomotive in the world – 330 tons with its tender. Against this the *King George V* weighed a modest 135 tons. One of the most impressive locomotives in the pageant was a brand new Canadian, the *Confederation*. This was a very large 4–8–4 of Canadian National, and in the daily parade of locomotives it steamed immediately behind the *King George V* and made a striking contrast in size.

Before the *King George V* was completed and had

begun the historic visit to the U.S.A. the competition for length of non-stop run had started. Until the summer of 1927 the record was held by the Cornish Riviera Express, not only in Great Britain but the world over. The distance was $225\frac{3}{4}$ miles, and it was covered in 247 minutes – 54·8 miles per hour. It was remarkable in one respect that the world record should still have been held by Great Britain, having regard to the size of the country; but the two principal competitors in quality and speed of passenger train service, France and the U.S.A., had limitations of their own. The French did not use water troughs; in the U.S.A. and in Canada too, the great weight of the trains resulted in such a high consumption of coal that intermediate stops had to be made to re-coal the tenders, from galleries built astride the main running lines in some cases. Upwards of 100 tons of coal was sometimes burnt in working a heavy express over the 970 miles between New York and Chicago. These limiting conditions enabled Great Britain, with its lighter trains and lower basic coal consumption of the high-grade indigenous fuel, to extend its hold on the record for length of non-stop run.

Then in September 1927 the L.M.S. scheduled the Royal Scot train non-stop in each direction between Euston and Carlisle–$299\frac{1}{4}$ miles. This was no special effort made during the height of the summer holiday season, but a run to be made day in, day out through the winter months, over a route that included the ascent over Shap, in wild Westmorland fell country.

The scene after the 'holing through' of the Great Northern Railway's Cascade Tunnel, the fulfilment of two-and-a-half years' tunnelling work beneath the Cascade Mountains. President Coolidge set off the final explosive charge by remote control from Washington on 1 May 1928.

The new 'Royal Scot' class of locomotive was used with great success in this tough assignment. But during that winter of 1927–8 the L.N.E.R. was preparing to carry the non-stop competition a stage further. Like the L.M.S., it had enough passengers, in the summer at any rate, to justify omitting all stops between King's Cross and Edinburgh, so why not, argued H. N. Gresley, make the run *actually* non-stop? It would be a magnificent piece of publicity, which the L.M.S. could not counter unless it ran the Edinburgh and Glasgow sections of the Royal Scot separately, because the point of division was at Symington, 366 miles from Euston. By the L.N.E.R. Edinburgh was 392¾ miles from King's Cross. It was of course much too long a run to be made by a single engine crew in the ordinary course, so Gresley conceived the novel idea of building tenders with a corridor connection to the train. Then, if two crews were carried, one could relieve the other half way through the journey, through the corridor of the

On the 2 foot 6 inch gauge of the Western Railway of India: three 'W' class 0–6–2s at Bilimora.

Below. The line of stately Pullman cars forming *La Flèche d'Or* in the Gare du Nord, Paris.

Opposite top. Union Pacific Railroad: this enormous westbound freight of sixty-eight cars near Sherman, Wyoming, requires *two* of the colossal 4–12–2 three-cylinder locomotives to haul it.

Opposite bottom. Italian State Railways: one of the unusual 2–6–0s with inside cylinders but outside valve gear leaving Milan (Porta Genova Station) for Alessandria.

tender. This run was introduced on 1 May 1928.

Despite all the glamour and excitement of new engine building, the running of prestige trains and the acceleration of some running times, the railway situation all over the world was increasingly disquieting. The one-time role of railways as the basic, pre-eminent means of long distance travel was being challenged by the prowess of the private motor car and by the motor lorry. The trunk roads were not crowded and although some countries had hampering speed limits, these were difficult to enforce generally. Where railways remained the most suitable means of transport, in commuter areas, the requirement for the provision of an intense service morning and evening, with very little traffic between times, was uneconomic in view of the poor utilisation of highly sophisticated equipment. In France at first the financial situation of the companies was unaffected by falling receipts and rising costs because they were still supported by the fixed dividends guaranteed to the shareholders by the Government. There was anxiety all the same, since the guarantees were due to expire in relatively few years. In Great Britain the railways were operating under legislation established largely in Victorian times; they were common carriers, and had to compete against rapidly developing and expanding road services on terms that were becoming increasingly disadvantageous. In the U.S.A. it was much the same, except that the decline in railway business seemed if anything to be more rapid than in Europe, with the further competition of civil aviation.

Then, to add to the difficulties, came the great worldwide slump, which had a paralysing effect on any kind of industry needing capital investment for its satisfactory continuance. On railways all over the world it was a case of 'making do'. No money was available for new locomotives or coaching stock or the modernisation of stations, some of which were sixty, seventy or eighty years old. But on all hands the principle of safety was uppermost, and share-

Above. The first locomotive on the Turksib Railway, U.S.S.R., with a crowd of interested onlookers.

Right. Narrow gauge in Colorado: a little Rio Grande 2–8–2 climbing to Cerro summit, west of Cimarron, Colorado.

Opposite. Narrow gauge in Colorado: mountain dwarfs train. A Rio Grande Southern 2–8–0 nearing the end of the Telluride branch.

holders came to accept the precept that what money was available should be spent in maintaining track, signalling and existing rolling stock in impeccable condition rather than for the paying of dividends. Very many people, with large investments in British, American and a variety of overseas railways, such as the British-owned companies in the Argentine, received no return on their capital. This section of the book has the heading 'Stress and Strain'. It began with the threat and onset of war; it continued through the difficult aftermath, and it ends pessimistically in the midst of the greatest slump in the world's history.

Above. A 2 foot 6 inch gauge Indian 'Pacific' (built by Kerr Stuart, Stoke-on-Trent, in 1922) leaving Yelahanka, on the morning train from Chintamani to Yesvantpur.

Above right. New Jersey Central Railroad: an enthusiastic crowd watching the departure of The Blue Comet from Red Bank in February 1929.

Right. The most powerful British 4–4–0: a 'Schools' class of the Southern, introduced in 1930, here seen near Reading, Berkshire. Engine No. 926 of this class is now working on the Cape Breton Railway, Nova Scotia.

Part 5

Resurgence: Towards a New Age

It is remarkable to recall that from the very depths of the great slump of the early 1930s there came some of the most enterprising and exciting developments that had been seen in the world of railways since the pioneer days of the nineteenth century. It seemed as though the well-nigh crippling financial stringencies acted as a challenge, both to the technical men and to those who planned train services. Certain it is that there were developments in the science of locomotive engineering more far-reaching than any witnessed since the earlier years of the twentieth century, and this was matched on the traffic side by an astonishing upsurge in speed. It was, however, significant of the general condition of world trade that the overwhelming bulk of new development took place in passenger business, and that the spectacular new services in the most advanced countries concerned no more than a few prestige trains, and not an acceleration of the services as a whole. In the high speed 'club' Britain, France and the U.S.A. were joined in no half measure by Canada and Germany. For a short time indeed Canada was operating some of the fastest start-to-stop schedules in the world. The earlier part of this concluding section of the book is therefore concerned mainly with express locomotive design and the steadily increasing speed of the crack trains.

In view of this it is perhaps a little odd that a new development that was later to prove of the utmost significance for the entire future of railways in most parts of the world had one of its earliest and most successful applications in the Argentine, on the Buenos Aires Great Southern Railway, and that a collateral development of scarcely less importance was in progress on the rejuvenated railways of Soviet Russia. This was the introduction of the diesel-electric locomotive. By the beginning of the 1930s the marked superiority of electric traction over steam for intensely-operated commuter services, and for working over heavily graded mountain routes, had been amply demonstrated in many lands. The St Gothard line had been electrified, and electrification of the Bombay suburban areas of the Great Indian Peninsula Railway had been extended to include the exceptionally steep gradients over the Western Ghats, thus exemplifying in one general project both the facets of train operation in which electric traction is seen at its most advantageous. But the capital cost of electric traction then, as now, was very high, and the slump years virtually precluded any appreciable extensions, except where the density of traffic

guaranteed a good and immediate return on the capital invested. The development of the diesel heavy-oil engine in marine practice seemed to offer a very attractive compromise between steam and full electrification. The diesel-electric locomotive provided the traction characteristics of a 'straight electric', while carrying its own power house. It could be introduced immediately on lines that had previously been entirely steam, and because it needed so little in the way of servicing it could do the work of at least two steam locomotives. Even in its earliest days it was claimed that a diesel-electric locomotive could be available for traffic for twenty out of every twenty-four hours.

At the same time the electric motors were relatively expensive, and design engineers sought other means of transmitting the power generated by the diesel engine to the road wheels of the locomotive. For units of small power a straight mechanical drive through a gear box similar to that of an ordinary road motor

vehicle was tried. The Russians did not stop at small locomotives, and applied a geared drive to a 1,200 horse-power heavy freight locomotive. The Germans tried compressed air transmission, and in 1930 figures were published to show that costs for the geared diesel were only 82 per cent of those for the diesel-electric, and those for the diesel compressed air only 63 per cent. In the end, however, it was the diesel-electric that proved most suitable for immediate

Railroading in the raw: a sulphur company's mixed train in the shadow of Volcan Tocora in the High Andes.

railway development, and the pioneer Argentine locomotive merits a special mention. At that time most of the principal officers of the Argentine railways were British, but the chief mechanical engineer of the B.A.G.S. was an exception. He was a brilliant, if violent-tempered, Italian named P. C. Saccaggio; and he took two standard 600 horse-power marine diesel engines of Sulzer manufacture and had them built in, by Armstrong, Whitworth & Co. of Newcastle-upon-Tyne, to what was called a 'power unit'.

The work that was then going on behind locked doors, as it were, at La Grange, Illinois, was in little more than ten years to sweep across the American railways like a forest fire. In the early 1930s, however, steam traction still seemed to be as impregnably established in the U.S.A. and Canada as it was in Great Britain and France.

It was in France, on the Paris–Orléans Railway, that the greatest breakthrough since the introduction of the Schmidt superheater came from the outstanding

This supplied power to an otherwise conventional five-coach multiple-unit electric train set. This, instead of drawing its power from a 'third rail' or overhead line, took it from the diesel generator sets in the power unit at the head of the train. It was an ingenious, if short-lived, conception, while in the meantime the Russians were developing a completely self-contained diesel-electric locomotive, also powered by Sulzer engines. In view of developments on the nationalised British railways thirty years later, this early association of the famous Swiss firm of Sulzer with diesel railway traction is most interesting.

It was natural at that time that no particular interest was shown in diesel traction by the home railways of Great Britain and France. In the slump years there was an urgent need to bolster up the sagging coal industries of both countries, and any development that would have meant importing fuel from abroad would have been unpatriotic, to say the least. In the two countries where diesel traction was being pioneered, fuel oil was more readily available. The situation in the U.S.A. was not so clear-cut. The eastern railroads had ready access to ample supplies of coal, but in the Middle West and western states many of the railways were making extensive use of oil-fired steam locomotives. Furthermore, the Electro-Motive Division of General Motors had now been set up, with men of outstanding technical ability and business acumen in the persons of the Ketterings, father and son, and the Dilworths, father and son.

genius of André Chapelon. The Orléans had been one of the earliest users of the de Glehn four-cylinder compound system. 'Atlantic' engines of the Orléans type had been purchased by the English Great Western Railway for trial, and it was on the Orléans that the first locomotive of the 'Pacific' type ever to run in Europe was introduced in 1907. These early compounds had been improved by the addition of superheaters, but the war years and the subsequent period of rehabilitation had precluded any major developments. Then, when André Chapelon took office, there was no money. Enhanced locomotive power was urgently needed, and the only course available to him was to see how the existing engines could be improved. Chapelon took one of the larger-wheeled Orléans 'Pacifics' first introduced in 1912, and fairly laid bare its innermost workings. In a compound locomotive the aim should naturally be to make the high and low pressure cylinders do an equal share of the work, but under scientific testing he found that at a moderate output of 1,000 horse-power, the low pressure cylinders were hardly doing any work at all. In the haulage of a 375-ton train at 66 miles per hour on level track the horse-power was 918 in the high pressure cylinders, and only 59 in the low. When working much harder, some power output was extracted from the low pressure cylinders, but even so the proportions were unacceptable to any scientifically-minded engineer: 1,460 horse-power for the high pressure and only 390 for the low pressure.

Above. French National Railways (S.N.C.F.): the Golden Arrow de luxe boat express for the English traffic passing Hesdignuel, between Etaples and Boulogne, drawn by one of the famous Chapelon 'Pacific' locomotives of the 'E' series.

Opposite top. The 'Heber Creeper' near Heber City, Utah, on a trip to Bridal Falls.

Opposite bottom. The first mountain cog railway in the world, built in 1869 up Mount Washington, New England.

The potential was there all right; the problem was to step up the output from the low pressure cylinders to something nearly, if not fully, equal to that of the high pressure. An enormous amount of power was obviously being wasted, and Chapelon found the reason in the out-of-date and ineffective design of cylinders, valves and steam passages.

The money he had for the reconstruction of one engine permitted the fitting of entirely new cylinders and all their associated equipment, while into the boiler he introduced an enlarged superheater and a twin-orifice blast-pipe and chimney. The original frames of the engine were massive and could be retained, while the boiler itself could be modified. One of the most important of the new features, which was nevertheless obscured, was the internal streamlining of all the ports and passages to give the freest possible flow of steam. The rebuilt engine still looked very French, with numerous pipes, reservoirs, valves and so on hung on outside; but in performance it was phenomenally transformed. While in its original form there was difficulty in getting an output of 1,800 horse-power, in its rebuilt form it topped the 3,000 mark, with an almost perfect distribution of the work between the high and low pressure cylinders. Then Chapelon went one better. He took one of the smaller-wheeled 'Pacifics' of 1907 vintage and applied all the techniques that had proved so successful on the transformed 'Pacific', but rebuilt the earlier engine into a 4–8–0. The results were even more astonishing, and yielded maximum horse-powers of around 4,000. The results of these tests were published in detail in the English technical press, and created something of a sensation. On the London and North Eastern Railway H. N. Gresley, who was on terms of intimate personal friendship with the leading French engineers, journeyed to France and saw the Chapelon rebuilds at work. Their outstanding performance lay in the haulage of very heavy trains at medium speed, since at that time railway speed in France was still limited by law to a maximum of 120 kilometres per hour (74·5 miles per hour).

The record average speed for a start-to-stop run then rested with the U.S.A., by virtue of a journey made as long previously as 1905, by the American express of the Philadelphia and Reading Railroad. With an observer of unquestioned international reputation on board, Sir William Acworth, the fifty-five-and-a-half miles from Camden, Philadelphia, to Atlantic City were covered in 42 minutes 33 seconds start to stop – an average speed of 78·3 miles per hour. On 16 September 1931 this was narrowly beaten by the Cheltenham Spa express of the G.W.R., when the 4–6–0 engine *Launceston Castle* ran from Swindon to Paddington in 58 minutes 20 seconds start to stop, an average of 79·5 miles per hour. In June 1932 the Great Western improved on its own world record with the engine *Tregenna Castle*, cutting the Swindon–Paddington time down to 56 minutes 47 seconds – 81·7 miles per hour. In the course of this run, with a trainload of 195 tons, it twice attained a speed of 92 miles per hour on level track. This was a most gratifying achievement, albeit made with a relatively light train. But before the end of the year 1932 the centre of interest in speed developments had begun to pass to Germany.

So far as daily booked speeds were concerned, apart from individual records like that of the G.W.R. on 5 June 1932, the winter timetables of 1932–3 gave the following results:

Aggregate European mileage scheduled daily at 55 miles per hour (start to stop) and over

Country	64 m.p.h. and over	62 m.p.h. and over	60 m.p.h. and over	58 m.p.h. and over	55 m.p.h. and over
Great Britain	235	634	2080	4422	18,155
Ireland	—	—	54	118	573
France	243	818	2373	5871	15,253
Germany	—	—	—	387	2,076
Italy	—	—	—	—	286

At that period also the fastest booked start-to-stop runs in Europe were:

Country	Railway	Route	Distance, *miles*	Time, *minutes*	m.p.h.
England	G.W.R.	Swindon–Paddington	77·4	65	71·4
France	Nord	Paris–St Quentin	95·1	88	64·8
Germany	State	Berlin–Hamburg	178·2	179	59·7
Italy	State	Milan–Verona	92·5	97	57·2
Ireland	G.N.R.	Dublin–Drogheda	54·3	54	60·3

The contemporary North American figures were:

Country	64 m.p.h. and over	62 m.p.h. and over	60 m.p.h. and over	58 m.p.h. and over	55 m.p.h. and over
U.S.A.	57	454	2022	5770	16,721
Canada	248	458	650	972	1,324

Opposite top. 'Castle' class locomotive climbing westwards out of the Severn Tunnel with the South Wales Pullman: a painting by Terence Cuneo.

Opposite bottom. Southern Pacific cab-forward 4–8–8–2 steam locomotive: a painting by Harlan Hiney.

The fastest scheduled start-to-stop runs were:

Country	Railway	Route	Distance, *miles*	Time, *minutes*	m.p.h.
Canada	Canadian Pacific	Smith's Falls to Montreal West	124	108	68·9
U.S.A.	Pennsylvania	Plymouth to Fort Wayne	64·1	61	63·0

Such an analysis could be very gratifying to British observers, but this situation did not last for long. All these runs were made with steam traction, but in the autumn of 1932 the German State Railways took delivery of a twin high-speed railcar set, of the articulated type, with two bodies resting on three bogies. It was almost completely streamlined, and powered by two diesel-electric engines, one at each end of the twin set. It was originally announced that it would run between Berlin and Hamburg to the same schedule as that quoted in the table above; but the year 1933 was not far advanced before some very much faster running was being regularly made. In the summer service the 'Flying Hamburger', as the diesel-electric railcar set was known, was booked to run the 178·1 miles from Berlin to Hamburg in 138 minutes, at a start-to-stop average speed of 77·4 miles per hour – a service unprecedented in world railway history.

It was then that H. N. Gresley of the London and North Eastern Railway invited the makers of the Flying Hamburger to submit details of the fastest service they could provide between London and

Above. Start of a new era of European high speed: the streamlined diesel railcar train The Flying Hamburger goes into service between Berlin and Hamburg, December 1932.

Right. The British streamlined era began in September 1935, with the inauguration of the Silver Jubilee service between King's Cross and Newcastle. Seen here is one of Sir Nigel Gresley's 'A4' 'Pacific' locomotives in British Railways livery.

Newcastle. Gresley quickly showed he could do better than this with steam, and tests with the engine *Papyrus* showed that an overall time of four hours between London and Newcastle was a thoroughly practical proposition. In the course of a magnificent day's work this engine and the crews that handled her broke at least three world records:

1. A distance of 12·3 miles run at 100·6 miles per hour.

2. 300 miles of one round trip at an average speed of 80 miles per hour.

3. A maximum speed of 108 miles per hour.

Authority was then given for the introduction of a four-hour service to Newcastle in the autumn of 1935, which would also include a brief intermediate stop at Darlington, providing connections to the important industrial conurbation on Teesside.

Hitherto the maximum demands upon the Gresley 'Pacific' engines had been made in hauling trains of 450 to 550 tons at average speeds of 55 to 60 miles per hour, but for the new train, which would weigh less than 250 tons, a cruising speed of 90 miles per hour on level track would be needed. Gresley felt that some modifications to his standard engines were desirable, and he applied the Chapelon technique of internal streamlining and improved valve design; the new engines were externally streamlined also. It was the year of the Silver Jubilee of King George V's reign, and not only was the new train named The Silver Jubilee, but it was finished throughout in silver – locomotives and coaches alike. The effect, when it

first came to London in September 1935, was breath-taking; but even more so was the trial run on the 27th of that month. A maximum speed of 112½ miles per hour was attained, and the train averaged 107½ miles per hour for twenty-five miles continuously – a new world record. This was a special trial made to see how much time was in hand on the new schedule, and the train went into regular service a few days later with complete success. In comparison with the Flying Hamburger which had seats for 102 passengers, the Silver Jubilee had seats for 122 in the compartments, and for another seventy-six in the restaurant cars. The booked time of 198 minutes for the 232¼ miles between King's Cross and Darlington involved an average speed of 70·4 miles per hour.

Since his installation as president of the executive in 1927, and his subsequent chairmanship of the L.M.S., Sir Josiah Stamp had become convinced that no real technical advances were possible so long as the London and North Western and Midland factions, brought together by the grouping of 1923, remained poised in a kind of balance of power. He decided that the only course was to bring in a complete outsider as chief mechanical engineer. The choice fell upon William Arthur Stanier, principal assistant to the chief mechanical engineer of the Great Western – a man of broad outlook, outstanding ability in all workshop techniques, but above all a charming personality. On 1 January 1932 he took office at Euston, with the most comprehensive mandate ever given to a British chief mechanical engineer.

Snow clearance at West Yellowstone, Montana, on the Union Pacific.

Sir Josiah Stamp looked at the locomotive department with the eye of an accountant and a statistician. If individual engines could work longer turns of duty, better utilisation could be obtained and the service operated with a reduced number of locomotives in commission. In three words Stanier's mandate was to 'scrap and build': to replace the heterogeneous collection of engines from the constituent companies with an efficient modern stud. Naturally and justifiably he took as the sheet anchor of his programme the

German State Railways: derailment of a Berlin–Cologne express.

trump card of the Great Western practice with which he was so familiar – the Churchward standard boiler, with its tapered barrel and highly specialised version of the Belpaire firebox developed at Swindon. These boilers were more expensive than the simpler forms used on certain existing L.M.S. types, like the Royal Scots, but from his Great Western experience Stanier knew that they paid for themselves over and over again in reduced maintenance charges and freedom from failure on the road.

While Sir Josiah Stamp naturally had his sights trained firmly on the 9,000 assorted and ageing locomotives of the constituent companies, the 'neon-lights display' of the L.M.S. passenger service was of course the Anglo-Scottish, over the West Coast main line from Euston. It was proposed to run straight through between London and Glasgow without a change. To prepare for this, in 1933, Stanier built two prototype 'Pacific' engines, *The Princess Royal* and *The Princess Elizabeth*. These two huge engines, the largest and heaviest yet seen in Great Britain for purely passenger service, were the prototypes of a famous series which from the autumn of 1935 were capable of doing the London–Glasgow run, not non-stop but with turn-round times of little more than three hours at each end. The high performance and mechanical reliability of these engines began to set new standards in British locomotive practice.

At first the L.M.S. made no attempt to counter the new-found high-speed service on the L.N.E.R.

exemplified by the Silver Jubilee train. But in Coronation Year, 1937, the L.N.E.R. was planning a six-hour service to Edinburgh and in face of this the L.M.S. could not well stand aside. West Coast supporters hoped that the L.M.S. would reply with six hours to Glasgow – a run nine miles longer it is true; and then in November 1936 came two astonishing trial runs. On the down journey a train of Silver Jubilee tonnage was conveyed, 230 tons; and with the 'Pacific' engine *Princess Elizabeth* this was taken to Glasgow *non-stop* in 5 hours 53 minutes 38 seconds – an average speed throughout of 68 miles per hour. On the following day, with an extra coach added, the return to Euston was made more than nine minutes quicker, at an average speed of 70 miles per hour exactly. Although this was easily a world record for steam, over such a distance as 401·4 miles non-stop, there were diesel developments in the U.S.A. which eclipsed it by a big margin. As in the case of the Gresley developments on the L.N.E.R. following the London–Newcastle trial runs with *Papyrus* in March 1935, the L.M.S. prepared a new design for the Coronation Scot service to be introduced in the summer of 1937. But while the new L.N.E.R. streamliner the Coronation provided the six-hour service to Edinburgh that had been foreshadowed, the L.M.S. felt that for their first essay in streamlined high-speed running, a six-hour service to Glasgow would have been too adventurous, and the new train had six-and-a-half hours instead.

While the new Coronation express of the L.N.E.R. wrested, by a few decimal points, the claim of the G.W.R. Cheltenham Flyer to be Britain's fastest train in running the 188·2 miles from King's Cross to York in 157 minutes at an average speed of 72 miles per hour, by the winter of 1937 British all-round supremacy in high-speed mileage had become a thing of the past. The U.S.A. was now taking its rightful place in relation to the size of the country and its railway mileage. But since development now took place so rapidly, both with steam and diesel-hauled services, I shall reserve comment for the time of the last pre-war year, which in most ways marked the zenith of American passenger train services, rather than refer to the increases chronologically. At this stage I may add that the fastest start-to-stop railway runs in the world were then made in Germany, by the *Fliegende Kölner*, a four-car diesel railcar set of the Flying Hamburger type, which ran from Berlin (Zoo) to Hanover, 157·8 miles, in 115 minutes (82·3 miles per hour) and from Hanover on to Hamm, 109·6 miles, in 80 minutes (82·2 miles per hour). This supremacy was, however, short-lived, for all the high-speed railcar trains in Germany were withdrawn in the winter of 1937–8. The nearest American approach to the Cologne train was the diesel-electric streamliner of the Union Pacific, the *City of Denver*, which ran the 62·4 miles from Grand Island to Columbus in 46 minutes start-to-stop – a speed of 81·4 miles per hour.

In total contrast to the breathless haste of railway travel in Europe and the U.S.A. was the leisurely progress on that immensely long highroad of Soviet Russia, the Trans-Siberian Railway, over which the speed of the one daily through train from Moscow to Vladivostok has not perceptibly increased in the last forty years. To the great majority of those who study railways in their multifarious aspects the Trans-Siberian Railway is a mere name. One can look it up in Cook's Continental Timetable and find that today the Russia express leaves Moscow at 10·05 hours and arrives in Vladivostok at 13·00 hours on the *eighth* day, having covered 5,778 miles. Allowing for the seven-hour difference in the clocks at each end the actual travelling time is six days and twenty hours, an average speed of 35 miles per hour. But what was the journey like? The greater part of the mileage is through Siberia, a name with a somewhat ominous ring about it. At the time of which I am writing, the mid-1930s, the eastern end of the line was in the throes of political unrest. The most direct line to Vladivostok had been over the one-time Chinese Eastern Railway, through the province of Manchuria; but the transfer of the province to Japan after the Sino-Japanese War and the change of name to Manchukuo, led to the purchase of Soviet interests in the Chinese Eastern Railway by Japan. Since then the through service between Moscow and Vladivostok has taken the longer, all-Russian route, skirting the northern frontier of Manchukuo. The two routes join at Chita (Siberia), about 1,900 miles out of Vladivostok.

and precipitous were the shores round the southern end of the lake that construction of the line was postponed and for five years, from 1899 to 1904, passengers and goods were shipped across the lake by ferry, or borne by train over the ice in the depths of winter. Such methods were, however, always regarded as a temporary expedient, and a remarkable line, including no fewer than forty-two tunnels, was blasted literally out of the solid rock along the shores of the lake. West of Lake Baikal is the beautiful city

Above. A high-speed streamlined 'Pacific' locomotive of the London Midland and Scottish Railway, being shipped to the U.S.A. for the New York World's Fair in 1939.

Left. Railways of Soviet Russia: one of the 'E' series of 0–10–0 locomotives, mass-produced from 1930, from Lugansk Works.

The country from there westwards has been compared to that of the Highlands of Scotland; here the line skirts the southern slopes of the Yablondi mountains, well-watered by numerous rivers and interspersed with pine forests. The scenic gem of the whole route comes in the approach to Lake Baikal, surrounded by mountains on all sides. From a railway construction viewpoint the line round Lake Baikal presents a parallel to the line along the northern shores of Lake Superior on the Canadian Pacific. So rocky

of Irkutzk, and from there the train makes its seemingly interminable way from forest lands to Steppes. The 1,540 miles from Irkutzk to Omsk take over forty hours, and there is still another 1,686 miles before Moscow is reached. The train stops at every station of any size, sometimes for twenty or twenty-five minutes since, in the 1930s, wood-fired steam locomotives were still in general use and time was taken in stacking fresh supplies of logs onto the tender. In summertime passengers could take a saunter into

Trans-Siberian Railway, with most of the route electrified, I am not in a position to say.

In the last few years before World War Two two things seemed to dominate the world railway scene. The first was the fight of the British railways to secure the amendment of statutory regulations which were proving a crippling handicap in their competition for traffic in modern conditions; the second was the phenomenal development of passenger train services in the U.S.A. The first was regarded with indifference by the press and public alike (where there was no outright hostility). The railways of Britain got little sympathy in their campaign for 'a square deal', and little had been achieved when all the railways in Great Britain were brought under government control for the duration of the war. The American evolution in high-speed passenger service was such as to draw forth panegyrics of praise from every branch of railway opinion throughout the world. It was remarkable also that while diesel traction claimed the fastest booked runs, reliance continued to be placed on steam for a high proportion of the total high-speed mileage. It is interesting to study statistically the passenger train situation as it existed in the summer of 1939, and see how strikingly it contrasted with the position that existed only seven years earlier. Two tables are presented, one showing the aggregate daily mileage covered respectively at 60, 64, and 70 miles per hour and over, and the other showing the fastest scheduled runs.

the forest during such stops, as ample warning was always given of impending departure. The first signal was one clang of the bell, the second two, and the final one three. If some passenger cut things a bit fine there was no need to worry; the acceleration was so slow that an active person could easily run after the train and catch it. How things are today on the

Aggregate mileage of runs at 60 m.p.h. and over, summer 1939, daily

Country	Traction	70 m.p.h. and over	64 m.p.h. and over	60 m.p.h. and over
Belgium	Steam	230	295	2525
Bohemia	Diesel	—	65	233
Denmark	Diesel	—	76	709
France	Diesel	936	2421	3006
,,	Electric	70	795	3180
,,	Steam	—	830	4341
Germany	Diesel	4694	6979	8321
,,	Electric	—	310	1142
,,	Steam	356	722	4151
Great Britain	Steam	730	1829	12,016
Holland	Diesel	—	599	3147
,,	Electric	—	1792	4235
Italy	Diesel	—	729	2609
,,	Electric	1187	2970	4510
,,	Steam	—	—	205
Poland	Diesel	—	28	107
Switzerland	Electric	—	—	150
U.S.A.	Diesel	3284	not	16,623
,,	Electric	240	separately	10,753
,,	Steam	1516	quoted	32,736

Fastest scheduled runs, summer 1939

Country	Traction	Railway	from	to	m.p.h.
Germany	Diesel	State	Hamm	Hanover	83·3
U.S.A.	Diesel	Union Pacific	Grand Island	Columbus	81·4
France	Diesel	S.N.C.F.	Nancy	Paris	73·0
Bohemia	Diesel	State	Pardubice	Prague	66·3
Italy	Diesel	State	Turio	Chivasso	66·0
Denmark	Diesel	State	Ostjyden	Roskilde	65·7
Holland	Diesel	State	Amersfoot	Zwolle	65·3
Poland	Diesel	State	Radomsko	Piotrkow	64·6
Italy	Electric	State	Rome	Naples	72·5
Holland	Electric	State	Driebergen	Ede	72·0
U.S.A.	Electric	Pennsylvania	Philadelphia	Newark	71·3
France	Electric	S.N.C.F.	Poitiers	Angouleme	70·1
Germany	Electric	State	Breslau	Konigszelt	66·9
U.S.A.	Steam	Milwaukee	Sparta	Portage	75·8
Belgium	Steam	State	Brussels	Bruges	74·9
Germany	Steam	State	Hamburg	Berlin	72·7
Great Britain	Steam	L.N.E.R.	London	York	71·9
France	Steam	S.N.C.F.	Valence	Avignon	67·2
Italy	Steam	State	Verona	Padua	62·8

Opposite top. Queensland Government Railways: this 3 foot 6 inch gauge Australian system had steam locomotives with a very distinctive look, arising from the shape of the sandbox closely spaced between the chimney and steam dome. The picture shows a group of them at a running shed in the environs of Brisbane.

Opposite bottom. Gulf, Mobile and Ohio: even in the throes of modernisation, old and well-tried methods still survived, such as this method of recoaling a locomotive en route with a tipping bucket.

The remarkable figures for diesel traction in Europe will be specially noted, made almost entirely with light-weight railcars, rather than by full-length trains. If it had been possible to analyse this high-speed service in relation to the seating accommodation in the trains there is no doubt that the steam-hauled trains of the U.S.A., France and Great Britain would have shown up to great advantage.

In respect of steam haulage in the U.S.A. special reference must be made to the remarkable position of the Pennsylvania Railroad, which by itself contributed an aggregate of 4,132 miles of runs scheduled at 60 miles per hour and over, and 551 miles at over 70 miles per hour. Much of this mileage was made by heavy sleeping car expresses on the New York–Chicago route, like the Broadway Limited, and for motive power the company was relying entirely on the relatively small, but very efficient, 'K4' 'Pacifics', the design of which dated back to the early 1920s. A large number of these fine locomotives was available, and on the heaviest trains it became customary to use them in pairs. The principal rival of the Pennsylvania on the New York–Chicago service was the New York Central, and at speeds of 60 miles per hour and over this company had the amazing aggregate of 10,615 scheduled miles. At 70 miles per hour and over, however, it had less than that of the Pennsylvania. The standard express train load on the New York Central was then something over 1,000 tons – roughly double the heaviest then being operated in

Great Britain – and the giant 'Hudson' 4–6–4 locomotives of the N.Y.C. tackled them single-handed. The most spectacular steam running in the U.S.A. at that time was being made over the highly competitive routes between Chicago and the twin cities of St Paul and Minneapolis, where the Chicago and North Western, and the Milwaukee, with steam, were competing against the Burlington – one of the earliest American railways to introduce diesel traction. The Milwaukee, in particular, ran the strikingly painted Hiawatha express, which regularly attained maximum speeds of more than 100 miles per hour.

Apart from daily service running at 100 miles per hour and over, several major spurts on special occasions had put the British speed record up to a momentary and not entirely convincing 114 miles per hour, achieved by the Stanier streamlined 'Pacific' engine *Coronation* in June 1937. In the following summer a series of high-speed brake trials on the L.N.E.R. provided an opportunity for attempting a new British record. One of the latest Gresley streamlined 'Pacifics', No. 4468, *Mallard*, was therefore driven to her limit on the lengthy descent from Stoke tunnel, near Grantham, towards Peterborough and attained the world speed record with steam traction of 126 miles per hour. This has not been surpassed and the locomotive, after her withdrawal from ordinary traffic more than twenty years later, has been preserved as an historic museum piece.

Nevertheless, the outstanding feature evident from a study of the tables of daily service is the advance of diesel traction, and the onset of war led to an interesting and significant manufacturing situation in the U.S.A. At first, of course, that country was involved neither in direct hostilities, nor in movement of war traffic, and it was the railways of Europe that bore the immediate burden and devastation. They were not unprepared. The civil war in Spain had given some of the eventual belligerents in World War Two an opportunity to try out new techniques, which were closely observed by others, so that when the tension in Europe began to mount preparations included the building up of an organisation to minimise the effects of aerial bombardment and provide for the rapid restoration of service after an attack. In Great Britain the preliminaries began as early as 1937. The actual opening of the war took the form that was generally expected, with a sudden and fiercely concentrated attack on Poland, with immense destruction of railway installations within a matter of hours. And when France and Great Britain, also within a very short time, declared war on Nazi Germany, the civil defence services of industry, the railways and the civilian population in general were keyed up to expect, within hours, just such an assault as had been made on Poland. In Great Britain the situation facing the railways on the eve of war differed greatly from that of August 1914. Then the Expeditionary Force of the British Army, with all its equipment, had to be conveyed to the ports of embarkation under railway traffic conditions differing

An impressive array of German *Kriegslokomotiven* (war locomotives), 2–10–0s of the '52' class.

little from those of a busy summer holiday season. In 1939 a large-scale evacuation of children from London and the big cities had to be carried out under the menace of imminent air attack.

The evacuation of the children was a remarkable piece of railway and social organisation. By far the largest movement was from London, involving the conveyance of 607,635 people in four days. It was an operation planned to the last detail. The long distance trains conveying their youthful passengers to what were then considered 'safe' areas were started from four outer-suburban stations – one on each of the four main line railways; to those stations the evacuees were taken either by Underground trains, or by special road transport. No fewer than 1,577 special trains were run. To provide the necessary rolling stock, locomotives and timetable 'paths' many ordinary trains had to be cancelled; but this was of little consequence at the vital weekend of 1–4 September 1939. With the threat of immediate air attack ordinary business travel had virtually ceased, and such ordinary trains as remained were very lightly loaded. The programme of evacuation specials had been planned with a view to minimising disturbance in the event of air raids. All defence services were fully prepared for a surprise attack, without any formal declaration of war; but fortunately none came, and the vast operation was completed by the evening of 4 September, without any casualties.

Nevertheless, although the British declaration of war had not been followed by an immediate attack on Great Britain, the railway system of the country was placed at once and drastically on a war footing. Quite apart from the stultifying effect of the 'blackout' during hours of darkness, the splendid express train service built up so assiduously disappeared overnight, and in its place there was provided a greatly decelerated service in which no train was required to average more than 45 miles per hour from start to stop. With the prospect of a lengthy and grim struggle, immediate steps were taken to avoid excessive wear and tear on track and rolling stock, and limitation of maximum speed was a first step towards this end. Preparations were made for the supply of rolling stock for the British Expeditionary Force sent to France in the late autumn of 1939. For tasks requiring no more than moderate power a number of the veteran Dean 0–6–0 goods engines of the Great Western Railway were equipped for continental service; but the larger 2–8–0s of Stanier L.M.S. design ordered by the War Office were only just beginning to roll off the production lines when the entire war situation was changed by the Nazi onslaught on Belgium and Holland in May 1940, the driving back of the Expeditionary Force to the beaches of Dunkirk, and the subsequent collapse and surrender of France.

The railway situation confronting Britain and her Allies now began to assume global proportions. There were desert lines in the Middle East; the railway lifelines of southern Africa were now of strategic

importance; while in Australia, just at this critical time, the great viaduct over the Hawkesbury river became in urgent need of complete renewal – this on one of the busiest and most strategic lines in all Australia! The British locomotive building industry was called upon to supply, with the utmost urgency, large new engines for Africa, Australia and New Zealand, as well as the requirements of the War Office at home. And in the late summer of 1940 there began the long-expected aerial attack on Britain itself, as a prelude to a full-scale Nazi invasion. One could write whole volumes on how British railwaymen carried on through this terrible period; of the prodigies of effort and improvisation by which lines were repaired and bridges and stations restored to workable condition, and how train crews calmly took precious freights through the danger areas. Above all there was the unsung heroism of countless signalmen who remained steadfastly at their posts, alone, in exposed signalboxes, while the bombs were falling all around them. Discipline at all levels of the service was as faultless as that of crack regiments in the heat of battle, and accidents other than through direct enemy action were few and far between.

The one really bad accident of 1940 was a tragic reminder of the conditions under which railwaymen were working. On the night of 4 November 1940, the driver of the 9.50 p.m. express from Paddington to Plymouth and Penzance was a London man. His home had been bombed, and he feared for the safety of his

Norfolk and Western Railway: for some time after World War Two this railway continued to rely entirely on steam traction and fine modern servicing facilities were installed, as shown in this view of the Williamson, West Virginia, locomotive terminal and yard.

wife and family; but he was booked on a 'lodging turn' which would keep him away for nearly two days, and so he set off to work through to Newton Abbot. Train working was much delayed on these anxious wartime nights, and he reached Taunton sixty-eight minutes late. He had a very heavy train, packed with naval, military and air force men, as well as many civilians, and owing to the lateness of the train the signalman at Taunton West decided to send him forward for the first two miles on the relief line, so as

Spectacular result of a bomb attack on a German locomotive yard at Munster, 1945: one of the Reichsbahn Class '52' 2–10–0s, heavily camouflaged, jacknifed by bomb blast.

to give a fast newspaper and mail train that did not stop at Taunton a clear run through. It was a perfectly normal and safe manoeuvre which the signalman judged would cause the minimum delay to both trains. By the time the 9.50 came to the end of the four-track section at Norton Fitzwarren he judged that the newspaper train would be almost clear.

When the time came for the 9.50 to leave Taunton the signals were 'off' for both trains, taking the 9.50 down the relief line, with the main line clear for the newspaper train. If it had been running on time the 9.50 would have been signalled to cross on to the main line, and its unfortunate and sadly worried driver saw the signals clear for the newspaper train and thought they were for him. He did not realise, after leaving Taunton, that he was on the relief and not on the main line. He saw further signals for the newspaper train as he drew away into the country and thought they were his own, and in this state of mind the automatic train control could not save him from his final and fatal error. At Norton Fitzwarren the four-track section ended, and he would have to take the cross-over track to the main line. The newspaper train had not yet passed, and the points could not be set for him to cross. The Norton Fitzwarren signals on the relief line were at danger, and as he approached the distant signal the siren of the automatic train control apparatus sounded its shrill warning in his cab. The tragedy was about to be consummated.

The Great Western had been ahead of the other British railway companies in the installation of a system of automatic train control. This provided an audible signal in the cab on the approach to each 'distant' signal at the lineside. If that signal was clear a bell was rung; if the signal was in the 'warning' position a siren was sounded, which the driver was required to acknowledge. If he failed to do this the siren went on sounding and the brakes were automatically applied.

All Great Western express drivers knew that occasionally the collector shoe on the engine did not make proper contact with the ramp in the track, and then one received a 'false alarm' – a siren, instead of the 'all-clear' bell. Still imagining he was on the main line, and duly observing the distant signal for the main line at clear he thought this was a false alarm, and duly acknowledged and cancelled the warning. Just at that moment the newspaper train came up, running fast and overtaking the 9.50. It was only then that the poor driver realised something was wrong. But it was too late. He ran through Norton Fitzwarren station and through the catch points at the end of the four-track section, and his 'King' class engine crashed on to the soft ground ahead and turned over. The leading coaches piled into the overturned engine and tender and smashed up, and in those crowded compartments there were twenty-seven killed and fifty-six seriously injured.

Bomb damage on the railways of Britain was to a large extent incidental. There was no precision bombing of specific targets, such as that meted out to the German railways in the attacks on marshalling yards and other railway installations; and as the extent of the war increased so also the scale and diversity of railway participation increased. By the summer of 1941 the involvement of the American railways was considerable, and the historic meeting between Winston Churchill and President Roosevelt at Placentia Bay, Newfoundland, in August of that year ensured a substantial step-up of American-made munitions to Europe. Traffic from many parts of the U.S.A. was turned towards the Atlantic ports. Then, on Sunday, 4 December 1941, the sudden and devastating attack on the unprepared Pacific fleet at Pearl Harbour brought instant realisation that the long Pacific seaboard of the U.S.A. was practically undefended, and that the catastrophe of Pearl Harbour could be repeated, against land targets at Los Angeles, San Francisco and elsewhere. The flow of war material was switched, in a matter of days, from the Atlantic to the Pacific coast, and troop movements had been switched even earlier than that. The great transcontinental routes of the Union Pacific and the Santa Fe became vital lifelines of war traffic, called upon to carry unprecedented tonnages; and in complete contrast to the situation in wartime Britain the emphasis was immediately upon *speed*.

It was not, however, a case of simply running hard. For many hundreds of miles in the Middle West and the western states these great lines were single-tracked. The passing loops were many miles apart, and traffic was regulated by the telegraphic train order system. This had been adequate – just adequate! – for the attenuated service of the slump years; but when the guns and the tanks began to roll, and service and business personnel were travelling to the west coast in such numbers as to require duplication of the principal express trains and the running of many specials, train orders were just not good enough. Fortunately a magnificent tool of operation was available represented by the magic letters C.T.C. – Centralised Traffic Control. This enabled long stretches of line, some well over a hundred miles, to be controlled solely by signal indication, not with written train orders, but through a central despatcher's office, where the traffic situation on the whole line was constantly displayed in coloured lights on a console diagram. The despatcher could arrange the 'meets' of trains at the passing loops according to the 'all line' position, set the points and clear the signals at stations fifty to a hundred miles away by thumb switches on his console diagram. C.T.C. was not available for instant application, but the signalling manufactories at Swissvale, Pennsylvania, and Rochester, New York, worked night and day, and it was soon being installed on lengthy stretches of line. It worked like a charm.

In the meantime locomotives were being worked as never before. The Chief of the Santa Fe, then considered to be one of the world's finest passenger trains, carried every day more high-ranking army and navy officials from Chicago to the Pacific coast than any other train, and for the distance of 2,226 miles only two locomotives were employed. One, a 'Hudson' type 4–6–4, worked the 992 miles from Chicago to La Junta, Colorado, and on the most westerly lap had to average 80 miles per hour over the 202 miles from Dodge City to La Junta. Here one of the giant 4–8–4s of the '3776' class took over and put in more than *twenty-eight hours* of continuous running over the remaining 1,234 miles to Los Angeles. These engines were handled by nine different crews in the course of the journey, crossed three mountain ranges at altitudes of more than 7,000 feet, pounded up the heavy gradients leading to them, and ran at 100 miles per hour elsewhere. All this was done with a train never weighing less than 1,000 tons. For the record, the Santa Fe '3776' class, introduced in 1938, weighed 228 tons without their tenders, and had a tractive effort of 66,000 pounds.

In 1941 the Union Pacific put on the road the largest steam locomotive ever built. They had a particular problem in fast freight haulage. It became a national policy during the war to maintain liberal supplies of citrus fruits, for distribution as juices – orange, grapefruit, etc. – which were considered vital to the health of men in the armed forces and of the civilian population. One of the major sources of supply was in the western states and supplies from various areas were concentrated at Ogden, Utah, for forwarding in huge block loads to the east. The trains of heavy refrigerator vans provided a major haulage task, across the mountains to Green River and

through the highly spectacular Echo Canyon, and these enormous articulated engines of the 4–8–8–4 type were specially allocated to what became known as the 'Vitamin C' trains. The loads were usually 3,000 tons and more. These engines became known as the 'Big Boys'; they weighed 345 tons without their tenders, which weighed another 195 tons. The tractive effort was no less than 135,400 pounds and despite the vast amount of coal and water carried, the supplies of both had to be replenished twice in

the course of the 6½-hour run from Ogden to Green River.

In the 'Big Boys' the steam locomotive was really approaching its physical limits. After all, the engine and tender together measured just over 120 feet from end to end; an American journalist who rode one of the 'Vitamin C' trains referred to the engine as a 'hungry brute'. The diesels were already making their mark, and during the war development, by Government decree, took a rather one-sided turn. In the national emergency there was naturally a desire, and indeed an urgent need, to use all manufacturing facilities and expertise to the best advantage, and in diesel locomotive production the electromotive division of General Motors had a considerable lead over its competitors. Rather than risk dissipation or duplication of effort in development, the government of the U.S.A. decided that for the duration of the war all orders for main line diesel locomotives should be placed with General Motors, whose policy of strict standardisation ideally suited the needs of the hour. The American Locomotive Company (A.L.C.O.) received orders for the smaller units. The handsomely-styled General Motors nose-cab units became an increasingly familiar sight on many American railways, ideally suited to massive freight hauls because two, three, or even four individual units could be coupled, according to the load of the train, and operated by a single engine crew. The diesels had an inherent advantage over steam in

Contra Costa, operating the Solano train ferry across San Francisco Harbour, between Benicia and Port Costa. The service was discontinued after the opening of the new bridge in 1930.

mountain country, for although locomotives like the Santa Fe '3776' class and the U.P. 'Big Boys' could equal or surpass them on a fast run, the tractive power of the diesels was considerably greater in starting and at low speed.

As the war developed the need arose for transporting vast numbers of troops, and troop train runs in the U.S.A. were something very different from the relatively short hauls in Great Britain. These trains ran through from Chicago to the Pacific coast,

Zero weather on the Delaware and Hudson, as a heavy freight pounds away near Plattsburgh.

usually involving at least two nights in the train, and for this duty 1,200 special 'troop sleepers' were built by the Pullman Standard Car Company. Externally they looked like box cars with a row of windows low down, square-sided, square-topped. But inside they were remarkably comfortable. There were thirty-nine men to a car. Two men slept in each lower berth, and one in each upper berth. The berths were well stocked with linen and blankets, and it was a tradition

that the negro porters made up the berths as carefully as for any Pullman passenger. Many young Americans made their last railway journey in these trains, bound for the deadly war across the Pacific from which so many of them never returned. A troop train could consist of more than twenty of these special 'sleepers', some of which were equipped as canteens, and others as office accommodation for the train commander. They were usually run as second portions of the regular express passenger trains, and at top express speed.

In the later stages of the war railways across the world played an increasingly diverse and desperate part. The fearful campaigns amid the jungles of Burma were fought along the line of the railway. New supply routes were built through primeval forest lands in the tropics, at a terrible cost in human life, and when the time came for liberation strategic bombing ahead of the advancing armies destroyed, almost to the point of complete obliteration, many key installations on the railways of South East Asia. The fine Malayan Railway locomotive works at Sentul, Kuala Lumpur, was a case in point. In Japan, even before the climax of the nuclear bomb attacks on Hiroshima and Nagasaki in August 1945, relentless bombing of the many industrial targets along the teeming eastern coast of Honshu had caused railway destruction sufficient to bring much of the system to a standstill. On the continent of Europe much of the most severe damage to railways came in the last year of the war. Strategic bombing prior to the great Allied landings in Normandy in June 1944 involved the destruction of numerous major viaducts and bridges on the main supply routes in France, while at the time of the actual landings, as part of the overall Allied strategy, Dutch railwaymen went some way towards completely immobilising their equipment before going 'underground'.

Across the world railwaymen of all nations toiled incessantly to keep their lines open and their trains running, and at times, on all sides, their devotion and heroism was sublime. In Britain, the springboard of the great assault of 1944, the statistics of operation may well sound unbelievable without any reference to the conditions of physical difficulty and danger in which they were achieved. The Greater London area was alone among the war zones of the world in experiencing the devastating effect of the V2 rocket attacks, of which more than 1,000 landed between September 1944 and March 1945. Many of these landed on railway property, and some did immense damage. The maximum haulage effort of the British railways occurred in the year 1943, when the build-up towards the invasion of 1944 was reaching its peak. By that time in the war there had been far less than the normal replacement of obsolescent rolling stock and fixed equipment, and between 20 and 30 per cent of the normal workshop capacity had been diverted to armament production. Above all, some 15 per cent of the staff had been released for National Service, and all working had been carried out in the black-out at night, and under the constant threat of bombing attacks. Yet in the face of what could well be imagined as crippling difficulties, the British railways succeeded in stepping up their output, in the vital matter of net ton-miles of freight haulage, from 16,669 million in pre-war years to 24,357 million in 1943 – a phenomenal increase of 46 per cent.

The fifteen years following the end of World War Two were perhaps the most critical in history for railways. Both as weapons and as targets they had played a major part on both sides of the conflict, everywhere; but how had the experience of total war furthered the science of railroading? It is easy to speak in terms of broad generalisations, but to my mind three widely dissimilar developments stand out which had an immediate influence on the post-war scene. Two of these originated in the U.S.A., the other arose from the export trade of the British locomotive building industry. The first was the very rapid advance of the diesel-electric locomotive, which had repercussions in the motive power field in many parts of the world. The second was the astonishing success of C.T.C., which led to many investigations into its possible application, from the Highlands of Scotland to some of the most remote parts of the British Commonwealth. The third was the demonstration in wartime service of the remarkable versatility and dependability of the Beyer-Garratt type of articulated locomotive.

To take these three aspects of railway working in detail: the success of the completely standardised General Motors type of diesel-electric locomotive on the railways of the Middle West in the U.S.A. was convincing beyond any doubt; but in the eastern states where there were ample supplies of good locomotive coal the case for the diesels had to be argued at some length. Railroads like the New York Central and the Norfolk and Western refused to be drawn into the false position of comparing the performance of new diesels with that of steam locomotives of pre-war vintage. A diesel then cost roughly twice as much as a steam locomotive of equivalent power, and that additional capital cost, with the associated interest on capital, had to be set against the increased availability of the diesels. In 1945 the New York Central took delivery from A.L.C.O. of the celebrated 'Niagara' class of 4–8–4s for service on the New York–Chicago run. These locomotives were slightly less powerful than those of the '3776' class of the Santa Fe, but they were ideally suited to the almost level track of the 'water level' route to Chicago. A long series of trials was made with these engines against diesel-electrics, with inconclusive results; but in the U.S.A., as in Great Britain, it was arguments other than scientific engineering ones that determined future policy. In the unsettled social conditions that prevailed in the U.S.A. the uncertainty of coal supplies loaded the case against the coal-fired steam locomotive, and in a very few years after the end of the war no more than a handful of railroads retained steam as their front line motive power.

In Great Britain the immediate outcome of post-

war conditions was the reverse. On the London, Midland and Scottish Railway the intention, in 1946–7, was to carry out exhaustive tests comparing diesel and steam locomotives, and two experimental units built by the English Electric Company were put into service in December 1947 for comparison with the latest version of the very successful Stanier steam 'Pacifics' of the 'Duchess' class. But the political somersault represented by the British General Election of 1945 had so perplexed opinion all over

The London–Paris Golden Arrow service: on the English side one of the Bulleid air-smoothed 'Pacifics' of the 'West Country' class, the *City of Wells*, climbs from London towards the crest of the North Downs, passing Chelsfield, Kent.

the world that facilities for foreign exchange were difficult to arrange and oil supplies severely restricted. So that when the British railways were nationalised in 1948, and the form of new motive power had to be decided, R. A. Riddles, the member of the newly constituted Railway Executive responsible for mechanical and electrical engineering, chose not only the form of power that gave the highest tractive effort per pound sterling, but also that which used indigenous fuel – in other words coal-fired steam. So, while the development and utilisation of diesel power went rapidly ahead in the U.S.A., in Great Britain it was halted for almost a decade, at any rate so far as the home railways were concerned. The British railways came under a considerable weight of criticism for their seeming unwillingness to adopt a modern development that was, to all outward appearances, an outstanding success in the U.S.A., though there were good enough reasons for the decision taken by Riddles in 1948.

The American success with C.T.C. had been equally outstanding, but in considering its application to British and European railways the particular circumstances that had ensured its success in the U.S.A. needed careful study. The transcontinental lines on which some of the more spectacular installations had been made up to then had no wayside signals at all, and C.T.C. was put in, at considerable expense, for the sole purpose of increasing the capacity of the line. On the long sections of single line in Great

Britain there is no doubt that C.T.C. would have improved operation, but the lines concerned were fully signalled and, even if all the mechanical signalling apparatus had been dispensed with, there could not, at that time, have been any reductions in staff. In the remote areas signalmen usually combined other duties at the stations, and even if there was no signalling to do the men would still have been required. In overseas territories, however, C.T.C. was introduced to great advantage in Africa, Australia and New Zealand, with British-built plants closely following the American pattern. At the same time the operational advantages of centralised control seemed to have a wider application than for long stretches of single line railway, on which the density of traffic even in the height of wartime activity in the U.S.A. was very low compared to that of the busiest inter-city routes in Britain and on the continent of Europe.

The immediate difficulty was the time taken to transmit the necessary remote controls. The essence of the original C.T.C. systems was that no more than two- or three-line wires were used from end to end of the section under control. The process which followed the operation of one of the thumb switches on the central console could be likened to the dialling of a number on the ordinary automatic telephone system. The despatcher 'dialled' the particular signal or pair of points he wanted to operate; and just as the telephone subscriber cannot dial two numbers at once, or receive an incoming call while he is dialling someone else, so the design of the original C.T.C. precluded the functioning of more than one control at once. It originally took about four seconds to send out a 'control' or to receive an 'indication', and it will immediately be appreciated that this put a limit on the number of trains that could be simultaneously controlled. When British railwaymen began thinking of applying the C.T.C. principle to certain areas where a centralised control would have been of advantage for the more efficient regulation of train movements, the time factor entered prominently into it. Then, however, the new science of electronics began to make its impact on electrical control methods of all kinds, and in the back rooms some highly important and significant researches were begun, the effect of which were only to be seen at a later date.

In America particularly, but to a greater or lesser extent in most parts of the world, there was a general consensus of opinion that the steam locomotive had reached the end of its useful life, and that the sooner it was replaced the better. Those who were most vocal in expressing such a view – apart from the engineers who had solid grounds for their opinions and preferences – could be broadly divided into the neophiles, who loved novelty for its own sake; those who were out to promote the interests of the oil industry; and those who had no more intelligent motivation than a desire to 'keep up with the Joneses', and made no attempt to probe beyond the spectacular facade and find out the very cogent reasons behind the breathtaking American transformation. In the meantime the British locomotive building industry, with its finger firmly on the pulse of railway operation in the far countries of the Commonwealth, developed the Beyer-Garratt articulated locomotive to a very high degree of efficiency. Experience in such a variety of overseas railways, with greatly differing running conditions and wide extremes of temperature, resulted in the perfecting of detail design to an extent probably unequalled elsewhere. This expertise built into locomotives of varying size, weight and rail gauge

Above. Eastern Railway of India: a 'WG' class broad-gauge 2–8–2 at Barauni Junction.

Left. German colour-light signalling, making a striking abstract composition at dusk. A green light showing on the upper board of the mast in the foreground gives the 'all clear' past this signal, while two green lights below indicate another 'all clear' at the next.

Opposite. Chesapeake and Ohio Railroad: a striking view of the roundhouse and turntable at Clifton Forge, Virginia.

179

Swiss Federal Railways: modernisation near Lausanne: an aerial view of the mechanised marshalling yard at Denges.

ensured reliability of performance that enabled exceptionally long monthly mileages to be obtained, without incidental casualties. Particularly in southern Africa the performance of some of these engines had to be seen from the footplate to be believed. The steam locomotives exported from Great Britain in the years following the end of World War Two have proved a magnificent investment for the railways concerned. Most of them are still engaged in the heaviest of duties today.

On the continent of Europe the emphasis was, from the outset, on electrification. In Holland, south and west of the Zuider Zee, the network was rebuilt from the ruins of the war to provide eventually a rapid service of multiple-unit electric trains. Compared to the diversity of steam locomotives in service before the war it was highly efficient, though rather dull for the connoisseurs of railway lore. Only the international express trains were hauled by individual locomotives, and these were powerful but rather soulless electrics. In France the rebuilding was on a more ambitious scale. Alone among the countries whose railways had been ravaged by the war, France at once set her sights on far higher speeds than had been customary in pre-war years. It was not only a case of track improvement on the open line. Big junctions like Montereau and Laroche were completely remodelled so that the non stopping trains could run through at maximum speeds, and as the trunk routes were rehabilitated so the line maximum speeds were raised. The old legal maximum of 120 kilometres per hour (74·5 miles per hour) became a thing of the past and, as one by one the lines were electrified and continuous colour-light signalling was installed, the speed limit was increased to 140 kilometres per hour (87 miles per hour). In pre-war years a considerable mileage of the Paris–Orléans Railway had been electrified, using the 1,500-volt direct current system of traction with current collection from an overhead line wire; and this system was used for the first installations made in post-war years, notably on the main line from Paris southwards to Dijon and Lyons. It was also standardised in Holland.

The early decision of the French railways to terminate all development of steam locomotive practice came as a great disappointment to that very distinguished engineer André Chapelon, who had already prepared a remarkable series of post-war

100 miles per hour on special tests. Another Chapelon design of which many were built and did splendid work was the '241-P' class four-cylinder compound 4–8–2. This was developed from a pre-war design of the Paris, Lyons and Mediterranean Railway. It was also a very large and powerful machine, having a tractive effort of 45,084 pounds against 47,077 pounds in the experimental 4–8–4, and the total engine weight was 129 tons, against 145 tons on the 4–8–4. In relation to their tractive effort and especially in

Above. German Federal Railways: an auto-carrier train from Hamburg to Westerland passing through Niebüll, drawn by a 'Pacific' locomotive of the '012' class.

Left. East African Railways: one of the huge 59th class Beyer-Garratt locomotives– most powerful locomotive on the metre gauge anywhere in the world–at Nairobi running shed. These locomotives are magnificently painted in crimson-lake.

designs which would have carried the development of the steam locomotive many stages forward. Only one of his great new 4–8–4 express passenger locomotives was built. It was a three-cylinder compound, capable of climbing a 1 in 125 gradient, as on the line through the Côte d'Or mountains north of Dijon, at 60 miles per hour with a train of 650 tons and, although normally restricted, when first built, to a service speed of 81 miles per hour, it reached

comparison with the largest American 4–8–4s these French compounds were not unduly heavy. Furthermore, the standard French rating for tractive effort of compound locomotives gave a rather modest estimate of their capacity. The very first Chapelon locomotive, the Paris–Orléans rebuilt 'Pacific' referred to earlier, for example, had a nominal tractive effort of only 28,440 pounds. Yet the maximum performance of this class was superior to that of any

181

of the pre-war British steam locomotives, some of which had rated tractive efforts of more than 40,000 pounds!

In Soviet Russia there was a great revival of spirit on the railways. Inefficient administrators were removed and, although the railways remained the Cinderella of the economy, railwaymen and women strove to increase output, in the form of ton-miles achieved. Women worked alongside men in the locomotive department; there were some women drivers and many women firemen. Husband and wife engine crews were not unusual. In 1941 Hitler, greatly underestimating the Soviet railways, expected an early collapse, as in 1916–17; but the railways did not fail. Nevertheless, though they made prodigious efforts, and kept the armies supplied with munitions and reinforcements, the war took a very heavy toll. Large numbers of locomotives were destroyed by retreating armies, lines were blocked, and on certain routes the wholesale destruction of communications led to permissive working – essentially at slow speed. Even after the war little finance was made available for railway development up until 1953, since when progress has been remarkable, particularly in the electrification of main lines.

By the year 1950 the problems besetting railways all over the world were more disturbing and serious than any connected with technical matters. During the war vast numbers of men and women serving in the armed forces of the nations involved had travelled

by train, often in very uncomfortable conditions, and with the return of peace and the switch-over of the automobile industry to private car and ordinary commercial vehicle production, there was a general and natural move back to the freedom in transport which people had been denied during the war years. In America the diesel 'honeymoon' was soon over and, with the advance of internal air lines and the popularity of the private car, people were talking freely about railways being 'on the way out'. In Britain those enjoying for the first time the pleasures of holidays with pay were not impressed with the crowded and unpunctual weekend trains in which they had to travel, and for the relatively short journeys involved were ready enough to turn to super-annuated and often unreliable old motor cars as soon as petrol rationing ended. The nationalised British Railways was insolvent, and with a facile glibness that was astonishing in persons of high authority, all the blame for this situation was every-where attributed to the continuance of steam traction. In most parts of the world the recession in practically all forms of traffic was all the more disturbing in view of what had been conveyed during the war. British railwaymen looked with something akin to envy on the rapid technical developments and improvements in service taking place on railways that had been devastated to the point of virtual standstill in the war, and yet had made phenomenally rapid recoveries.

Above. Breathtaking snow scene on the Rhaetian Railway in Switzerland. This electric train is bound for St Moritz in the Engadine, and has just passed through Celerina. The Rhaetian Railway is metre gauge.

Opposite top. A wintry Japanese scene, with a 'C58' class 2–6–2 in spectacular surroundings between Dogosan and Bingo-Ochiai.

Opposite bottom. An electrically-hauled express train on the Tauern line of the Austrian Federal Railway, which branches southwards from the Salzburg–Innsbruck line through the Tauern Tunnel into Italy, crossing the spectacular modern bridge.

183

The extent to which British Railways was being starved of capital was scarcely appreciated, but it had the effect of keeping the brake on all forms of development. One of these was the vital matter of automatic train control. In dealing with the Norton Fitzwarren accident we saw the G.W.R.'s developments in cab signalling; and the L.M.S. and L.N.E.R. had jointly been working on a development of this. In post-war years the nationalisation of the railways, and the upheavals connected with integration of technical staffs and so on, had tended to slow up development; but by the year 1952 progress had almost reached the stage of a trial installation when a terrible accident threw the whole question of automatic train control into the blinding glare of national publicity. On the morning of 8 October 1952, in weather that could be described as seasonable, though not foggy, the up Perth sleeping car express was running one-and-a-half hours late and was nearing the London outer-suburban area when commuter traffic was at its height. A train from Watford to Euston was making its usual stop at Harrow, fully protected to the rear by all signals correctly in the danger position. Then suddenly, inexplicably, out of the mist came the Perth train at full speed. Hardly had it crashed, with terrible effect, into the standing local train when the 7.55 a.m. express from Euston, double-headed, came from the other direction and crashed into the wreckage of the first collision. The result was the most terrible wreck ever seen on a British railway.

Among the 112 people killed were the driver and fireman of the Perth express, and as a result the reason why they passed all the up line signals at danger will never be known. But what was certain was that if the line had been equipped with the automatic cab signalling used on the Great Western, or the development then on the point of trial, the enginemen would have been alerted and in all probability the catastrophe would have been avoided. It is sad to think that a disaster of this magnitude had to occur before British Railways was jerked into a sense of urgency over what is now known as the Automatic Warning System. Yet such it was, and the reliability and effectiveness of 'A.W.S.' on the present high-speed routes is the result.

In 1955 the epoch-making Modernisation Plan for British Railways was launched. For the first time in its history finance on a large scale was made available for modernisation. It is perhaps an exaggeration to suggest that the technical departments were not ready, and that a rather uncoordinated 'spending spree' resulted. But on one point the directive from the highest level was crystal clear – get rid of steam traction as quickly as possible. While some busy lines were marked down for electrification, diesel locomotives and railcars were to constitute the backbone of the new motive power, and in the first excitement of the launching of the plan a considerable body of opinion – albeit quite outside the railway industry – urged that the only way to secure rapid and reliable deliveries was to make bulk purchases from the U.S.A. Fortunately for British industry other counsels prevailed, but at the same time the orders for new locomotives were widely spread around and went to some firms with little previous experience of railway work. These found to their surprise that diesel engines standardised in road haulage took ill to the strenuous usage demanded on railways. On the credit side of this anxious period of all-too-rapid transition must be set the success and solid reliability of the English Electric 2,000 horse-power units, which had been developed from the pre-nationalisation move towards diesels by the L.M.S., and which included the fruits of the builders' experience in a vigorous furthering of Britain's export trade in locomotives. The new units on British Railways were first introduced on the London–Norwich service of the former Great Eastern Railway, and were later brought successfully into traffic on many different routes.

By far the most important development of the mid-1950s was in electric traction, though its significance in Great Britain was to some extent obscured by the fuss surrounding the shipwreck hurry in which the diesels, of all shapes and sizes, were being put on the rails. But electrification must be considered against the entire European scene, by which British practice was profoundly and fortunately influenced at that time. There was first of all the form of the new standard locomotives for high-speed express service. At one time it was generally considered that for such service a locomotive should have a leading pair of wheels, or truck, like the bogie of a steam loco-

British Railways. The last-ever steam locomotive to be built for service on main lines in Great Britain: the Class '9F' 2–10–0 No. 92220 *Evening Star*, here seen working a Bath to Bournemouth express near Chilcompton, Somerset, on the now closed Somerset and Dorset Joint Line.

Left. Russia: locomotives for the new electrified lines under construction at Novocherkassk works.

Below left. Workmen erecting overhead wires on a stretch of line under electrification between Lvov and Sambor in the Ukraine, U.S.S.R.

motive, to ensure smooth riding. In the later stages of the war, however, the Lötschberg line in Switzerland introduced a new type of locomotive of maximum power, carried on two eight-wheeled bogies, all axles of which were powered. It meant that all the weight of the locomotive was available for adhesion – an important consideration on a line so heavily graded as the Lötschberg, but on which maximum speeds were not high. Not only the Swiss Federal Railways but also the French followed this precept, and there was no doubt that the French locomotives were required to run fast. Their success was studied closely by British engineers, not least when in 1955 one of the twelve-wheeled series, No. CC7107, reached a speed of 206 miles per hour on a special test run between Bordeaux and Dax. A short time afterwards this world record was closely paralleled by one of the eight-wheeled locomotives, No. BB9004, on the same route. The maximum speed on this second occasion was 205½ miles per hour. These locomotives were operated on the standard Paris–Orléans system of traction, 1,500 volts direct current. These exceptional speed records seemed to confirm beyond any doubt the suitability of the 'all-adhesion' type of locomotive for fast running, while the success of the locomotives in ordinary traffic led to the builders' receiving many repeat orders from other railway administrations.

At this time the question of traction system, which seemed set for standardisation at 1,500 volts

per second, led to studies in the use of such a supply for railway traction with the minimum of step-down transforming, and the outcome was an experimental French installation at 25,000 volts A.C., 50 cycles, on the Geneva–Chamonix line between Aix-les-Bains and La-Roche-sur-Foron. This proved successful, and the decision was taken to adopt 25,000 volts A.C., 50 cycles, as the future standard.

This striking decision had immediate repercussions in Great Britain. The Modernisation Plan provided for electrification of the main line from Euston to Liverpool and Manchester, and for extension of the Eastern Region network in the London suburban area to Colchester and Clacton-on-Sea. The heavy responsibility for deciding whether to continue with the 1,500-volt system of the Eastern Region, also installed on the heavily used freight line between Sheffield and Manchester, or to adopt instead the latest French system with the very real advantages it possessed, fell upon S. B. Warder, the chief electrical engineer of the Railway Executive. The decision was all the more difficult since, if 25,000 volts A.C. was adopted for the Clacton line, it would mean extensive conversion work in the London area. The Sheffield–Manchester line was isolated from other projected electrification schemes, and could remain as it was. Warder decided for the 25,000 volt A.C. system, and work commenced from the Manchester end of the London Midland line. It could not be a rapid process, and while other parts of the Modernisation Plan

D.C. in Britain as well as in France and the Netherlands, was being exposed to some considerable controversy. It was by no means standard all over Europe. Belgium and Italy were using 3,000 volts D.C., while Switzerland, Austria and West Germany used 15,000 volts A.C., at $16\frac{2}{3}$ cycles per second. In France yet a fourth system was being projected. The rapid extension of national electricity supply networks at very high voltages, and at a frequency of 50 cycles

were proceeding, especially with the wholesale introduction of diesels and the equally wholesale scrapping of steam, the finances of British Railways as a whole were falling still deeper into the red. The high cost of electrification was called in question, and for one critical period work on the line between Euston, Liverpool and Manchester was stopped.

The recession in railway business was indeed worldwide, but nowhere was it more severe than in the U.S.A., and nowhere was the situation dealt with more drastically. Train services were reduced to a shadow of their former selves and standards were unfortunately lowered, thus acting as a further deterrent to the promotion of first class travel. There was a period when no one seemed to go by train in the U.S.A. for choice, while in England the modernisation work involving track renewals caused such extensive disruption of service, despite deceleration of schedules, as to tarnish still further the somewhat dulled image of the railway industry. In June 1961 Dr Richard Beeching, Technical Director of Imperial Chemical Industries, was appointed to succeed Sir Brian Robertson as Chairman of the British Railways Board, with a simple mandate to restore the profitability of the railways. It was simple enough as a directive, but complex beyond measure in the difficulties that lay athwart the path to its achievement, and many years of frustration and near-failure were to lie ahead.

It was, in unhappy fact, not in the country of their origin, nor yet with those who had followed so quickly in the wake of Great Britain 130 years earlier, that the astonishing new era of railways began. It is however the year 1951, rather than 1961, that can be seen in retrospect as one of the milestones in world railway history; for it was then that the potentialities of modern equipment were first put to a new and vital test. For more than fifty years the Mesabi Range in Minnesota had supplied roughly three-quarters of the entire steel needs of the U.S.A. Until the end of World War Two it was one of the

Above. British Railways: first of the new standard steam classes, the 'Britannia' Class '7MT' 4–6–2. Engine No. 70050 of this class is shown passing through the arch in the town wall of medieval Conway, North Wales, with the Irish Mail.

Right. British Railways: the Mayflower express, Plymouth to London (Paddington), here seen near Reading, Berkshire, drawn by a diesel-hydraulic locomotive, named *Bulldog*, of 2,200 horse-power.

Opposite top. One of Japan's famous high-speed Shinkansen trains passes in front of Mount Fujiyama.

Opposite bottom. A Class '50' diesel leaving Bath with a London express amid springtime blossom.

Overleaf. Classic snow-clad scene on the Canadian Pacific: the tail end of the *Canadian* as it enters the Connaught Tunnel in British Columbia.

largest known deposits of iron ore anywhere in the world, but the tremendous demands made upon it during the five years of war had brought in sight its inevitable exhaustion, and a search for new supplies had begun. They were found in north-eastern Canada, on the borders of Quebec and Labrador, where a deposit of some 400 million tons of iron ore was shown to exist at a site then known as Knob Lake. There, far from being any nearby habitation, there was literally nothing for many hundreds of miles. For the ore to be mined, econo-mically, everything had to be imported – equipment, personnel, and means of transport. The whole project was planned as a single integrated enterprise, and that included the transport of *ten million* tons of ore every year. There was only one conceivable form of transport – a railway. It would need to be at least 300 miles long, from Knob Lake to a natural harbour on the St Lawrence estuary, about 500 miles down-stream from Montreal, called Seven Islands, and a railway was duly planned to carry loaded trains of no less than 14,000 tons running at 30 miles per hour, and take the empty cars back from Seven Islands at 40 miles per hour.

It was an economically planned utilisation of a railway: a steady regular flow of traffic day and night, year in, year out, using all equipment to the best advantage. It is perhaps an exaggeration to say that nothing like it had previously been seen anywhere in the world. But on the great majority of the world's railways the lines had been projected and opened for

Above. West German Federal Railways: the impressive front end of a TEE luxury diesel express train.

Left. Canadian National Railways: a famous member of the 'U-2-g' 4–8–4 class, No. 6218, hauling a Toronto-bound express, shortly after leaving Montreal. This locomotive is now preserved.

Opposite top. One of France's crack high-speed electric locomotives on *Le Capitole*, the 125 miles per hour flyer, bound for Toulouse.

Opposite bottom. America's latest contribution to the rejuvenation of railways, the new high-speed Amtrak train.

business, and the equipment had to carry whatever traffic was offered, whenever it was offered. It was inevitably a hit and miss affair. Sometimes the line was swamped with custom, at times it was starved; the management could do little to even things out. But the Quebec North Shore and Labrador Railway, as the line to Knob Lake was called, was like a 300-mile long conveyor belt in a steady flow-line production unit. It was built to the most massive main line standards, worked by powerful diesel electric locomotives, and controlled by C.T.C. sig-nalling from a panel machine at Seven Islands. Although there were colour-light signals at appro-priate locations throughout the line their operation was all controlled from the one traffic centre. By the early summer of 1954 the ore trains were running between Knob Lake and Seven Islands. The way in which Knob Lake has blossomed out into the city of Schefferville, and the cities of Wabush and Labrador City have grown up beside another enormous iron ore deposit some 220 miles from Seven Islands, and equally deep in the primeval forest lands, is one of the modern romances of Canada; and to ride 'The Express', the thrice-weekly passenger train which makes its way from Seven Islands to Labrador City and Schefferville amid the numerous ore trains, is to experience something of what railroading was like in pioneer days, except that the journey is made in the comfort of modern equipment.

The Quebec North Shore and Labrador was, unwittingly perhaps, the precursor of a new conception of railways. Yet perhaps it was only in its truly global scale that it was new. The very first railways in north-eastern England were built to convey minerals, and the industries grew up near to where the mineral deposits lay. In the latter half of the twentieth century, with the working out of many of the original sources of mineral wealth, coal and iron ores and other minerals are having to be brought to the industries from far afield. Newly-constructed or modernised railways are taking part in some immensely long hauls. Coal is being conveyed from the inland areas of north-western Queensland; iron ore from the Hamersley Range in north-western Australia, and again from Koolyanobbing – not too distant, as Australian mileages go, from the gold fields of Kalgoorlie – to the great refinery at Kwinana, on the coast near Fremantle. In Canada there is a brand new railway 385 miles long, begun

in 1962 and built specially to convey lead-zinc ore concentrates from the Pine Point mine, on Great Slave Lake, to the Northern Alberta section of the Canadian National Railways at Roma. This magnificently engineered and equipped railway is one of the very few built recently that is not connected with the transport of coal and minerals to Japan. That country's intake at the moment is indeed phenomenal, taking account of the tonnage of coal passing over the Queensland lines, the iron ore from Hamersley, and the traffic of the neighbouring Mount Newman private railways and the Western Australian Government Railway to Kwinana. But one of the greatest projects of all is on the historic Canadian Pacific.

The shades of Sir William Van Horne, and the other great men of ninety years ago whose courage and resolution ensured the completion of the C.P.R., must indeed be stirred by the astonishing modern development through the mountains of British Columbia which involves the haulage of six coal trains a day, each consisting of 105 cars, from mines in the Crowsnest Pass to Roberts Bank, near Vancouver. *Sixty thousand tons of coal a day* – all bound for Japan. These great trains have to be hauled through some of the most severe mountain areas of British Columbia, and in climbing from Beavermouth to the Connaught Tunnel – well, let me tell what I saw one autumn morning, when I was riding in the locomotive cab of the Canadian, the luxury express from Vancouver to the eastern cities. Both

The *Flèche d'Or*, double-headed with two Class 'K' 'Pacifics' of the former P.L.M. Railway, passing through the suburbs of Boulogne.

portals of the Connaught Tunnel are set in mountain scenery that is sublime. There is no other word for it, with an array of great peaks, some topping the 10,000 foot mark, raising their snowy summits to the clear blue sky of a cloudless dawn. But there was much more than scenery to rivet my attention. We came to Stoney Creek loop: why so many sidings here, in the mountains? But for nearly fifteen miles beyond this point the line drops down the Beaver Hill, on an almost continuous gradient of 1 in 45, and when we ourselves got to Beavermouth one of the great coal trains from the Crowsnest was waiting to go up the hill. It must have been a little below maximum tonnage for it was powered by only eleven locomotives – *only eleven*, each of 3,000 horse-power! The maximum-load trains need *thirteen*, four at the front, five robot-controlled at mid-train, and four pushing at the rear. Even so, coal from the Crowsnest is not the only freight passing over this difficult route. In the ninety miles of the 'Mountain' sub-division from Revelstoke to Golden we passed three other 100-car freight trains, going west. These trains have to be re-marshalled at Stoney Creek, with the worst incline surmounted.

The carefully ordered pattern of regular mineral trains on these 'conveyor-belt' railways overseas could well be the envy of the British or continental European operator faced with a common carrier business. The sorting and marshalling of goods trains can be the biggest time- and money-waster in the whole sphere of railway operation. In the years

between the two World Wars the American railways made great progress towards the mechanised marshalling of freight trains. Indeed the constantly increasing size of the conventional U.S. box car was making ever more hazardous the age-old custom of shunters riding on individual cars to apply the brakes. Outside the U.S.A. development was slow until after

Above. Southern Railway of India: a 'ZP' class 2 foot 6 inch gauge 'Pacific' (Japanese-built in 1954), leaving Yelahanka.

Left. British Railways: English Electric prototype of the latest and most advanced diesel-electric locomotives in Great Britain – the 'DP2', from which the Class '50' was developed – here seen at King's Cross Station, London.

World War Two, though the vital nature of all marshalling yards was emphasised by the repeated aerial attacks made on those on the continent of Europe during the war itself. British development was individual and rapid after the Modernisation Plan was launched in 1955, and some fine new fully-mechanised yards were built, notably at Middlesbrough, Lamesley (near Newcastle), Millerhill (near Edinburgh), Carlisle, and Margam (near Port Talbot). British practice and equipment was also used in large installations in Australia, New Zealand, South Africa and Sweden. In Great Britain itself, however, the rapidly changing pattern of freight traffic, from individual consignments to block loads and regular trains chartered by traders such as the Ford Motor Company (which has a continuous service of trains carrying car bodies from Merseyside to Dagenham) has greatly lessened the flow of freight vehicles requiring the specialised attention of a mechanised marshalling yard, and some of those commissioned

Right. South Australian Railways: the semi-streamlined lightweight 4–8–4 locomotive *Sir Malcolm Barclay-Harvey* leaving Adelaide with an excursion train of vintage passenger coaches. This locomotive is now preserved and used for hauling special trains.

Below right. Colour-light signals on the Southern Pacific, silhouetted as the setting sun gilds rails and the Salton Sea beyond.

less than twenty years ago are now closed.

The British position so far as freight traffic is concerned is nevertheless rather exceptional, and the great marshalling yard, with increasingly sophisticated control equipment, is an outstanding feature of modern railways in many lands. One of the most remarkable among recent installations is at Alyth Yard, near Calgary, on the Canadian Pacific, built to the latest standards with equipment developed and manufactured in the U.S.A. Traffic converges on Alyth from four main routes, and the majority of the trains arriving require a general sort-out. Today the word computer is all too often a catch-phrase conveying some form of modern control which the user does not really understand. But at Alyth Yard all the manifold activities of a yard mechanised in the sense understood forty years ago are combined with the latest North American concept of automatic car identification, locomotive and crew rostering, and the forecasting of train movement, in one central 'brain'. At Alyth there are no men making lists of the cars in each train and their destinations; this is done by photo-electric scanners. There is no hump yard-master; no operator in the control tower controlling the car retarder; no hump foreman, pressing buttons. Once the process of hump shunting begins, it is continuously monitored by the master computer. It is indeed one of the world's classic examples of the integration of all aspects of practical railroading in to one instrument of electronic machinery.

As the time is now approaching when the 150th anniversary of the inception of passenger travel on railways is to be celebrated, in England in September 1975, it is fitting that we should turn in conclusion to a survey of passenger travel today; and while some of the most remarkable recent developments have been in freight traffic, a new age has already dawned for passenger travel in many parts of the world. It is certainly so in the country where railways were born. The whirlwind economic excision of unprofitable facilities that hit British Railways when Dr Beeching got into his stride, threatened the plan for electrification of the London Midland main line from Euston to Liverpool and Manchester; but the halt was fortunately no more than temporary, and when the full electric service was operated from 1966 it proved a real money-spinner. Apart from its reliability, punctuality and smoothness of travel, it carried the trump card of SPEED. Travelling times of roughly one-and-a-half hours between London and Birmingham and two-and-a-half hours between London and both Liverpool and Manchester, could not be matched on a city centre to city centre basis by any other form of transport. The service was frequent and at regular intervals, and businessmen came to travel between London and Birmingham as they might have used their own cars to get from one part to another of the same city. Although trains travelling at 100 miles per hour were now following each other at five-minute intervals, the highest degree of safety was ensured by the use of continuous colour-light signalling and the highly efficient automatic

warning system in the locomotive cabs.

The use of electronic methods of remote control has enabled the basic advantages of centralised regulation, as demonstrated so effectively by the C.T.C. installations commissioned in the U.S.A. during World War Two, to be realised also on what is the busiest main line in the world. During the first phase of the London Midland electrification, re-signalling in the south of England with electronic remote control provided only four signal boxes in

the eighty-two-and-a-half miles between Rugby and Euston; but the development of these techniques in the extension of the electrification between Weaver Junction, Cheshire, and Glasgow to its completion in May 1974, has resulted in the control of this 230 miles of very busy main line being vested in no more than five signal boxes. These highly sophisticated power plants are at Warrington, Preston, Carlisle, Motherwell and Glasgow Central, and some idea of the degree of remote control now effected can be appreciated from the distances between some of these new signal boxes. Preston and Carlisle are ninety miles apart, and Carlisle and Motherwell eighty-seven-and-a-half; and yet throughout the intervening stretches, some of them in desolate mountain country, the trains are under continuous surveillance on the illuminated track diagrams in the central signal boxes, and as safely controlled as though they were never out of sight of a signalman.

While the electrified London Midland line provided the most outstanding example of passenger train service development in Great Britain, it was certainly matched for speed by the diesel-hauled trains on the East Coast route. There the twenty-two special diesel-electric locomotives with the 3,300 horse-power 'Deltic' type high-speed engines have established a remarkable record, not only of individual performance but of overall reliability, while being subjected to some of the most intense utilisation ever attempted in a high-speed passenger service. Like the London

A fine example of German station architecture. The large German city terminals were given a grandiose, and sometimes even ponderous, treatment. This photograph shows the main station at Leipzig, East German State Railways, today.

On the continent of Europe the network of TEE (Trans-Europe Express) trains has been developed on an international basis. These provide high-speed trains and rolling stock of maximum comfort, between major centres of population and industry. Not all of them are international, and indeed some of the best known run entirely within one country. Unlike the great majority of British fast trains, however, they require the payment of supplementary fees, in addition to the basic first class fares. A few of these luxury services may be quoted:

Train name	Route
Blauer Enzian	Hamburg–Salzburg–Zellam See
Etoile du Nord	Amsterdam–Brussels–Paris
Edelweiss	Amsterdam–Zurich
Ligure	Milan–Avignon
Parsifal	Paris–Cologne–Hamburg
Rheingold	Hook of Holland and Amsterdam to Geneva and Milan
Roland	Bremen–Basle–Milan

Midland electric locomotives, they also have a maximum rated speed of 100 miles per hour, and it was indeed the success of these locomotives that led certain commentators to suggest that electrification was not really necessary. Aided by some notable improvements in track alignment at previously difficult locations, these locomotives have reduced the London–Newcastle journey time to considerably less than four hours.

To these may be added the celebrated purely French trains the Mistral, from Paris to Nice; the Capitole, from Paris to Toulouse; and the Aquitaine, which covers the 360 miles from Paris to Bordeaux in exactly four hours (that is an average from start to stop of 90 miles per hour). This train, like the Capitole and certain trains in Germany, runs regularly at

125 miles per hour. Some of these trains, like the Mistral, are no lightweights. The Mistral is in fact very heavy and requires a locomotive capable of 8,000 horse-power to haul it. The smoothness and general comfort of these 'super' trains on the continent of Europe is indeed very enjoyable to experience, though for my own part I would always exchange the most luxurious seat for a place in the driver's cab! To ride the head-end of the Mistral from Paris to Dijon and cover ninety-eight miles in a single hour is an experience not readily forgotten. Not less so was the sight of the dials in the cab when we were climbing a 1 in 125 gradient into the Côte d'Or mountains and still doing 95 miles per hour with fourteen of those heavy *grand-confort* air-conditioned coaches behind us! Another deeply impressive French experience was to ride in the locomotive cab of *Le Capitole*, covering lengthy stretches of the run from Paris to Toulouse at 125 miles per hour with eleven of those same luxurious coaches behind us.

The different systems of electrification on the railways of Europe could have caused some embarrassment in the running of international trains, particularly where it was desired to maintain old traditions. Before World War Two the French and Belgian railways co-operated in running certain non-stop expresses between Paris and Brussels. From the locomotive point of view this was a prestige job, operated by steam 'Pacifics' of the Northern Railway of France. Then, however, the French decision to adopt the 25,000 volt A.C. system of traction involved the electrification of the line from Paris to the Belgian frontier near Mons, while the Belgians had already standardised with 3,000 volts D.C. In France the ingenuity of electric locomotive designers evolved the remarkable quadri-current locomotive, which not only is able to run on any of the present standard systems of electrification in Europe, but can change from one to another at the international frontiers without stopping. I had the privilege of riding in the cab of the locomotive working the Etoile du Nord TEE train, non-stop from Brussels to Paris, and saw what was involved at the Franco-Belgian frontier. These locomotives carry four pantographs, one for each of the different electric systems. We were running in Belgium and as we came to the frontier station power was shut off and the 3,000 volt D.C. pantograph lowered. Then we coasted through the change-over point at about 70 miles per hour with all pantographs down and, having come into the French sphere, raised the 25,000 volt A.C. pantograph. Still, however, the power was not re-applied. We had to receive electrical proof that we had raised the correct pantograph, which was obtained by contact with the French overhead line. Only then did the electric interlocks permit our driver to re-apply power for traction. Actually the process of changing over at the frontier was a matter of seconds rather than minutes, and we were soon running at 100 miles per hour.

And what of Great Britain? For the electrification to Glasgow, opened in May 1974, the remarkable new 'AL7' electric locomotives were introduced. At a casual glance they look little different from their 'AL6' predecessors but they have numerous important technical improvements. They can accelerate an eleven- or twelve-car train from rest up to 100 miles per hour in less than four minutes, and take these same loads up the steepest gradients on the line at 90 miles per hour. The heavy road through the Westmorland fells, and through the Lowland hill ranges of Scotland, which taxed both steam and diesels so severely, has been virtually ironed out. The gradients are no longer of any consequence, and one can travel from London to Glasgow at an average speed of 80 miles per hour – all at standard first and second class fares. There is no supplement for high speed on these splendid trains. Still it is evident from developments in many parts of the world that there is a definite, if limited, demand for super-luxury passenger trains, in countries where internal airlines can provide immeasurably faster city-to-city service than any conventional form of train could possibly do – whatever the motive power, however straight and perfect the track. It is *distance* that beats the train, in a straight commercial competition. But I will mention here just three world-famous, very long distance trains that continue to draw a handsome patronage. These are the Blue Train of the South African Railways, running between Pretoria and Cape Town; the Canadian of the Canadian Pacific, crossing the continent from Montreal and Toronto to Vancouver; and the Indian Pacific, running right across Australia, from Sydney to Perth, and operated by four different railways – those of New South Wales, South Australia and Western Australia, and the Commonwealth system.

Of these three the Blue Train has the shortest run, a mere 1,000 miles, and through passengers have only one night in the train. As to its appointments, one is reminded of the remark of King Edward VII, when the management of the London and North Western asked him how he would like the new royal train equipped. He replied simply, 'Make it like a yacht'. Passengers travelling from the eastern cities to Vancouver by the Canadian spend two nights in the train, and its greatest feature, apart from the spacious bedroom accommodation, is the dome car on the rear end: a buffet lounge, an 'Admiral's stern walk', and an elevated observation 'dome', from which one can look ahead as well as to the rear, high above the rest of the train. It is a fascinating place, when the train is snaking its way through the deep canyons of British Columbia. As for the Indian Pacific on its three-day journey across Australia, it is like embarking on a sea voyage. Inside the air-conditioned coaches one is shut off from the world outside; one lives a kind of ship life, meeting fellow travellers again and again at meals, listening to the pianists among them playing in the lounge car, and taking

coffee after meals in that same lounge – a pleasant touch of gracious living – while the fierce sun of inland Australia burns up the seemingly endless solitude of the Nullabor Plain.

Yet for all the luxury of these special trains, for all the incomparably faster service provided by the diesels and the electrics on the inter-city routes in all countries, there are many, even among regular travellers, who strive to keep evergreen the memory of steam. Beautifully equipped museums have been set up in many lands. One thinks of Utrecht, Stockholm, Lucerne, Melbourne, Brisbane, Kyoto, Delson near Montreal, Munich – not to mention the British collections at York and Swindon. But today mere museum pieces are not enough. Sections of line must be preserved, and train services operated solely by steam run daily. Steam-hauled excursions are organised on what are otherwise diesel railways and young people, many of whom are too young ever to have seen the original steam railways, flock to the linesides and to the booking offices. Older enthusiasts join trans-world safaris to see railways where steam is still in regular use; to Southern Africa, to Japan, to India, to Taiwan – to capture for their future enjoyment the sight and sound of steam, by camera, cine, and tape-recorder. Some use special duplex-controlled double cameras so that they can record the passing of steam trains in both colour and black and white at the same time. One treasures memories of *Puffing Billy* on the Victoria Railways, carrying its

narrow-gauge load into the Dandenong Range; of giant East African Beyer-Garratts hauling 1,000-ton freights up to Nairobi, on a line so curved that in places the rear of the train is travelling parallel to the engine but in the opposite direction; of the Prairie Dog Central making its decorous way out of Winnipeg, and of the repatriated *Flying Scotsman* grinding round the curves on the Dart Valley Railway from Paignton down to Kingswear.

But for all the fascination of steam, it is no longer in her old and trusted hands that the future of railways lies. Nor is it wholly in the gargantuan conveyor-belt hauls of minerals that the money-making is to be found. Ten years ago the Japanese National Railways introduced to the world their New Tokaido Line. It had been long contemplated because, even before World War Two, the administration had decided that the existing main line from Tokyo to the south was saturated. More important was the decision that any relief should not merely take the form of laying down more tracks parallel to the old ones. The route took a sinuous course never far from the shores of the Pacific, and in the cities it was closely encompassed by buildings on all sides. No, relief should take the form of an entirely new line, practically straight, gradeless and, most significant of all, to the European and American standard gauge, instead of the old 3 foot 6 inch one. Nothing could be done until some years after the end of the war, but then work began on the New Tokaido Line – a railway speedway the like of which had never previously been seen anywhere. On immense viaducts it strode its way over the rooftops of the cities; it spanned the great rivers, plunged straight as a die through any hill or mountain that was in the way, and when it was finished Japan began to operate the fastest train service the world had ever known. At first there were some who considered it little more than a stunt, a railway built regardless of cost as a symbol of national prestige. I would not suggest that prestige did not play some part in the overall conception; but the public flocked to travel on it, and today it is the New Tokaido Line that is getting within measurable distance of saturation.

It could be described as a conveyor-belt railway for passengers. On the original section, from Tokyo to Osaka, there is a sixteen-coach 'lightning' train every quarter of an hour, from 6 in the morning till 9 at night. The distance between these two great cities is 320 miles, and the time is 3 hours 10 minutes. Seven days a week, all the year round these trains carry an average of 1,000 passengers each, so that roughly 55,000 people are travelling at 100 miles per hour from Tokyo to Osaka every day, while another 55,000 are going in the opposite direction. All the trains are exactly alike; all run at a maximum speed of 130 miles per hour with immaculate smoothness and safety on a line that has no wayside signals. I have had the fascinating experience of riding in the driver's cab. One may be thrilled by the roar and rough glamour of a hard-worked, coal-fired steam locomotive, and entranced by the effortless 100 miles per hour running of the electrically-hauled Royal Scot from Euston to the north. But to stand beside a Japanese driver, doing 130 miles per hour, and to have nothing but an illuminated indicator in the cab telling the driver at what speed to run, held me spellbound. Of course I knew that some of the most advanced signalling techniques lay behind the presentation to us of that cab signal, and if we did not react quickly when it changed to a slower speed the brakes would have been automatically applied, but to travel thus was the experience of a lifetime.

The New Tokaido Line has proved a magnificent success, commercially as well as technologically, and today the network of such lines is being extended throughout Japan. There is good reason for railway travel to be popular. Few Japanese own cars; the cities are too crowded to make them worthwhile, and if taxis can be readily chartered for getting about where underground and local railways are not convenient, one could hardly take a taxi for a business visit to Osaka, from Tokyo. The network now under construction is known as the 'Shinkansen', or new lines, and some of the routes will be far more spectacular in their engineering than the original New Tokaido Line. The line to the south end of the main island of Honshu will, for nearly half its total mileage, be in tunnel beneath the central 'backbone' mountain range, and the line going north into the island of Hokkaido will pass under the sea in a tunnel longer than the proposed Channel Tunnel between England and France. The boldness of the engineering is tremendous. So is the cost; but with the experience of the line between Tokyo and Osaka in mind, all expectations are that the resulting traffic will make it all worthwhile. And all these new lines are being planned for regular service speeds of 160 miles per hour.

So, with the 150th anniversary of passenger railways approaching, one finds railways not 'on the way out', but in vigorous and exciting evolution. In the summer of 1973 a new British train, on a line adjacent to that of the very first passenger railway, set up a new record for diesel traction by attaining a maximum speed of 143 miles per hour, and on 2 August that same train ran from Darlington to York, 44·1 miles, in 27½ minutes. For 39·9 miles of this journey the average speed was 121·8 miles per hour, with a maximum of 137 miles per hour. But one of the most reassuring features, to me at any rate, of a truly striking demonstration was the way in which this hurricane progress could be halted if necessary. Going north, just beyond Thirsk, we made an emergency stop. The speed was then 128½ miles per hour and the train was brought to rest with the most uncanny smoothness, with no disturbance of the glass and crockery on the tables, in just *fifty-eight seconds*.

Railways, then and now, indeed! One salutes the intrepid courage of the pioneers; the vision of those who made them the pre-eminent form of transport on land; the men of our own younger days, who weathered the years of depression, carried them through the inferno of World War Two, and still did not lose faith amid all the cynical prophesies of demise that came in the 1950s. Now, as the 150th anniversary draws near, it would perhaps be mixing metaphors to say that railways in most parts of the world will be passing that milestone going 'full steam ahead'; but the idiom is apt enough, whether it be with the phenomenal increase of the Shinkansen lines in Japan, in the running of prodigiously heavy mineral trains in Canada, Australia and Southern Africa, or in the prospect of the super-speed British expresses being linked with the TEE network via the Channel Tunnel. In Europe new lines are under construction for regular running at 300 kilometres per hour (186 miles per hour) in both France and West Germany. Railways are 'right-away' to ever more impressive achievements.

U.S.A.

Railway network c.1950

•••–•••–•••– Norfolk and Western	———— Missouri Pacific
✕✕✕✕✕✕✕✕✕ Erie	•••••••• Southern Pacific
+++++++ Seaboard Airline	++++++++ Santa Fe
––––––– New York, New Haven and Hartford	•••+•••+ Texas and Pacific
–‖–‖–‖–‖– New York Central	✕✕✕✕✕✕✕✕ Illinois Central
–ı–ı–ı–ı– Wabash	‖‖‖‖‖‖‖‖ Katy
•ı•ı•ı•ı• Chesapeake and Ohio	•✕•✕•✕•✕ Louisville and Nashville
•‖•‖•‖•‖ Baltimore and Ohio	———— Union Pacific
–––––––– Pennsylvania	–•–•–•– Southern
––––– Chicago, Milwaukee, St Paul and Pacific	═══════ Chicago, Rock Island and Pacific
✹✹✹✹ Chicago, Burlington and Quincy	–••–••– Western Pacific
✱✱✱✱ Northern Pacific	✕✕✕✕✕✕✕ Chicago North Western
–•–•–•–• Great Northern	•‖•‖•‖•‖ Denver and Rio Grande Western

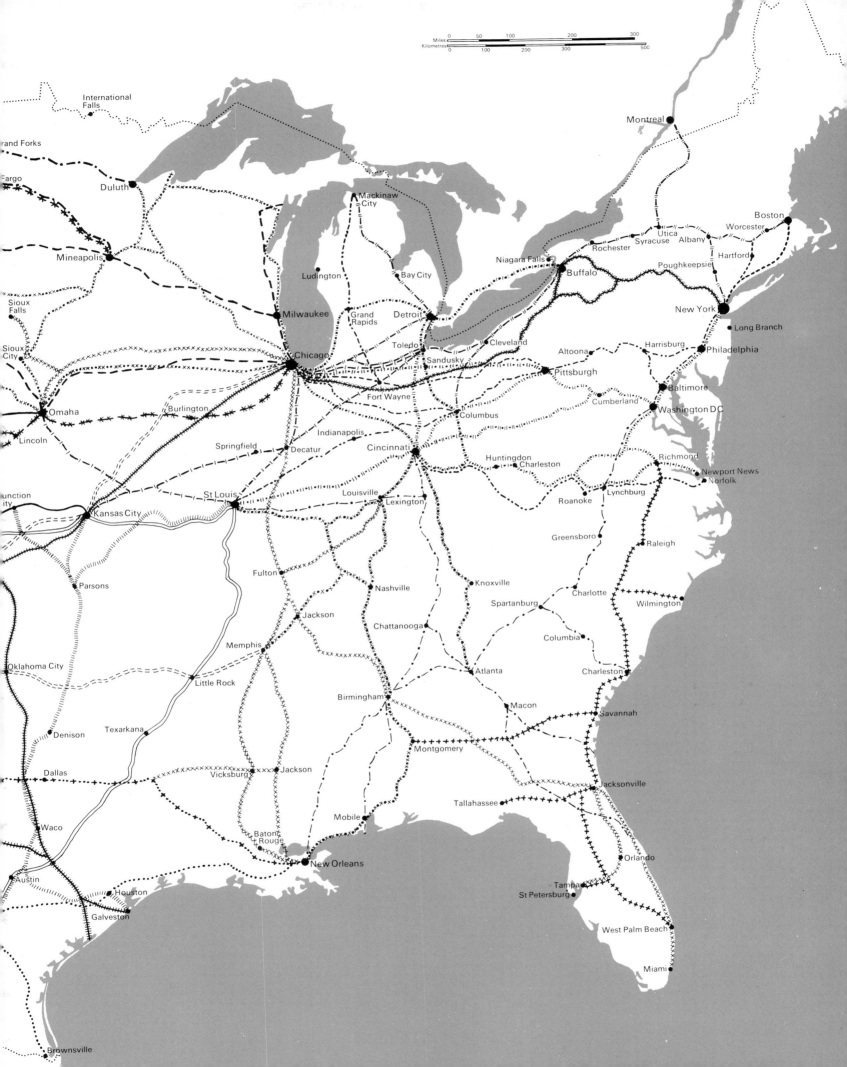

Europe
Railway network before 1914

France
- Nord
- Ouest
- Paris-Orléans
- Etat
- PLM
- Midi
- Est

Holland
- State
- Holland
- Netherlands Central
- Dutch Rhenish
- North Brabant

Germany
- Baden State
- Wurttemberg
- Saxon
- Bavarian
- Elsass-Lothringen Imperial
- Prussian State

Switzerland
- Swiss Federal
- Bern-Lötschberg-Simplon
- Swiss Federal Gothard Line

Austria-Hungary
- Austrian State
- Southern
- North Western
- Austro-Hungarian State
- Kaiser Ferdinand's Northern
- Hungarian State

Spain
- Norte
- Madrid, Zaragoza & Alicante
- Oeste
- Central of Aragon
- Andalusian

SWEDEN

Copenhagen

Gedser

Warnemünde
Neumünster Rostock
Lübeck Stralsund

Hamburg

Wittenburg

Hanover
Brunswick
Magdeburg

M   A   N   Y

Halle   Leipzig

Würzburg

Nuremberg

Regensberg

Augsburg

Munich

Worgl

Feldkirch
Innsbruck

Brescia

Vicenza

Verona   Padua
Venice

Modena
Bologna

Pisa
Leghorn

Civitavecchia

Rome

ITALY

Florence

Rimini

Ancona

Foggia

Naples

Bari

Taranto

Brindisi

Otranto

Messina
Reggio

Stettin

Berlin
Frankfurt an der Oder

Dresden

Eger

Prague   Bohm
Truban

Gmund

Linz

Salzburg

St Michael   Bruck

Graz

Klagenfurt
Villach

Ljubliana

Udine

Trieste

Fiume

Zagreb

AUSTRIA

Vienna

Bruck   Pozsony

Neustadt

Amstetten

Breslau

Oderberg

Brunn

Zsolna

HUNGARY

Gyékényes

Marburg

Budapest

Szolnok

Miskolez

Cracow

Lvov

Temesvar

Belgrade

SERBIA

MONTE
NEGRO

A
L
B
A
N
I
A

Nisch

Skopje

GREECE

Salonica

Athens

Königsberg

Danzig
Marienburg

Torun

Warsaw

POLAND

To Riga
and St Petersburg

Smolensk

Minsk

RUSSIA

Kiev

Odessa

RUMANIA

Pitesti

Turnu-Severin

Craiova

Bucharest

Constanta

BULGARIA

Sofia

Philippopolis

Adrianople

Constantinople

TURKEY

Miles 0   25   50   75   100
Kilometres 0   25   50   75

Great Britain
Railway network before 1922

–··–··–··–	London & North Western
– – – –	Great Northern
–·–·–·–	Great Eastern
·||··||··||·	South Eastern & Chatham
– – – – –	London Brighton & South Coast
|||||||||||||	London Tilbury & Southend
– – – – –	London & South Western
————	Great Western
+++++++++++	Metropolitan
–··–··–··–	Great Central
············	Midland
||–||–||–||	Cambrian
–·–·–·–	North Eastern
=========	Cheshire Lines
========	Lancashire & Yorkshire
xxxxxxxxxxxxx	Hull & Barnsley
·||·||·||·||·	Furness
++++++++++++	Caledonian
–·–·–·–·–·	North British
+++++++++++	Great North of Scotland
– – – – –	Highland
·|·|·|·|·|·|·	Glasgow & South Western
············	Others

Miles 0   25   50   75
Kilometres 0 25 50 75 100

List of Plates

Acknowledgments

The author and publishers would like to express their gratitude to the following for their assistance in the preparation of the book: Susan Burns of The Oakland Museum, Freeman Hubbard of *Railroad Magazine*, F. Page of the Crown Agents, Martha Phemister of the Public Archives of Canada, J. Garvey of The Transport Trust, R. H. Kindig, T. Taber, H. Uematsu and K. H. Vignoles. They are also indebted to the following individuals, libraries, museums and organizations for permission to reproduce illustrations: Leicester Museum and Art Gallery, Stretton Collection, half title, Newton Collection, 111 above and below, 125 below, 126 below; By courtesy of the Post Office, title page, 26 top, 28 above; British Rail, verso title, 15, 33, 44, 47, 51 left, 86 below, 87 above, 105 above, 129 above, 135 above, 169 above; Photos Science Museum, London, 8, 9 left and right, 10 above and below, 11 above, 12 above, 13 above, 16 left, 17, 18 above, 21 above and below, 29, 30 above, 43 right, 49; Crown Copyright, Science Museum, London, 18 below right; Radio Times Hulton Picture Library, 11 below, 64 below, 68, 91 above, 98 above and below, 99, 107 below, 129 below, 134 above, 149; Ullstein Bilderdienst, Berlin, 12 below, 22 below, 23 above and below right, 24 above, 28 below, 35, 46 above and below, 64 left, 130 above and below, 132 above, 172, 193 above, 197; Kodak Museum, Wealdstone, 13 below; *Railroad Magazine*, 14, 20, 24 below, 32 left, 63 below, 77 above, 101 below, 107 above, 117 below, 124 above left, 151, 153 below, 160 above right, 161, 167, 186 above, 196 below; J. and J. May Antiques, London, 16 right; Reading Company, 18 below left; Bibliothèque Nationale, Paris, 19, 37 below, 48 below; Courtesy of the Coverdale and Colpitts Collection, New York, 22 above, 55 above and below, 79, 81 below; Illinois Central Gulf Railroad, 23 below left, 95, 119 below, 170 below; Mr and Mrs M. G. Powell, 25 above and below, 38 below; Museum of British Transport, 26 centre, 56 above, jacket back; By courtesy of the Institution of Civil Engineers, 26 bottom; Great Western Railway Museum, Swindon, 30 below, 34 below, 74 below, 89, 112 below right; British Transport Commission, Historical Relics Section, 31 above; Smithsonian Institution, Washington, 31 below, 34 above, 56 below, 118 top right, 141; O. S. Nock, 36, 40 below, 42, 66 above, 69 right, 73 below, 84 above, 96, 112 below left, 113 below right, 117 above, 118 left above, 119 above, 126 above, 133 above, 134 below, 136, 138, 148 above and below, 154 below, 163 below, 166 below, 169 above, 170 above, 173, 175, 181 below, 192 above, 193 below, 194; The Parker Gallery, London, 37 above; Museen der Stadt, Vienna, 38 above; *La Vie du Rail*, 39 above and below, 48 above, 52 below, 66 below, 80 below, 97 top, 123 above left; Nederlands Spoorweg Museum, Utrecht, 40 above; Italian State Railways, 41; Union Switch and Signal Company, 43 left; Deutsches Bundesbahn, Zentrales Bildarchiv, 45, 179 below; Reproduced by permission of The British Library Board, 50 above, 51 right, 120; Milwaukee Road, 50 below, 78 above, 133 below; SNCF/DIF, 52 above; Greenwich Local History Library, 53 left above and below; The Public Archives of Canada, Ottawa, 53 right, 76 above and below, 77 below; Union Pacific Railroad Museum Collection, 57, 59 above and below, 62; Photographs courtesy of The Oakland Museum, Ca, 58 above and below, 60, 61; Association of American Railroads, 63 above, 106; Austrian Federal Railways, 65, 182 below, 187; J. M. McMillan, 67; Burlington Northern Inc., 69 left; Locomotive Publishing Company, 70, 87 below, 97 centre and bottom, 100, 121 above, 123 above right, 135 below; New Zealand Railways publicity photograph, 71; Japan Transportation Museum, Tokyo, 72, 73 above, 114, 115 left and right, 150; Pictorial and Feature Services, 74 above; Old Print Shop, New York, 75; Kennedy Galleries Inc., New York, 78 below; SNCF/*La Vie du Rail*, 80 above; Colonel Rixon Bucknall, 81 above; Royal Holloway College, London, 82; Barnaby's Picture Library, London, 84 below, 163 above; Thomas Cook and Son Ltd, London, 85, 91 below left and right, 113 above, 156 below; Swiss National Tourist Office and Swiss Federal Railways, 86 above, 102, 104, 105 below, 142, 143, 183; Olney Collection/Peter Gerhold, 88; Great Northern Railway, 90 above, 155 below; Järnvägsmuseum, Stockholm, 90 below, 103, 121 below; Public Transport Commission of New South Wales, 92 above; Photos South African Railways, 92 below, 93, 108 above; Pennsylvania Railroad, 94, 153 above; Colin Garratt, 109, 110 above and below, 127 above and below, 128 above and below, 145 below; Crown Agents, 108 below, 125 above, 131; V. G. Jackson, 101 above; Elizabeth Menzies and R. B. Green, 112 above; Central Library, Newcastle-upon-Tyne, 113 below left; C. W. Jernstrom, 116; R. H. Kindig, 118 bottom, 157 above, 158 below, 159; Novosti Press Agency, 123 below, 158 above, 169 below, 185 above and below, 199 above; India Office Library and Records, 124 above right; Central Library, Gateshead, 124 below; Bundesarchiv, Koblenz, 132 below, 166 above, 168; Imperial War Museum, London, 140, 174; J. E. Dayton, 144 above; The Mitchell Library, Glasgow, 144 below; L. G. Marshall, 145 above, 156 above, 160 above left, 179 above, 195 above; Victor Hand, 146 above; Nils Huxtable, 146 below; Ango Brehme, 147; M. W. Early, 152, 160 below, 188 below; Burlington Route Photo, 154 above; Dr P. Ransome Wallis, 157 below; Y. Broncard, 162; National Museum of Wales, Cardiff, 164 above; Harlan Hiney, 164 below; Delaware and Hudson Railway Company, 176; Derek Cross, 177, 188 above, 200; Chesapeake and Ohio Railway, 178; Swiss Federal Railways, 180, 199 below; P. H. Boot, 181 above; Japanese National Railways, 182 above, 201; Ivo Peters, 184, 189 below; East African Railways, 186 below; Japan Information Centre, London, 189 above; Canadian Pacific, 190; Amtrak, 192 below; English Electric Company, 195 below; South Australian Railways, 196 above; Don Wood, 198; Australian News and Information Bureau, 202; The Metropolitan Museum of Art, New York, Bequest of Moses Tanenbaum, 1937, jacket front. Colour transparencies were kindly loaned by: The Cooper-Bridgemen Library, 26 centre, 56 above, 82, jacket back; Scala/Sven, 37 below; Weidenfeld and Nicolson, 38 above. The items in the Coverdale and Colpitts Collection were photographed by Brenwasser, New York; those in Mr and Mrs M. G. Powells' collection and at the Institute of Civil Engineers by Gordon Roberton of A. C. Cooper Ltd, London; those from the Great Western Railway Museum by Maylott Studios, Swindon; and those from The Parker Gallery and The British Library by John R. Freeman Ltd, London. Bob Loosemore photographed 16 right; Harvey Uecker, 50 below and 133 below; D. Bristow, 74 above; Geoffrey Harfield of Simon Field Ltd, 81 above; D. C. Harrod, 88; Lambert Weston, 96; R. F. Corley, 136; Stanley Travers, 164 above; P. H. Groom, 166 below; Jim Shaughnessy, 176; and William M. Rittase, 178. The reference maps have been drawn by Harold Bartram.

Index